THE COMPLETE STORY

FORMULA ONE

THE COMPLETE STORY

FORMULA ONE

TIM HILL

Photographs
Daily Mail

Transatlantic Press
First published in 2008

Transatlantic Press
38 Copthorne Road, Croxley Green, Hertfordshire. WD3 4AQ

©Transatlantic Press
All photographs ©Associated Newspapers Ltd

A catalogue record for this book is available from the British Library.
ISBN 978-0-9558298-2-6

Printed in China

Contents

Introduction

The Quest for Motor Sport's Greatest Prize

On 22 July 1894, 21 new-fangled horseless carriages lined up for an 80-mile dash from Paris to Rouen, the world's first motor race. The winner barely exceeded 10 mph, yet the template was laid down for the grand sporting theatre of the modern Formula One extravaganza: man testing himself and his machinery to the limit; pitting his wits against his fellow competitors; risking all for the 'great prize'.

Grand Prix racing had been established for almost half a century when the FIA introduced the World Drivers' Championship in 1950. The legendary '3 Fs' – Farina, Fangio and Fagioli – gave Alfa Romeo a clean sweep in that inaugural year. Since then, a host of illustrious drivers and marques have battled it out for the annual blue riband. Ascari, Brabham, Clark, Stewart, Prost, Senna, Schumacher – just some of the 29 titans to scale the heights, though three of those paid the ultimate price for courting danger. In 2008, Fernando Alonso and Kimi Raikkonen launched their bid to don the crown again, while the rest of the grid cast a covetous eye to becoming the 30th member of one of sport's most exclusive clubs.

This lavishly illustrated book recreates the drama of almost six decades of F1 history, detailing the triumphs and tragedies that have attended the quest for motor sport's greatest prize.

Acknowledgements

The photographs from this book are from the archives of the Daily Mail. The pleasure this book will give to the many fans of Formula One is a tribute to the dedication of the staff, past and present, in the Picture Library at Associated Newspapers.

Particular thanks to Steve Torrington, Alan Pinnock, Dave Sheppard, Brian Jackson, Katie Lee, Paul Rossiter and all the staff.

THE COMPLETE STORY
FORMULA ONE

The birth of Formula One

In the years before 1950, motor racing had been dominated by individual Grands Prix competitions. However, during the forties the decision was made to link together several of these in order to create a single championship competition. In 1949, the Fédération Internationale de l'Automobile, or FIA, announced that the following year would see the inauguration of the Formula One World Championships, the name making clear that it was to be viewed as the ultimate competitive event in motor racing. The term itself related to the rules, which had been standardised by the FIA in 1946.

Seven races were granted Championships status, with six European rounds and one American, the Indianapolis 500. Although technically part of the World Championships, the 500 was slightly separate in that it did not run to Formula One rules, and it was rarely contested by Europeans.

Farina wins first Grand Prix

The inaugural race was held at Silverstone in May 1950, in front of a 150,000-strong crowd which included the British Royal family. It was won by Italian driver Nino Farina, racing for Alfa Romeo – one of three drivers who were to dominate the first decade of the competition. Juan Manuel Fangio came second, with Reg Parnell coming in at third place. Both were team mates of Farina and the clean sweep confirmed Alfa's place as the top marque with their supercharged 158.

The three 'F's'

Alfa's three star drivers, Farina, Fagioli and Juan Manuel Fangio, were already legends on the circuit. Luigi Fagiola, at 53, was a veteran, brought into the team following Consalvo Sanesi's injury in the Mille Miglia. Farina, aged 43, had been born into a family whose name was synonymous with quality coach-building and had already enjoyed a successful racing career before the war. Fangio, the youngest of the three at 38, was a product of Argentina's state-sponsored driving academy and was already a star in his homeland. The other notable driver that year was Alberto Ascari, son of Antonio Ascari, who had reigned in the sport during the 1920s. Ascari raced with Ferrari in their 4500cc V-12, but it was no match for the Alfas. During that first season, the six European titles were shared by Farina and Fangio.

There was plenty of drama to be had during the first year. At Monte Carlo, following the Silverstone race, a multiple pile-up on the first lap saw Farina spin out of the race that Fangio went on to win. In the Swiss Grand Prix, it was Farina's turn to beat his team mate into second. That race was dominated by disaster for Ferrari as their three cars all blew up. The next race, at Spa, saw Fangio beat Fagioli, with Farina limping home to fourth with transmission problems. At this stage, however, Farina still led on points: Farina 22, Fagioli 18, Fangio 17.

When Fangio won the French Grand Prix, it was Farina who was now in trouble, pulling in at seventh place and thereby missing out on any points. As the final race, Monza, loomed, Farina had been overhauled by his team mates and the pressure was now on.

Farina beats Fangio to the title

For Alfa, Monza was home territory, and so they fielded an additional two cars, driven by Piero Taruffi and Sanesi. Ascari put pressure on the two Alfa drivers in the early rounds, lying in second. His car only needed the one fuel stop to the Alfas' two, but his eventual lead was temporary and his car expired in a cloud of smoke. On the 24th lap, Fangio's gearbox failed and Taruffi handed over his car, only for it to drop a valve and leave the race. Instead, first position went to Nino Farina. The year belonged, however, to Alfa, who had secured all six of the European races in the first World Championships.

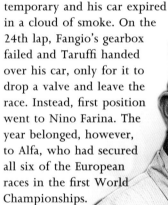

1950

THE DRIVERS' WORLD CHAMPIONSHIP

1	GIUSEPPE FARINA	ITALY	ALFA ROMEO	30
2	JUAN MANUEL FANGIO	ARGENTINA	ALFA ROMEO	27
3	LUIGI FAGIOLI	ITALY	ALFA ROMEO	24
4	LOUIS ROSIER	FRANCE	LAGO-TALBOT	13
5	ALBERTO ASCARI	ITALY	FERRARI	11
6	JOHNNIE PARSONS	USA	KURTIS OFFENHAUSER	8
7	BILL HOLLAND	USA	DEIDT OFFENHAUSER	6
8	PRINCE BIRA	THAILAND	MASERATI	5
9	MAURI ROSE	USA	DEIDT OFFENHAUSER	4
	REG PARNELL	GT BRITAIN	ALFA ROMEO, MASERATI	4
	LOUIS CHIRON	MONACO	MASERATI	4
	PETER WHITEHEAD	GT BRITAIN	FERRARI	4

Farina claims the first world title

OPPOSITE: Nino Farina of Italy and Argentinian Juan Manuel Fangio were both team-mates and rivals. At this practice session at Silverstone in August the two Alfa Romeo stars started their challenge to become world champion.

TOP: The Alfa Romeo team prepares for the inaugural World Championship race at Silverstone on 11 May, 1950 – the first race of the 1950 World Drivers' Championship.

BELOW FAR LEFT: Fangio, nicknamed 'El Maestro' (The Master), had graduated from Argentina's famous state-sponsored driving academy and went on to win the Drivers' World Championship with four different teams. Farina, also a well qualified individual with a doctorate in political economy, was the first ever Formula 1 World Champion.

BELOW LEFT: Giuseppe 'Nino' Farina secured his place in the record books by becoming the inaugural world champion.

BOTTOM: A mechanic checks the tyres on the stylish Alfa Romeo 158 – one of the most successful racing cars ever produced, it dominated the first two seasons of the Formula One World Championship.

Alfa Romeo dominate Formula One

BELOW: In the first of his three wins of the 1950 season, Farina takes the chequered flag in the British Grand Prix. His other victories in Switzerland and Italy secured the 1950 Championship.

RIGHT: Members of the victorious Alfa Romeo team after the finish of the race at Silverstone. Farina is flanked by Luigi Fagioli of Italy (right) and Reg Parnell of Britain (left), who came second and third respectively.

OPPOSITE BELOW: Silverstone staged the British Grand Prix for the first six years of the championship before the race moved to the Aintree circuit in 1957. The former airfield first hosted the British Grand Prix in 1948 and was renowned as a very fast but basic circuit.

OPPOSITE ABOVE: Mechanics working on the famous Alfa Romeo 158. This car, together with its successor the 159, dominated Grand Prix racing between June 1946 and July 1951.

Farina continues to excel

RIGHT AND BELOW: Farina holds the International Trophy, a prize awarded annually by the BRDC, after his victory at Silverstone on 26 August 1950. He had beaten Fangio into second place driving at an average speed of 90.15 mph.

BELOW RIGHT: Farina finished the 35 laps of the race in one hour, seven minutes and 17 seconds in his Alfa Romeo. Fangio later commented that Farina had driven 'like a madman'.

OPPOSITE BELOW: The International Trophy was the second big race to be held at Silverstone in 1950. It followed the British Grand Prix held in May when an estimated crowd of 150,000 packed the circuit. It was the first major motor racing event attended by members of the Royal Family, including King George VI, the Queen and Princess Margaret.

OPPOSITE ABOVE: Raymond Sommer is pushed out the race before even completing a lap. Two BRM cars were entered for the International Trophy Race; unfortunately neither car was able to finish as the mechanics struggled to overcome problems with reliability.

The rise of Ferrari

Juan Manuel Fangio was to enjoy plenty of his own success during the next season. He took the Championship title again for Alfa, despite the increasingly threatening performances of the Ferrari team. His victory in 1951 was the first of five World Driver's Championships, a record which remained unbeaten for 46 years; 'El Chueco' was to dominate motor racing throughout the decade.

Fangio fights back

The season started in May with the Swiss Grand Prix and Fangio took the prize, with the injured Ascari only managing sixth place. Fangio was not to win the second race in Belgium; instead the honours went to Farina, another crucial victory for Alfa. Although Fangio's car had suffered technical difficulties during a pit stop, it did manage to set the fastest lap later on, winning a useful point as a result. Ascari and his Ferrari teammate Villoresi came in behind Farina, but his winning margin of three minutes was still significantly great.

Alfa versus Ferrari

It was at Rheims that the competition between Alfa and Ferrari really began to bite. Fangio had failed to shake off Ascari, and it was only the failure of the Ferrari's gearbox that relieved the pressure. As senior driver, Ascari was given a new car, that of Jose Froilan Gonzalez, and when Fangio's car began to experience problems, he was given Fagioli's motor. The race was eventually Fangio's, with Ascari only a minute behind and Villoresi closing in at third.

The Alfas' need for two refuelling stops, in contrast to Ferraris' one, was to contribute to their undoing at Silverstone. Fangio, unable to establish a good lead, was under threat from Ascari's team mate Gonzales, 'the Pampas Bull', who, taking advantage of the technical weakness, eventually romped home a full minute ahead of his rival fellow countryman.

Alfa undone by shortcomings

The German Grand Prix saw Ferrari almost take a clean sweep of the top six finishers; only Fangio's second place thwarted them. The Alfas' shortcomings were becoming more apparent, with the times set by the Ferrari cars outclassing the them. Fangio's genius saved him; he knew that he had to maintain a regular, but fast, pace, keeping the car within its limits but at the top of the pack. His extra fuel stop put paid to a brief spell in the lead, but he remained in second place until the flag, again taking the point for the fastest lap. Although Ascari had won, Fangio still took seven points.

The Spanish Grand Prix, held at Barcelona was the final race of the season, with Fangio holding a three-point advantage over Ascari. The Italian was dogged by his tyres; Ferrari had introduced smaller diameter wheels for the race but they were unable to cope with the rough treatment meted out by the track and repeatedly needed changing. Fangio took the race and the title.

Alfa forced to withdraw from Formula One Despite Fangio's achievements, the year was to see a shift in supremacy away from Alfa. Ascari may well have accumulated only 12 points during the previous year, but his performance during the final round at Monza heralded the beginnings of a serious threat. Ferrari's new, unsupercharged 4.5-litre cars were impressive and Alfa's ageing 158 model, which had been designed in the late thirties, needed replacing. Without financial support, Alfa Romeo had no choice but to withdraw from Grand Prix racing, a decision which was potentially disastrous for the sport, since it opened the way for Ferrari to dominate. In order to restore the element of competitiveness, the FIA announced that the 1952 series would run to 2-litre Formula Two rules.

Rising British star

The year was also to see some significant British success, despite the dominance of the European drivers. At Switzerland, the young Stirling Moss finished a respectable eighth in his HWM, while the British Grand Prix in July saw Reg Parnell come in fifth, with Peter Walker at seventh, both racing BRMs.

1951
THE DRIVERS' WORLD CHAMPIONSHIP

1	Juan Manuel Fangio	Argentina	Alfa Romeo	31
2	Alberto Ascari	Italy	Ferrari	25
3	Jose-Froilan Gonzalez	Argentina	Lago-Talbot and Ferrari	24
4	Giuseppe Farina	Italy	Alfa Romeo Alfetta	19
5	Luigi Villoresi	Italy	Ferrari	15
6	Piero Taruffi	Italy	Ferrari	10
7	Lee Wallard	USA	Kurtis Offenhauser	9
8	Felice Bonetto	Italy	Alfa Romeo	7
9	Mike Nazaruk	USA	Kurtis Offenhauser	6
10	Reg Parnell	Gt Britain	Ferrari, BRM	5

Alfa Romeo and Ferrari reign supreme

MIDDLE: Farina and Fangio relax as they prepare to do battle again. Fangio took first place in three of the Grand Prix races in 1951 whilst Farina only won the Belgian Grand Prix

BOTTOM: The first four places in the 1951 European Grand Prix were shared between Ferrari and Alfa Romeo. The BRM team continued to struggle with the British pair, Reg Parnell and Peter Walking finishing 5th and 7th respectively. Parnell had just joined BRM after leaving Alfa Romeo where he had been the fourth works driver.

ABOVE LEFT: Farina with his cups following a victory in the Goodwood Trophy race in his supercharged Alfa Romeo.

ABOVE RIGHT: Alberto Ascari biggest successes came after he left Maserati and joined the Ferrari team.

OPPOSITE: Stirling Moss with socialite Josephine Lowry-Corry in 1951. Moss was a pioneer in British racing but his first Formula win did not occur until 1955 when he won the British Grand Prix at Aintree driving the Mercedes-Benz W196.

The Three Fs...

BELOW: Farina was the team leader of Alfa Romeo's legendary '3 Fs'. 52-year-old veteran Luigi Fagioli achieved six podium finishes in seven races in the first World Championship season and earned the distinction of being the oldest person to ever win a Formula One race. Argentinian Juan Manuel Fangio was the 'baby' of the team at 39 and won all three of the races that he finished in the inaugural Championship.

OPPOSITE ABOVE: A young Stirling Moss poses behind the wheel of his HWM. He was known during his career as 'Mr Motor racing' and firmly believed that the manner of a victory was as important as the outcome.

OPPOSITE BELOW: Alfa Romeo drivers Fangio, Bonetto, Sanesi and Farina chatting as they prepare for the impending race at Silverstone in July 1951. Fangio was beaten into second place by Ferrari's Jose Gonzales.

RIGHT: Farina joined the dominant Alfa Romeo team driving alongside Fangio and fellow countryman Luigi Fagioli in 1950 where he notched up three vicories. However he only won one championship race for the team in 1951 at the Belgian Grand Prix and then joined Alberto Ascari at Ferrari in the next season. He was a striking character noted for a petulant streak and a driving style which involved him in many accidents. It was ironic that he finally lost his life while driving to spectate at the 1966 French Grand Prix.

Ferrari dominates

Despite Formula Two cars being less powerful than their Formula One counterparts, the decision to run the championship under F2 rules was made with a view to opening up the field of competing marques. Since the larger, more powerful Formula One cars were so much more expensive to build only the top manufacturers such as Alfa Romeo and Maserati were able to compete. Now smaller companies, including Cooper, Connaught and HWM, were able to enter alongside the top flight. Yet despite this new blood, Ferrari's domination seemed inevitable; they ran their lightweight 4-cylinder 500s and in the 1952 series Alberto Ascari won six times, with his team mate Piero Taruffi taking the seventh European event.

Fangio heads to Maserati

Ferrari had welcomed several of Alfa's former stars into its ranks, among them Nino Farina, who was now destined to take second place to Ferrari's reigning star. Unlike Farina, however, Fangio wanted to be the undisputed number one in any team he drove for and so chose to drive for Maserati, who were offering him their new 6-cylinder car. Yet Fangio was not to enjoy success. On the car's debut race at Monza, having driven through the night to reach the circuit, the tired and somewhat accident-prone Argentinian flipped on a corner, was flung out and broke his neck – bringing an abrupt end to his season.

Mike Hawthorn makes debut

Britain's own rising star, Stirling Moss, had pinned his hopes on a new Bristol-engined ERA. He too crashed out on the car's debut at Spa, and likewise, his season was not one to be fondly remembered. His countryman Mike Hawthorn, in a Cooper-Bristol, was to be more successful. He finished the Belgian Grand Prix in a highly creditable fourth place, having spent much of the race at third behind the Ferraris. It was his Grand Prix debut, the finest debut placing ever achieved by an Englishman. Known as 'Papillion', the butterfly, the dapper, bow-tied Yorkshireman was to go on to even greater success before his untimely death in 1959.

Ascari victorious

Ascari seemed to be unstoppable, despite early failure across the Atlantic. He won all six of the European races that he entered, missing only the Swiss Grand Prix at Berne in May. His absence was a result of the decision to take part in the Indianapolis 500, held during the same month. It gave Ascari the chance to race in a Formula One car again, a 375, but Ascari had little success; he was forced to retire from the race having been kept to twelfth position.

At the Belgian Grand Prix, Ascari finished almost two minutes ahead of Farina then in France he would keep Farina and Taruffi to second and third place respectively. At Nürburgring, Farina, Fischer and Taruffi took supporting roles behind the usual star performer. It was much the same story in

1952
THE DRIVERS' WORLD CHAMPIONSHIP

1	Alberto Ascari	Italy	Ferrari	36
2	Giuseppe Farina	Italy	Ferrari	25
3	Piero Taruffi	Italy	Ferrari	22
4	Rudi Fischer	Switzerland	Ferrari	10
	Mike Hawthorn	Great Britain	Cooper Bristol	10
6	Robert Manzon	France	Gordini	9
7	Troy Ruttman	USA	Kuzma Offenhauser	8
	Luigi Villoresi	Italy	Ferrari	8
9	Jose-Froilan Gonzalez	Argentina	Maserati	6
10	Jim Rathmann	USA	Kurtis Offenhauser	6

the sand dunes of Zandvoort, a new championship venue in Holland. Farina and Villoresi took the minor placings in yet another Ferrari clean sweep.

Gonzalez challenges

It was only at Monza that Ascari was to be provided with some stern opposition, and that was after the world title was already in the bag. Jose Froilan Gonzalez finally had the new Maserati and he fought Ascari hard for the final win of the season. The Argentinian roared into an early lead, but an overlong pit stop for refuelling was to be

costly. Ascari took advantage and came through for his sixth victory in a row. Gonzalez was almost a minute behind, but at least he had the twin consolations of beating the Ferraris of Villoresi and Farina, and of sharing the fastest lap with the world champion.

With the new Maserati having grabbed everyone's attention, the coming season was now keenly awaited, when a fully fit Fangio would be back to challenge Ferrari's supremacy. But 1952 belonged to Ascari. His 36-point maximum haul was something that not even Fangio would quite match in any of his five title successes.

Mike the mechanic

ABOVE LEFT: Yorkshireman Mike Hawthorn poses with his proud father Leslie, a trained engineer and racing enthusiast.

ABOVE: The Ferraris reigned supreme in 1952 finishing first, second and third in the Championship. Hawthorn also enjoyed considerable success in his Cooper-Bristol. He built on the success of his fourth place in the Belgian Grand Prix and ended the season joint-fourth in the Championship.

LEFT: Mike helps out at the family business in Farnham. Leslie Hawthorn bought the Tourist Trophy Garage in 1931 when Mike was two years old. Mike grew up working on engines and was never happier than when tinkering under a bonnet.

OPPOSITE: Alberto Ascari had an incredible season in 1952, winning six out of the seven European Grand Prix, only missing out on the Swiss race where he had not started.

A natural!

OPPOSITE BELOW RIGHT: Mike Hawthorn's enthusiasm for motor racing was evident from a very early age.

BOTTOM: Moss was involved with the new Bristol-engined ERA in 1952, but the results were disappointing and the car never realised its potential.

OPPOSITE: Stirling Moss was optimistic about the ERA prior to the British Grand Prix at Silverstone, but the car failed to deliver and had to retire after 36 laps.

RIGHT: Alfa Romeo were unable to fund a new car and had to withdraw from racing in 1952 leaving Ferrari as the main Championship contender. Farina then moved to Ferrari, where he finished runner-up to Ascari.

OPPOSITE ABOVE RIGHT: Many people believed that Mike Hawthorn was a natural born driver – a view shared by father Leslie who commented: 'You need three things for success in motor sport: a good car, meticulous preparation and a good driver. We are lucky in having all three'.

Moss continues to struggle

OPPOSITE BELOW: Stirling Moss at the wheel of his ERA in 1952. His insistence on driving for British teams hampered his early career and it was not until 1955 that he achieved his first Formula One victory.

OPPOSITE ABOVE LEFT: Mike Hawthorn looks on as the scrutineers examine his Cooper-Bristol before the British Grand Prix at Silverstone.

RIGHT: Fangio testing his BRM before the season starts in May 1952 with the Swiss Grand Prix.

BELOW: Mike Hawthorn in action at Goodwood. The 23-year-old Yorkshireman became famous overnight after winning two races at the Easter Goodwood meeting.

OPPOSITE ABOVE RIGHT: Alberto Ascari was the only European driver to compete in the Indianapolis 500 during its 11 years as part of the World Championship.

Ferrari versus Maserati

In 1953 as with the previous year, the series was to be run as a Formula Two competition, and the inclusion of the Argentine Grand Prix made it a nine-event championship where the four best finishes would be counted. Now the competition was between Ferrari and Maserati, and consequently the season was a nail-biter; with the top six places being shared between the marques. Ferrari was headed by Ascari, Farina and Villoresi, but their number had been bolstered by the inclusion of Mike Hawthorn. Having made such a favourable impression on Enzo Ferrari during the previous season, he had been seduced into joining the Italian team and committing to full-time professional racing. Meanwhile, Maserati now had the fully recovered Fangio leading fellow countrymen Jose Froilan Gonzales and Onofre Marimon, Fangio's protégé.

Fangio disappointed

The tone was set for the season as Ascari and Fangio battled it out in the opening round. The new Maserati wasn't quite ready, and Fangio started the race in the 1952 model; however, the engine blew up, leaving the field open for Ascari, who won with a lap to spare over Villoresi. The story was the same in the Dutch Grand Prix, with Fangio again having to withdraw, this time owing to an axle problem. It was Farina who took second place to Ascari, but a close third was shared between Maserati's Felice Bonetto and Gonzalez

Gonzalez seemed on course to steal even more of Ferrari's thunder in Belgium until his accelerator pedal broke. More bad luck was to thwart Maserati when Fangio skidded and crashed out of the race. Ascari took his ninth consecutive win.

Hawthorn steals win

The French Grand Prix, held at Rheims, was the stage for a dramatic battle between Fangio and Hawthorn. The two had been racing wheel to wheel, but Hawthorn's stylish late application of the brake in the final corner saw him steal the win by a car's length. Fast tracks like Rheims clearly suited the powerful Maseratis, but on slower circuits, such as Silverstone, the Ferraris, which handled better, remained superior. Ascari easily took the British Grand Prix in July.

Last win for Farina

Farina won at Nürburgring, managing to maintain Ferrari's unbroken series of victories. But it was to be his last Grand Prix win; an accident the following year would end to his championship career. Although Ascari had not finished the German Grand Prix, he still managed to impress the crowds with a fine performance. He was thwarted first by the loss of a wheel, then finally with third-placed Hawthorn in his sights, his car expired. Yet Ascari had managed to set a Formula Two record for the Nürburgring beforehand.

The Swiss Grand Prix at Bremgarten sealed Ascari's championship title. He and Fangio were yet again vying for the lead, when both were forced into the pits. Fangio was forced to take over Bonetto's Maserati which he then drove so hard that it burned out. Ascari, meanwhile, had needed only a change of plugs and rejoined the race in fourth place. With the mark of a true champion he battled his way back to the front to take the chequered flag from team mates Farina and Hawthorn.

1953
THE DRIVERS' WORLD CHAMPIONSHIP

1	Alberto Ascari	Italy	Ferrari	34.5
2	Juan Manuel Fangio	Argentina	Maserati	28
3	Giuseppe Farina	Italy	Ferrari	26
4	Mike Hawthorn	Great Britain	Ferrari	19
5	Luigi Villoresi	Italy	Ferrari	17
6	Jose-Froilan Gonzalez	Argentina	Maserati	13.5
7	Bill Vukovich	USA	Kurtis Offenhauser	9
8	Emanuel de Graffenried	Switzerland	Maserati	7
9	Felice Bonetto	Italy	Maserati	6.5
10	Art Cross	USA	Kurtis Offenhauser	6

Ascari wins the crown

At Monza, with the title settled, Fangio and Maserati finally got it right. Fangio fought hard for the lead with Ascari and Farina, and right into the last lap it was anybody's race. Then, after 313 miles of close slipstreaming, Ascari made a rare mistake and spun his car at the last corner. Farina mounted the grass to avoid a collision, and the Argentinian coolly slipped through and won his only race of the season. He finished runner-up in the final table, on 28 points. But for the second year running, the crown went to Alberto Ascari.

Alberto Ascari claims his second crown

Opposite: Alberto Ascari remained as the lead driver for Ferrari in the 1953 season.

Top far left: The renowned Ferrari 500 contributed to Ascari's second Drivers' World Championship in 1953.

Top left: Following a year recuperating from his accident at Monza, Fangio returned to drive for Maserati in the 1953 season.

Centre: Alberto Ascari relishes his success after the inaugural French Grand Prix at Pau, where he beat Hawthorn (right) and Harry Schell. Hawthorn later came of age in the championship race at Rheims, where he fought a sensational duel with Fangio and beat Ascari into fourth place.

Bottom: Ascari takes the chequered flag at Silverstone, beating Fangio into second place by one second. He shared the fastest lap time of one minute 50 seconds with another Argentinian, Jose Gonzales.

Ascari dominates at Silverstone

MAIN PICTURE: The start of the British Grand Prix where Ascari was in unbeatable form and completely dominated the race..

LEFT: Ascari had followed up his six Grand Prix wins in 1952 with five more in 1953 which helped him to his second World title in consecutive years.

Fabulous Ferrari...

BOTTOM: Mike Hawthorn whipped round the 12 mile course at the Goodwood International Auto Racing Meeting setting a new lap record of 93.91 mph on 26 September 1953.

ABOVE RIGHT: In the race for cars of unlimited capacity at Goodwood, Hawthorn roared to victory driving a Ferrari 'Thin Wall' Special.

BELOW RIGHT: Ascari continued his winning streak in 1953. He beat Fangio into second place on his way to victory at Silverstone, and in the Championship overall.

OPPOSITE TOP: Hawthorn, Ascari and Farina took three of the top four places for Ferrari in the championship that year – only missing out on second position taken by Fangio for the Maserati team.

OPPOSITE MIDDLE RIGHT: Farina and Hawthorn are given a lift by a gendarme as they rush to catch a plane to Italy in time for the Grand Prix at Monza.

OPPOSITE MIDDLE LEFT: Mike Hawthorn at Silverstone as he prepares for the British Grand Prix two weeks after his impressive victory at Reims-Geuex in the French event.

OPPOSITE BELOW: The busy pit-lane attracts many visitors as the crowd watches on from above.

Mercedes–Benz returns

1954 saw the return of Formula One regulations to the championship and 2.5-litre engines were now the order of the day. Although the Italian marques had dominated post-war racing, the Germans had enjoyed pre-war success thanks to their well-financed manufacturers, including Auto Union, which would evolve into Audi, and Mercedes-Benz, whose return was eagerly anticipated. Lancia also joined the circus, and along with Mercedes they introduced new cars which were to push racing in an exciting new direction.

Mercedes had been managed by the great Alfred Neubauer during the thirties, and he was now in charge of their return. When Neubauer brought Fangio onto the team, anticipation that the Italians would finally be put to the test was high. In fact, Ascari took the threat so seriously that he changed his allegiance from Ferrari to Lancia, who were developing a new car designed by former Alfa Romeo engineer Vittorio Jano.

Maserati win with Fangio

The opening race of the season was again in Argentina and with neither the Mercedes nor the Lancia ready, it was a somewhat predictable result: Fangio, in the Maserati, was to celebrate a win over the Ferraris of Farina and Gonzales. The win was not without some controversy, however. The Scuderia lodged a protest against a pit stop on Fangio's car, which they claimed had included more than the permitted three mechanics, but their protest was in vain.

Fangio also took the flag in the Belgian Grand Prix, despite racing to the end with a collapsed suspension. Fangio had spent much of the race battling with Farina, who was sporting an arm in plaster, but Farina's engine blew up and Ferrari were yet again forced into the runner-up position with Maurice Trintignant in second. In third place at Spa was Stirling Moss, who, unlike countryman Mike Hawthorn, had resisted the temptation to join an Italian marque. However, desperate for success, he entered the 1954 in a privately owned Maserati, and took third place as a result.

Mercedes makes inauspicious debut

The French Grand Prix saw the long-awaited return of the Mercedes team with their streamlined cars sporting new desmodronic valves, fuel injection and alloy parts. Both Fangio and team mate Karl Kling dazzled the crowd, finishing the race a lap ahead of Ferrari's Robert Manzon. Although the cars were fast, they were not so adept at holding the road and the design flaws became apparent at Silverstone, where Fangio struggled to take corners without hitting the oil drum barriers. Ferrari celebrated once again, thanks to Gonzalez and Hawthorn.

Success on home soil

Nürburgring was of course home turf for Mercedes and so they produced an unstreamlined W196. Despite the distressing death of friend Onofre Marimon during practice, Fangio dominated the race and won. Gonzalez, however, was too distraught, and handed over his car to Hawthorn, who finished in second place. There was more success for Mercedes and Fangio at Bremgarten, this time back in the streamlined W196, but it was not a comfortable victory. Stirling Moss, who had impressed at Spa, was given a works car and despite a ruptured oil tank he pushed back. his engine gave out before the line, but he crossed it in a typical show of grit and determination, taking 10th place.

When Fangio took the win at Monza in September, his six victories were more than enough to secure the title and confirm his place in racing history. At the final race of the season, however, Ferrari could take some cold comfort, with a win for Mike Hawthorn. The big contenders, Fangio, Ascari and Villoresi, hadn't made it to the finish, and victory for Hawthorn had secured a runner-up place in the Drivers' Championship. The race was also marked as being the debut for the new Lancia D50 with its V8 engine.

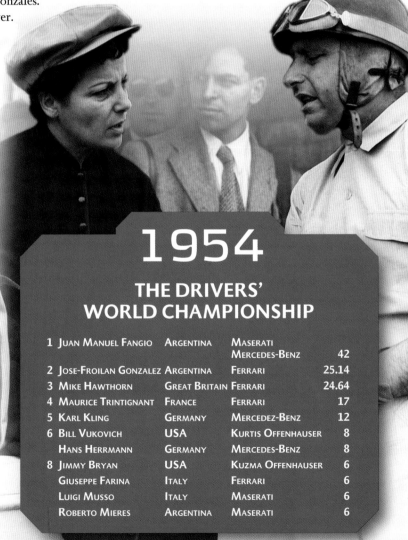

1954

THE DRIVERS' WORLD CHAMPIONSHIP

1	JUAN MANUEL FANGIO	ARGENTINA	MASERATI MERCEDES-BENZ	42
2	JOSE-FROILAN GONZALEZ	ARGENTINA	FERRARI	25.14
3	MIKE HAWTHORN	GREAT BRITAIN	FERRARI	24.64
4	MAURICE TRINTIGNANT	FRANCE	FERRARI	17
5	KARL KLING	GERMANY	MERCEDEZ-BENZ	12
6	BILL VUKOVICH	USA	KURTIS OFFENHAUSER	8
	HANS HERRMANN	GERMANY	MERCEDES-BENZ	8
8	JIMMY BRYAN	USA	KUZMA OFFENHAUSER	6
	GIUSEPPE FARINA	ITALY	FERRARI	6
	LUIGI MUSSO	ITALY	MASERATI	6
	ROBERTO MIERES	ARGENTINA	MASERATI	6

Team Mercedes and Fangio

TOP LEFT: It was all change in 1954 as Mercedes returned with the streamlined W196 showing off its revolutionary looks as well as exceptional performance. It is in stark contrasts with the British-built Connaught just behind.

MIDDLE LEFT: Argentinean Gonzales takes the chequered flag at Silverstone. At one stage Fangio had passed Hawthorn for second place, but after frequent collisions with the oil drums lining the track he dropped back and finished in fourth place.

BELOW: Ferrari take first and second place at the British Grand Prix as Gonzalez beat his team-mate Hawthorn. This was only the second, and last, Grand Prix victory for Gonzales. He had been the driver to break the Alfa stranglehold with his Ferrari in the 1951 British Grand Prix three years earlier.

BELOW LEFT: Fine-tuning before the race as mechanics carry out their final checks.

OPPOSITE: Fangio 's long-time partner Donna Andreina usually attended his races.

Collins, Hawthorn and Vanwall

OPPOSITE BELOW: Peter Collins driving a Ferrari in the rain. He joined Ferrari's team after spells with Vanwall, Maserati and a very brief outing with BRM.

OPPOSITE ABOVE: Mike Hawthorn sits in the new British hope, the Vanwall Special at Aintree. Peter Collins was driving the 'Thinwall Special' at the meeting organised by the Aintree Automobile Racing Company and the British Automobile Club.

TOP LEFT: Fangio chats with Peter Collins. Collins participated in a total of 35 World Championship Grands Prix, winning three races, achieving nine podiums and scoring 47 championship points,

MIDDLE FAR LEFT: Hawthorn was known as 'Le Papillon' on the Continent because of his flamboyant dress style. He usually sported a bow-tie as his outward trademark and had a reputation for extrovert good humour and bonhomie.

MIDDLE LEFT: Mike Hawthorn and Tony Vandervell, look over the new Vanwall. Vandervell, also known as the 'Old man', was one of the original backers of BRM. Hawthorn's stay at the Vanwall camp was short-lived as he fell out with Vandervell after only three races and returned to Ferrari for the end of the season.

BOTTOM: Mike Hawthorn sits in the Vanwall Special at an international motor racing meeting at Aintree. Driver Peter Collins offers advice as he had been actively involved during the car's development.

Moss changes tack

OPPOSITE LEFT: Moss clutches the Daily Telegraph Trophy following his win at Aintree. After this success he was rewarded with a place in the Mercedes team alongside Fangio in 1955.

OPPOSITE ABOVE RIGHT: Stirling Moss was at home on any motor vehicle, but he was finally able to demonstrate his skills and talent on four wheels when he gave up on British cars and drove a Maserati 250F to achieve his first podium place in the 1954 Belgian Grand Prix.

OPPOSITE BELOW RIGHT: Fangio is seen with his long-time partner Donna Andreina, who could be seen in the pits during the maestro's European races.

LEFT: Hawthorn drove brilliantly throughout the season and his win at the Spanish Grand Prix contributed to his third place in the 1954 championship. However, the year was not a happy one on a personal level; his father was killed in a road accident and he was hospitalised following a mid-season accident which had left him badly burned. He had also been unfairly accused of trying to avoid National Service, although he had in fact been rejected because of a chronic kidney complaint.

BELOW: Crowds overlook the pit-lane during practice for the British Grand Prix. The Mercedes W196 was the focus of much attention, although it was Jose Froilan Gonzalez who won the race in his Ferrari.

Hawthorn's nightmare

RIGHT: Hawthorn was severely burned when his car crashed during a race in Syracuse, Italy. Still heavily bandaged, he hoped to be out of hospital in time to compete in the Rome Grand Prix in May.

MIDDLE RIGHT: Hawthorn is helped from his Ferrari as he was overcome by heat and fumes in the Belgian Grand Prix at the Francorchamp circuit. Despite his difficulties he was able to keep control of his Ferrari until he reached the pits.

BELOW: Hospital director G F Randegger examines Hawthorn's heavily bandaged legs as he lay in hospital following the horrific crash in Sicily on 11 April.

OPPOSITE ABOVE: Peter Collins looks on with founder of the Vanwall Formula One racing team, Tony Vandervell, as mechanics check the fuel level.

OPPOSITE BELOW: Wearing dark glasses Britain's Mike Hawthorn prepares to take his Ferrari on a practice spin before the Belgian Grand Prix on 20 June, 1954. Fellow Ferrari drivers Farina (adjusting his helmet) and Frenchman Trintignant look on.

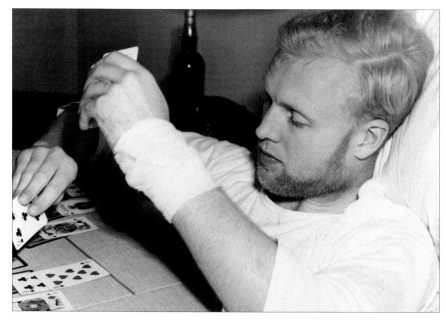

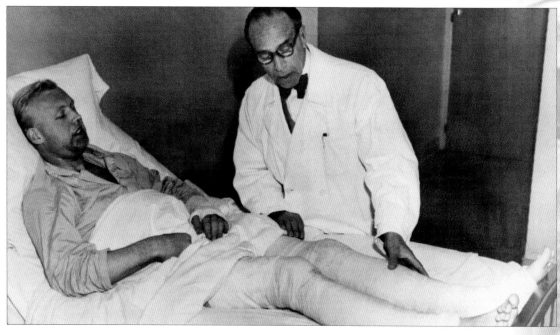

Tragedy forces change

Mercedes were the now the team to beat, and the 1955 season started with more shifting allegiances. It was Stirling Moss's turn to join the German outfit supporting Fangio. There were now eleven Grands Prix, with the addition of the Monaco race, but tragedy at Le Mans led to the cancellation of the scheduled final four. The whole of the season was dogged with disaster and would lead to significant changes in the championship fraternity.

Point allocation nightmare

The opening race in Argentina was a nightmare for both the drivers and the race organisers. Intense heat led to the exhausted withdrawl of almost all the drivers. Only Fangio and Roberto Mieres completed the race without handing over to other drivers. Fangio won, and Mieres was fifth in his Maserati, but allocating the points beyond those two was a mathematical headache with the incessant swapping of cars and drivers. Fangio's point allocation was clear: he had won and set the fastest lap.

Death of Ascari

At Monaco, Ascari's luck ran out yet again. He had led for most of the race until he missed a chicane and plunged straight into the harbour. Despite the spectacular nature of the accident, the Italian emerged apparently unscathed. However, on a practice run at Monza, just a few days later, an unaccountable error led to a fatal crash, causing some speculation that he had sustained undetected injuries. Alberto Ascari had died at the age of 36. Following his death, Lancia withdrew from racing: Ascari had been testing one of their sports cars at Monza.

The Belgian Grand Prix was a one-two for Mercedes, with Fangio leading his 'eternal shadow' Stirling Moss to the chequered flag. Despite this, Moss was now Britain's number one driver, eclipsing Mike Hawthorn. Hawthorn had parted with Ferrari for the 1955 season, joining Vanwall, but a stormy relationship with boss Tony Vandervell saw him return to Ferrari for the remainder of the season.

Disaster at Le Mans

The next scheduled Grand Prix was at Zandvoort, but before this took place the 24-Hour competition at Le Mans attracted a number of top drivers. The accident that occurred here had a significant effect on the World Championship. When Levegh's Mercedes smashed into Macklin's Austin Healey, it somersaulted over the barrier and into the packed crowd. Eighty-three people, including Levegh himself, were killed. As a result, the Grands Prix of France, Germany, Spain and Switzerland were cancelled, and only the Dutch, British and Italian rounds were left to run. It also signalled the end of racing for Mercedes, who decided to withdraw at the end of the season, in

part to concentrate on their road car production, but no doubt influenced by the role their vehicle had played in the disaster.

Mercedes did take the final three wins before their departure. Fangio and Moss yet again took the first two places at Zandvoort and at Aintree's introduction to Formula One they occupied the top tier. However, Moss was victor on home soil, with Fangio at second. The poetry of the placing led some to question whether Fangio had allowed Moss to win, but there was no doubt that Moss had performed with excellence.

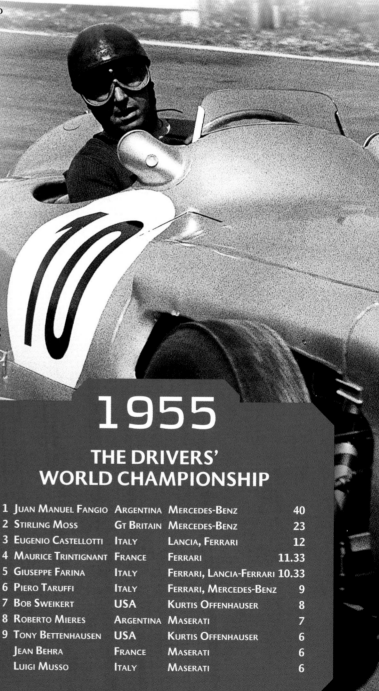

1955

THE DRIVERS' WORLD CHAMPIONSHIP

1	Juan Manuel Fangio	Argentina	Mercedes-Benz	40
2	Stirling Moss	Gt Britain	Mercedes-Benz	23
3	Eugenio Castellotti	Italy	Lancia, Ferrari	12
4	Maurice Trintignant	France	Ferrari	11.33
5	Giuseppe Farina	Italy	Ferrari, Lancia-Ferrari	10.33
6	Piero Taruffi	Italy	Ferrari, Mercedes-Benz	9
7	Bob Sweikert	USA	Kurtis Offenhauser	8
8	Roberto Mieres	Argentina	Maserati	7
9	Tony Bettenhausen	USA	Kurtis Offenhauser	6
	Jean Behra	France	Maserati	6
	Luigi Musso	Italy	Maserati	6

Mercedes dominates

At Monza, Moss failed to finish but did set the fastest lap of more than 134mph. Taruffi was left to follow Fangio home in yet another one-two for Mercedes. The Italian driver, Castellotti, finished less than a minute behind Taruffi in third place, which was also his placing in the final championship table. Castellotti took just 12 points, emphasizing the dominance of Mercedes and its two premier drivers. Moss had finished on 25, but Fangio reached 40 points for the second successive season, and with it his third world title.

With the loss of Ascari, it seemed that Fangio was unbeatable. Yet both Fangio and Moss were now without Mercedes, and with both needing new cars, competition between the two would hot up. The Briton looked for a car that would help him depose the undisputed champion.

First taste of Grand Prix success

Opposite: Fangio at The British Grand Prix held at Aintree for the first time. Stirling Moss had his first Formula One win with Fangio finishing second. It has been debated whether the Argentinean yielded the lead at the last corner to allow his young team-mate to win in front of his home crowd – an allegation always firmly denied by Fangio.

Left: The dapper Hawthorn sits in the Vanwall before the International Trophy Race. Unfortunately, the patriotic car failed to finish.

Below: Mike Hawthorn maintains his competitive streak as he enjoys a ride on the dodgems at Battersea Funfair.

Bottom: Moss finished a distant second to Fangio the 1955 championship. He achieved three podium wins in the season compared with Fangio's five – which included four first places.

El Maestro takes his third world title

OPPOSITE ABOVE: His four wins assured the incomparable Fangio of his second successive world title, and his third crown in five years.

OPPOSITE MIDDLE: The tragedy at Le Mans which cost 83 lives was the most catastrophic accident in motor racing history and deeply affected many of the drivers. Mike Hawthorn, seen here during practice for the British Grand Prix at Aintree, was one of those racing on that fateful day on 11 June and had to be persuaded to continue to drive.

OPPOSITE BELOW: Moss was an intensely patriotic driver who proudly displays the Union Jack on the bodywork of his Silver Arrow. As Mercedes decided to withdraw from competitive racing Moss was eager to find a competitive British car.

LEFT: Peter Collins from Kidderminster, England, started his Formula One career with the British HWM team.

BELOW: Hawthorn joined the Vanwall team for a brief', unproductive spell; but his views conflicted with Vanderwell who remained hopeful that his car would be able to compete with the German and Italian teams.

BOTTOM: Peter Collins drove for both Vanwall and Maserati after he left HWM, He is pictured here driving a privately owned Maserati.

Marvellous Maserati

BELOW LEFT: Stirling Moss driving his Maserati

LEFT: Victory drink from the trophy for the garlanded winner. Mike Hawthorn takes a well earned drink after winning the non-championship International Trophy Race at Crystal Palace on 30 July.

OPPOSITE: Mike Hawthorn drove Stirling Moss's Maserati in the International Trophy Race as Moss arrived too late to practice. Hawthorn beat Harry Schell in a Vanwall and set a new lap record of 78.93 mph.

Collins saves Fangio

The former team mates Fangio and Moss went their separate ways. Fangio finally joined Ferrari, who were actually fielding modified Lancias this season. Although in some respects this was a good move for Fangio, he was unhappy with his treatment at the Maranello outfit, and 1956 was to be his only year with the Scuderia. Moss chose Maserati, despite his patriotic allegiances. He had tried out the three British contenders, Connaught, BRM and Vanwall, but none was really up to the mark. Moss was keen to beat Fangio, and his best chances were with the Italians.

With the battle lines clearly drawn between the rival Italian camps, the season promised to be full of drama, both on and off the circuit. Alongside Fangio, Ferrari had Luigi Musso, Eugenio Castellotti and the young Englishman Peter Collins. Jean Behra and Cesare Perdisa provided strong support to Moss at Maserati.

Fangio sets the pace

Argentina was yet again the host for the opening round, and the win went to Fangio. He beat Behra into second place. Moss had started well, but when his engine gave out his race was all but over. Although Fangio too had faced engine trouble, he was in a far better position to overcome the problem, always taking a car from a team mate and going on to reap points.

Fangio in desperate battle

Such was the case at Monaco, where Moss gained his second Grand Prix win with a textbook race, and Fangio took over Collins's car to take second. Fangio had spun his Lancia-Ferrari and then, in desperation, repeatedly hit barriers and kerbs, battering his car in the process before swapping again. Behra brought his Maserati home third, while the unfortunate Castellotti drew the short straw by having to take over Fangio's battered machine. He finished fourth.

Collins sees success

The 1956 season proved to be a turning point for another British driver, Peter Collins. Collins had been racing at Formula One since 1952, replacing Moss at HWM, then moving to Vanwall. With Ferrari, Collins was finally able to join the pack, and he won at both Belgium and France. He had benefited from technical difficulties experienced by Fangio and Moss at Spa, while at Rheims a lengthy pit stop for Fangio gave Collins the edge. Collins was now leading the title race on 19 points, but everything would change after the British Grand Prix at Silverstone. Both Hawthorn and Tony Brooks made a dramatic impact early in the race, leading for the first ten laps, but both then had problems. When the Maserati driven by Moss succumbed to axle trouble, Fangio came through to snatch victory and Collins grabbed second.

Championship wide open

Although Colllins still led on points, the championship was now wide open; at only one point short, Fangio was breathing down his neck as they entered the German Grand Prix. The Argentinian's victory there was convincing and Moss had returned to his usual second position. But Collins was out of the points and out of luck. He had been lying second when his fuel tank fractured, and he was now eight points adrift of his Argentinian team mate going into the final round at Monza.

Collins helps Fangio

Collins still had a chance of taking the title, needing a win in Italy to overhaul Fangio, and things seemed to be going the right way when Fangio was forced out with steering problems. Yet Collins, despite being in a strong second position, pulled over and handed his car to the reigning champion. It was a magnanimous gesture. Fangio took the car and came in behind Moss, to share second position with Collins. It was enough to secure Fangio the title again, but he always acknowledged the debt he owed to Peter Collins for the honour. Collins reputedly said that he had made the gesture because he would have plenty of other opportunities to take the title. Sadly, that was not to be the case.

1956

THE DRIVERS' WORLD CHAMPIONSHIP

1	Juan Manuel Fangio	Argentina	Lancia-Ferrari	30
2	Stirling Moss	Gt Britain	Maserati	27
3	Peter Collins	Gt Britain	Ferrari, Lancia-Ferrari	25
4	Jean Behra	France	Maserati	22
5	Pat Flaherty	USA	Watson Offenhauser	8
6	Eugenio Castellotti	Italy	Lancia-Ferrari	7.5
7	Sam Hanks	USA	Kurtis Offenhauser	6
	Paul Frere	Belgium	Lancia-Ferrari	6
	Francesco Godia	Spain	Maserati	6
10	Jack Fairman	Gt Britain	Connaught -Alta	5

Struggle for the title

BELOW: A smiling Moss looks on as the windscreen of his D-type Jaguar is cleaned. He finished a close runner-up to Fangio in the Drivers' World Championship.

ABOVE: Fangio (right) chats with Spanish racing driver and aristocrat Alfonso de Portago.

ABOVE LEFT: Mike Hawthorn looks forlorn after his BRM car faded in the Daily Express Trophy race at Silverstone in May. Hawthorn had led for the first 14 laps but the race was won by Stirling Moss.

OPPOSITE: Stirling Moss discusses strategy with Maserati team-mate, Frenchman Jean Behra.

A remarkable gesture from Peter Collins

BELOW: Peter Collins at Stow corner during the RAC British Grand Prix at Silverstone on 14 July. The 303 mile race was won by Fangio; Collins shared the drive with Alfonso de Portago and their second place earned them three points each. The final race of the season, the Italian Grand Prix in Monza, saw one of the most selfless and generous actions in sporting history. Collins was on the verge of becoming Britain's first Formula One World Champion when he relinquished his car to Juan Fangio after the team leader suffered steering problems. Fangio finished second, thus sharing his points with Collins. This was enough to hand the Drivers' title to Fangio and demoted Collins to third place. Collins reputedly believed that he would have many other opportunities to take the title – but this was sadly never to be.

RIGHT: Moss enjoys a cigarette in the cockpit. He won the final race of the season at Monza and finished in second place in the World Championship.

OPPOSITE BELOW: Australian Jack Brabham was mechanically inclined from an early age and learnt to drive his father's truck when he was 12 years old. He made his debut in a Cooper, but had to retire with engine problems. He later drove an old Maserati 250F with little more success.

OPPOSITE ABOVE: John Surtees was equally at home on two or four wheels. Mrs Geoff Duke, wife of the British multi-time World Motorcycle Champion, presents him with his latest motorcycling trophy after winning at Oulton Park, May 1955. Surtees won seven world titles on two wheels before he expanded his motorsport horizons.

Fangio celebrates fifth title

The eighth season of Formula One racing was to be a disaster for Ferrari, with no wins for the Scuderia to celebrate. In contrast, British manufacturing appeared to be on the ascendant, with Vanwall finally providing a creditable challenger, the VW8 designed by Colin Chapman. As ever, the drivers were the crucial element for success – or failure. Whereas Vanwall were finally able to secure Moss and Brooks, Ferrari lost Fangio, who left for Maserati. Although the title would go to Fangio for the fifth time, British racing could consider the year a key success: they won three of the eight Grands Prix.

Difficult times for Ferrari

The first victory was another home turf celebration for Fangio. He crossed the line ahead of Behra following a fierce battle between himself, Behra, Collins and Castellotti. Another Argentinian, Carlos 'Charley' Menditeguy, finished third. Maserati collected all four top positions; the Ferraris had suffered badly with technical problems, but ultimately they seemed unable to compete with Maserati's new 250F cars. Even the fastest lap eluded Ferrari, going instead to Moss who was driving a borrowed Maserati.

Ferrari lost two of their key drivers just weeks later: firstly Castellotti, who was killed while testing a car at Modena, then the popular Alfonso de Portago, who was killed while competing in the Mille Miglia.

Jack Brabham impresses at Monaco

A multiple pile-up at Monaco took out a number of drivers in the next event, but it couldn't stop Fangio's winning streak. Typically, he carefully avoided the melee and finished just ahead of a battered Brooks. In sixth place was Jack Brabham, who had pushed his 2-litre Cooper-Climax to the line despite a failed fuel pump, his pluck and determination earning him particular praise.

British Vanwall finally wins race

Fangio took the win at Rouen in July, but Ferrari secured second, third and fourth position courtesy of Musso, Collins and Hawthorn. Moss missed the race through illness but he was raring to go for the British Grand Prix, held at Aintree later that month. When his Vanwall began to suffer, he swapped with Tony Brooks, shifting from first position to sixth place, but despite this he carved his way to the lead and stole a magnificent victory. It was the first significant win by a British car since 1923. Although the Vanwalls were to be hampered by suspension problems in the following race, their star was destined to rise further in the final two rounds.

Fangio breaks then rebreaks lap record

At the German Grand Prix Fangio took his final and arguably best win in a Grand Prix race. With only ten laps to go he overcame a gap of 45 seconds behind Hawthorn and Collins, in each lap breaking then re-breaking the record until he passed both drivers. It is still considered to be the finest drive in the sport's history. Fangio crossed the line 3.6 seconds ahead of the Farnham Flyer with customary style and panache.

Moss finishes second – again

The Pescara circuit was added in order to compensate for the loss of the Belgian and Dutch venues, but Ferrari withdrew from the race, leaving Musso, Hawthorn and Collins without drives. Musso managed to borrow a Ferrari and led during the early stages but was eventually overtaken by Moss and retired on the tenth lap, ending his title hopes. Fangio followed Moss home, confirming his fifth world crown, a feat which would not be repeated for another 46 years. Moss won again at Monza, following an epic battle with Fangio. Despite his two consecutive victories, his final tally of 25 points ensured him second place for the third year; the title remained elusive.

For almost a decade, Formula One had been dominated by the Italian marques, yet now both Ferrari and Maserati appeared to be in decline. Ferrari were struggling and Maserati announced its withdrawal from racing. Again, hopes were high that the successor to the Italians could be British.

1957
THE DRIVERS' WORLD CHAMPIONSHIP

1	JUAN MANUEL FANGIO	ARGENTINA	MASERATI	40
2	STIRLING MOSS	GT BRITAIN	MASERATI, VANWALL	25
3	LUIGI MUSSO	ITALY	LANCIA FERRARI	16
4	MIKE HAWTHORN	GT BRITAIN	LANCIA FERRARI	13
5	TONY BROOKS	GT BRITAIN	VANWALL	11
6	HARRY SCHELL	USA	MASERATI	10
	MASTEN GREGORY	USA	MASERATI	10
8	PETER COLLINS	GT BRITAIN	LANCIA FERRARI	8
	SAM HANKS	USA	EPPERLY OFFENHAUSER	8
10	JEAN BEHRA	FRANCE	MASERATI	6

Home Success

Bottom: Vanwall team-mates Stirling Moss and Tony Brooks hold the trophy after their shared win in the British Grand Prix at Aintree on 20 July. This was the first occasion that a British-built car won a World Championship race, a feat achieved with two British drivers at their home Grand Prix.

Left: Hawthorn chats to model Jean Howarth, the daughter of a wealthy textile owner. They were engaged to be married in April 1959, but sadly this would never happen.

Far left: Mike Hawthorn joined Ferrari again after an unproductive time with BRM.

Left: Fangio and Hawthorn in animated conversation before practice for the upcoming British Grand Prix.

Opposite: When Mike Hawthorn returned to Ferrari in 1957 he found a kindred spirit in fun-loving team-mate Peter Collins.

Fangio and his magnificent Maserati

OPPOSITE BELOW: In 1957 Fangio returned to the Maserati fold for his final full World Championship season. He was to celebrate his 46th birthday during this time, but was still regarded as a dominant force. Four wins in the mighty Maserati 250F ensured he stormed to his fifth world crown.

OPPOSITE ABOVE: John Surtees was at home at the Isle of Man TT. The motorcycle ace won 6 TT races and was the first man to win the Senior TT three years in succession.

RIGHT: Ferrari's Mike Hawthorn chats to Vanwall's number two driver Tony Brooks.

Problems for the 'Prancing Horse'

OPPOSITE: Mike Hawthorn is pushed out in his Italian Ferrari for a practice spin at Aintree before the British Grand Prix. He was to finish in third place behind Fangio (first) and his team-mate Luigi Musso.

LEFT: The ice-cool British driver Peter Collins prepares for the first race of the next season, the Argentinian Grand Prix. Collins' love of autos stemmed from an early age when he helped out in his father's garage and took the wheel for the first time when only nine years old.

BELOW: Another member of the 'Prancing Horse' team, Collins prepares for practice prior to the British Grand Prix. As Ferrari's problems with reliability continued, he had to retire from the race owing to a water leak.

Watershed season

In many respects, 1958 was an important watershed in Formula One's history. The regulations of the competition were changed, so that although the Formula One engine capacities remained the same they were to be fuelled by commercial-grade petrol instead of alcohol-based fuels. Race distances were shortened and the competition was opened up to include not only a driver championship but a constructor's title also. The season was also technically the last for Fangio; he only participated in two further top flight events – the Argentine and French Grands Prix.

Moss wins in Cooper-Climax

For Stirling Moss, the loss of Fangio was a boon. He would no longer be a mere shadow, and could seriously compete for the coveted title. He scored the victory in a Rob Walker 2-litre Cooper-Climax rather than his usual drive; Vanwall had not completed the adjustments necessary for the fuel change.

Diasappointment for Vanwall

By Monaco, the Vanwalls were ready, but all three cars failed to finish. The disappointment was ominous: technical problems dogged the team throughout the season. In contrast, the Cooper Climax was victorious yet again; this time Maurice Trintignant was the winner.

British cars sweep the board

Moss finally won at Zandvoort in a victorious Vanwall, although both Brooks and Lewis-Evans were unable to finish. Other British successes included Harry Schell and Jean Behra in BRMs at second and third and a Cooper-Climax driven by Roy Salvadori in fourth. Driving a Ferrari, Mike Hawthorn was fifth with fellow Briton Cliff Allison for Lotus in at sixth.

Vanwall took first and second with Brooks and Lewis-Evans at Spa. The race also saw the first woman driver to compete, Italy's Teresa de Filippis. Driving a Maserati, she finished in tenth position.

Musso and Collins killed

Fangio made his final appearance at Rheims, finishing fourth in a race that was won by Mike Hawthorn. However, Ferrari's delight was muted by the death of Luigi Musso, who crashed at Muizon while challenging Hawthorn for the lead. The British Grand Prix saw Moss finish in a cloud of smoke yet again, this time after just 24 laps. Hawthorn took the upper hand in the championship by finishing second to team-mate Peter Collins. The story seemed all too familiar at Nürburgring a fortnight later, when magneto trouble put Moss out after just four laps. The Ferraris of Collins and Hawthorn again looked likely to prevail, but Brooks passed both of them. Then tragedy struck as Collins, in a heated duel with Brooks spun off the track and was killed. Hawthorn devastated by the loss of a team mate and close friend, retired from the race and, soon after, from the sport.

McLaren makes debut

Nürburgring was also host to a parallel Formula Two class event, and making his debut that same day was a new name to the sport, New Zealander Bruce McLaren driving his Cooper into fifth place.

Oporto saw Moss win for a third time, yet, despite this, Hawthorn was still challenging him on points. His second place kept him well in contention for the title. When Moss fell out at Monza thanks to a failed gearbox, Hawthorn's second place earned him enough points from his six best finishes. Moss, having only finished five times, was now eight points adrift of his rival.

Hawthorn wins title

The final round was another new venue, the Ain Diab circuit in Casablanca. Moss had to both win and set the fastest lap to have any chance of taking the championship. Unfortunately he also needed Hawthorn to finish no better than third. Although Moss managed the win, Hawthorn's team mate Phil Hill pulled back from second position to allow the Papillion through. Despite winning only once during the series, on points alone Hawthorn was the victor. Moss, who had won four races, lost out by just one point.

Death of Mike Hawthorn

Tragedy was to strike the sport once more before the start of the next season. Mike Hawthorn had decided to retire – not jubilant with his success, but instead mourning the loss of Peter Collins. At the age of just 29 he was killed behind the wheel of his Jaguar, in a collision with a lorry.

1958

THE DRIVERS' WORLD CHAMPIONSHIP

1	MIKE HAWTHORN	GT BRITAIN	FERRARI DINO	42
2	STIRLING MOSS	GT BRITAIN	COOPER, VANWALL	41
3	TONY BROOKS	GT BRITAIN	VANWALL	24
4	ROY SALVADORI	GT BRITAIN	COOPER	15
5	PETER COLLINS	GT BRITAIN	FERRARI DINO	14
	HARRY SCHELL	USA	MASERATI	14
7	LUIGI MUSSO	ITALY	FERRARI DINO	12
	MAURICE TRINTIGNANT	FRANCE	COOPER, MASERATI	12
9	STUART LEWIS-EVANS	GT BRITAIN	VANWALL	11
10	PHIL HILL	USA	MASERATI, FERRARI	9
	TAFFI VON TRIPS	GERMANY	FERRARI, PORSCHE	9
	JEAN BEHRA	FRANCE	MASERATI	9

Moss loses out by one point

BELOW: Stirling Moss won the first championship race of the season in Buenos Aries, his seventh Grand Prix victory and his first of four wins in the 1958 season. However, it was still not enough to take the Championship title as Mike Hawthorn beat him into second place by one point.

ABOVE LEFT: A pensive Peter Collins sitting in his Ferrari. Collins achieved his third and final victory at the British Grand Prix at Silverstone in the new Ferrari Dino.

BOTTOM LEFT: Mike Hawthorn is surrounded by spectators after finishing in second place behind team-mate and compatriot Peter Collins, putting him at the top of the World Championship table.

LEFT: Graham Hill initially joined the Lotus Team as a mechanic but eventually managed to persuade founder and chief designer, Colin Chapman, to let him have a place as a driver on the team.

OPPOSITE: Hawthorn and British racing driver Bruce Halford have a confab before a race at Brands Hatch, December 1958.

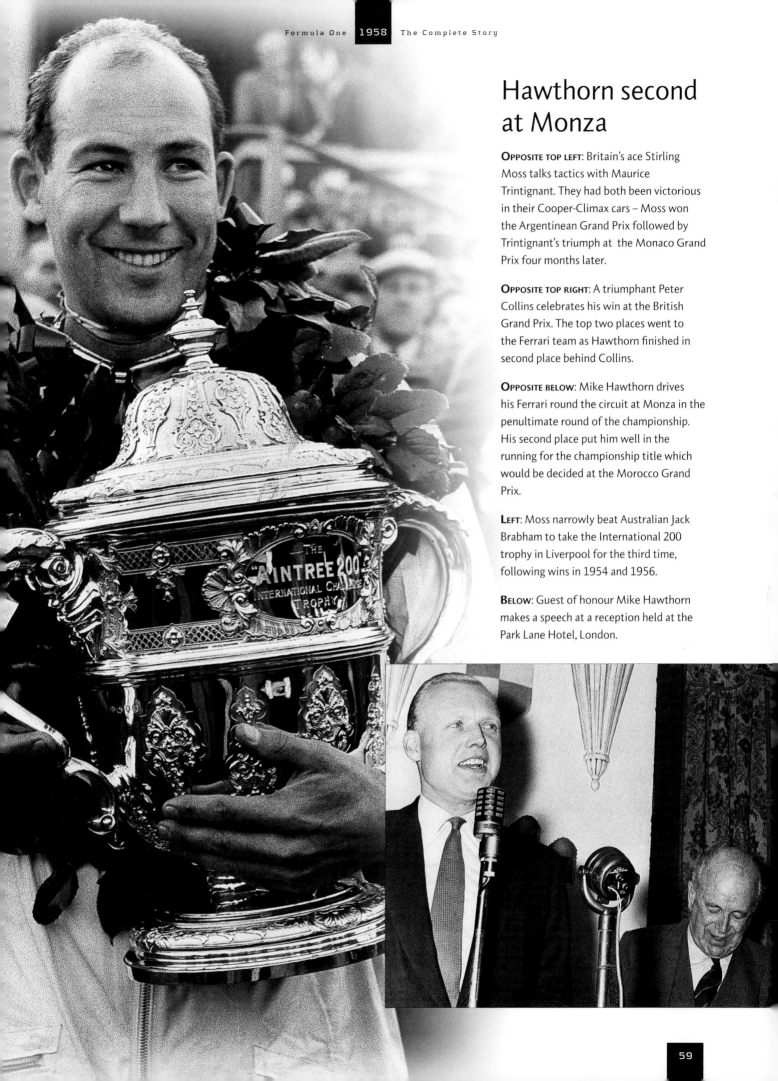

Hawthorn second at Monza

OPPOSITE TOP LEFT: Britain's ace Stirling Moss talks tactics with Maurice Trintignant. They had both been victorious in their Cooper-Climax cars – Moss won the Argentinean Grand Prix followed by Trintignant's triumph at the Monaco Grand Prix four months later.

OPPOSITE TOP RIGHT: A triumphant Peter Collins celebrates his win at the British Grand Prix. The top two places went to the Ferrari team as Hawthorn finished in second place behind Collins.

OPPOSITE BELOW: Mike Hawthorn drives his Ferrari round the circuit at Monza in the penultimate round of the championship. His second place put him well in the running for the championship title which would be decided at the Morocco Grand Prix.

LEFT: Moss narrowly beat Australian Jack Brabham to take the International 200 trophy in Liverpool for the third time, following wins in 1954 and 1956.

BELOW: Guest of honour Mike Hawthorn makes a speech at a reception held at the Park Lane Hotel, London.

Peter Collins wins British Grand Prix

Above: Jack Brabham's best finish in 1958 was at the Monaco Grand Prix when he achieved fourth place in his Cooper-Climax.

Right: Brabham tunes his Cooper- Climax engine. 1958 was the Cooper's first full season in Formula One, and although it wasn't a particularly successful year for the Aussie, the rear-engined Cooper was soon to make its mark.

Opposite above left: Peter Collins celebrates victory in his Ferrari (opposite below) at the British Grand prix.

Opposite above right: Moss scorches round the course at Goodwood where he was triumphant in an Aston-Martin; however, in the 1958 championship series he once again drove all but one of the races for Vanwall.

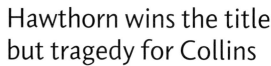

Hawthorn wins the title but tragedy for Collins

OPPOSITE: Stirling Moss and Mike Hawthorn lark about in a mock quarrel over the World Championship as they prepare for the British Grand Prix. They both lead the field with 23 points well ahead of their nearest rival Harry Schell with 11 points.

ABOVE: Hawthorn moved closer to his first World Championship title after finishing as runner up to his friend and team-mate Peter Collins at the Silverstone circuit in July. This put Hawthorn seven points ahead of rival Stirling Moss who was forced to retire his Vanwall with engine problems. A fortnight later disaster struck when Collins lost control of his car and spun off the track at the Nürburgring. He was thrown clear of his Ferrari but died from the resulting injuries.

LEFT: Mike Hawthorn leaves St Mary's Church near Kidderminster, Worcestershire after attending a private funeral service for his close friend Peter Collins who had been killed at the German Grand Prix. He walks beside Collins' uncle David Jones.

New blood

Vanwell had enjoyed significant success in 1958, yet its drivers were staggered to learn that Tony Vandervell had decided to withdraw from racing for the next season. Tony Brooks headed to Ferrari, but Moss, still itching to win a championship, decided to hedge his bets between two teams: BRM with their front-mounted engines and Cooper-Climax. BRM would record their first championship win, but not with Stirling Moss behind the wheel. The decade was to end with a host of new talent joining the field and more frustration for Moss.

Brabham's Cooper wins at Monaco

The cancellation of the Argentinian Grand Prix meant that Monaco hosted the first race of the season. Although Moss got away well, he was soon forced to retire and Cooper-Climax scored a victory with Australian Jack Brabham. Cooper also took third position, sandwiching Brooks in the Ferrari at second place. The rear-engined Cooper was a much better car than the one in which Moss had won the Argentine Grand Prix the year before, and Brabham had been the team's top driver since its move to Formula One in 1957. Their victory had been anticipated by many.

BRM enjoyed their first success at Zandvoort, thanks to the skill of Swede Joakim Bonnier. It was to be his only championship win, but he had mastered the somewhat unreliable BRM to beat off the challenge of Cooper's Brabham, Moss and Gregory.

Ferrari had to be content with Jean Behra's fifth place, but to recompense, Tony Brooks and Phil Hill made it a one-two for the Scuderia at Rheims, with Brabham having to settle for third.

Cooper reap points at Aintree

Ferrari were absent from the British Grand Prix at Aintree, and so it was a home win for Cooper again, with Brabham beating Moss in the BRM to second place. In third position was Bruce McLaren, now racing in Formula One for Cooper. The German Grand Prix, held this year at Avus in Berlin, saw another driver's life lost: this time Jean Behra was killed during a pre-championship event. Tony Brooks for Ferrari won the main event which was split into two 30-lap heats. New Ferrari driver Dan Gurney came second, with Phil Hill making it a clean sweep for the team in third.

Moss victorious

In Portugal, Moss was the out-and-out winner, finishing a lap ahead of team mate Marsten Gregory in second. He had now abandoned the BRMs, deciding to remain with Cooper, and at Monza his success continued. Whereas the more powerful Ferraris were at the mercy of their rapidly worn tyres, Moss drove smoothly enough to be able to take advantage of their need to stop: he won again. In third position was Brabham, still

collecting vital points, and once again, Moss found himself battling to gather enough points for victory. With just one round to go, the competition was wide open, with Moss, Brabham, and Brooks all in contention.

Moss loses out on championship title

The decider was in December, at the Sebring airfield track in Florida. It was the first championship race held in the United States with the exception of the Indianapolis 500. The contenders had three months to plan and prepare. For Moss, the showdown was anti-climactic; transmission failure put him out of the race after just six laps. Brabham took over in front and held it to the last lap, until he ran out of fuel and his car ground to a halt 500 yards from the line. He pushed his Cooper to the finish, earning fourth place. McLaren and Trintignant, both with Cooper, crossed the line first and second, but it was Brooks's placing that was critical. Third place and four points was enough for him to snatch second from Moss, but not enough to keep Jack Brabham from taking his first, deserved, world crown.

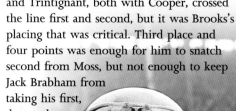

1959

THE DRIVERS' WORLD CHAMPIONSHIP

1	JACK BRABHAM	AUSTRALIA	COOPER	31
2	TONY BROOKS	GT BRITAIN	FERRARI DINO, VANWALL	27
3	STIRLING MOSS	GT BRITAIN	COOPER, BRM	25.5
4	PHIL HILL	USA	FERRARI DINO	20
5	MAURICE TRINTIGNANT	FRANCE	COOPER	19
6	BRUCE MCLAREN	NEW ZEALAND	COOPER	16.5
7	DAN GURNEY	USA	FERRARI DINO	13
8	JO BONNIER	SWEDEN	BRM	10
	MASTEN GREGORY	USA	COOPER	10
10	RODGER WARD	USA	WATSON OFFENHAUSER	8

Cooper battles it out with Ferrari

Opposite: Stirling Moss with Maria Teresa Filippis, the first female Formula 1 driver in the sport's history. Although she participated in five Grand Prix races, she was unable to score any points.

Top left: Going into the last round at Sebring in Florida Jack Brabham, Stirling Moss and Tony Brooks were all in with a chance of taking the World Championship. Brabham ran out of fuel 500 yards from the line and had to push his car home in fourth place – enough to win the crown as Moss had retired and Brooks' third place was not enough to secure the title.

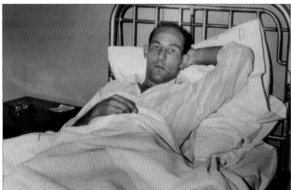

Centre left: Stirling Moss lies in a hospital bed in Newport Cottage Hospital with cut legs and bruises. He and his wife were injured when the Austin 7 Moss was driving collided with a van at Chetwynd near Newport.

Below left: The coffin containing the body of Mike Hawthorn is carried into Farnham Cemetery in Surrey after his funeral at Farnham parish Church. Hawthorn had been killed in a road accident after crashing his Mark One Jaguar on the A3 Guildford bypass in January.

Bottom right: After both Luigi Musso and Peter Collins were killed in 1958, Phil Hill had been promoted to Ferrari's Formula 1 team. Working with team mate Tony Brooks the pair provided the driving force behind the Maranello cars.

Bottom left: Huge disappointment for Stirling Moss as he prepared for the decisive last round of the championship at Sebring. He led the race from the beginning but his title hopes were dashed after only five laps when he was forced to retire with a broken gearbox.

Brabham's first title

RIGHT: Australian Jack Brabham had been a flight machanic in the Royal Australian Air Force before his love of racing led him to Britain in 1955.

BELOW: Moss had to wait until the Portuguese Grand Prix in Monsanto before he scored his first win of the season. A successive win at Monza to gave him a fighting chance of winning the World title.

RIGHT: Jack Brabham led the victorious Cooper team to win the Formula One World Championship in a rear-engined vehicle – a feat which revolutionised future car designs.

OPPOSITE ABOVE: Brabham holds the winning trophy at the British Grand Prix. His team-mate Bruce McLaren finished in third place. Stirling Moss, driving a BRM, split the two Coopers to claim second place and rekindle his hopes of becoming champion.

OPPOSITE BELOW: Jack Brabham and the car which changed the shape of racing cars forever: the rear-engined Cooper-Climax.

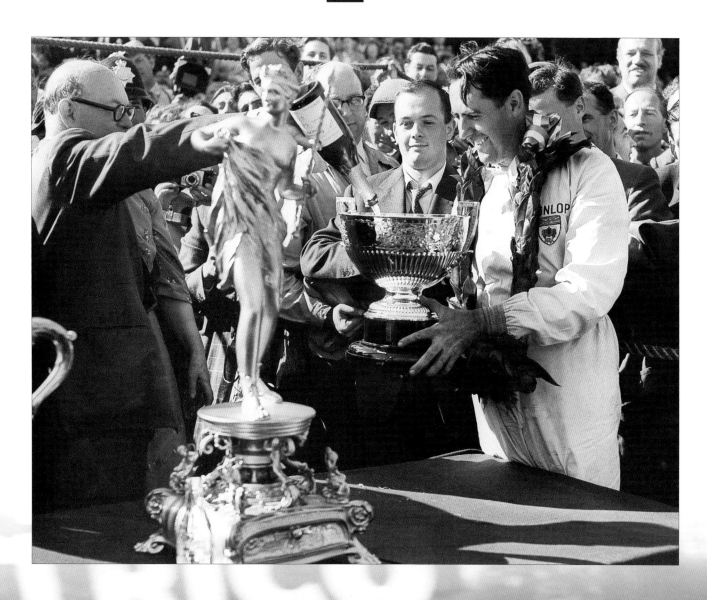

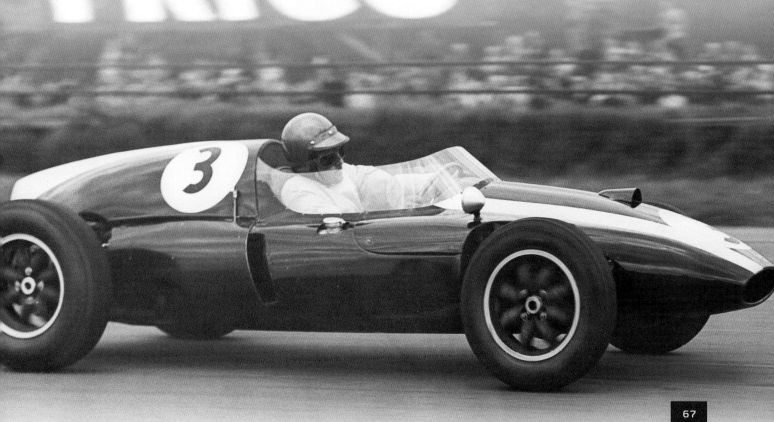

Brabham wins again

The new decade began with the Cooper cars now at the top of the heap. Their mid-engines were the work of English engineers John Cooper and Colin Chapman, who together would revolutionize the design of racing cars. The back-to-back championship wins of Cooper and Jack Brabham in 1959 and 1960 heralded British domination of Formula One for the next ten years. During the 1960 season, Climax-engined cars won every race bar one and Ferrari certainly saw the writing on the wall. Their dogged persistence with front-engined cars was about to come to an end.

McLaren wins again
At the opening race in Argentina, Brabham failed to impress, with transmission troubles forcing an early retirement. His young team mate, Bruce McLaren, was more fortunate: both of the early leaders, Moss and Bonnier, ran into mechanical trouble, giving McLaren the chance to edge to the front. He won the race, his second consecutive win, beating Cliff Allison in the Ferrari into second. Moss, in Trintignant's Cooper, finished third.

Moss performs brilliantly
At Monaco, Moss drove in the new rear-engined Lotus 18, the brainchild of Colin Chapman. Despite the wet conditions, Moss and the car performed brilliantly and won the race ahead of McLaren. Despite sustaining a puncture at Zandvoort, Moss delivered another excellent performance, pushing the car from twelfth place to fourth at the finish. Brabham, who had led all the way, took the win, the first of five in a row.

A run of terrible accidents
Although Brabham was to collect the winner's points for a further four races, Moss's fortune was quite the opposite. At Spa, during preparation for the the main event, a wheel came off his Lotus and in the ensuing crash he broke both of his legs, although he returned just weeks later to race at Oporto. It was the first of a number of terrible accidents. During the race itself, Briton Alan Stacey was hit by a bird, while countryman Chris Bristow shot off the road in his Cooper-Climax. Both men were killed. The race was won by Brabham, with McLaren second. In fifth place was Jim Clark, collecting his first championship points. He had already debuted at Zandvoort, racing against Graham Hill, who had made his own debut at Monaco two years previously.

Brabham profits from misfortune
Brabham's fourth victory was at Silverstone; however, it was Hill who took most of the plaudits. Despite stalling his BRM on the line, Hill took the lead, only to spin off with just seven laps to go. Brabham profited and gratefully accepted maximum points, while John Surtees, who was also in his debut year, took second place. Surtees had already been dominating the motorcycling Grand Prix circuit, and

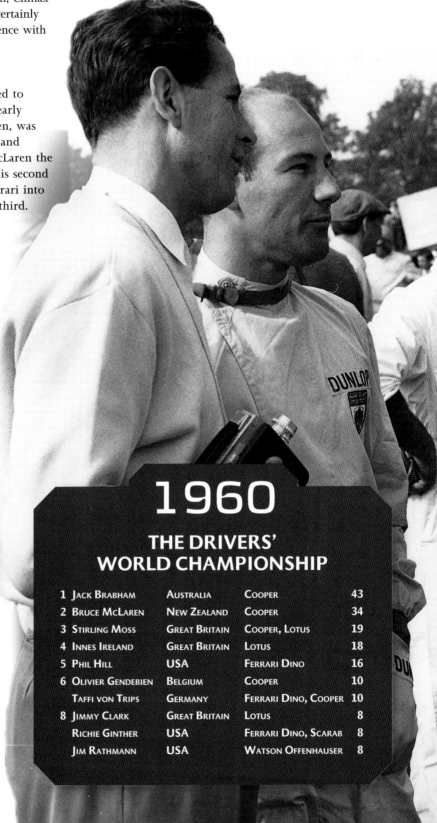

1960
THE DRIVERS' WORLD CHAMPIONSHIP

1	JACK BRABHAM	AUSTRALIA	COOPER	43
2	BRUCE MCLAREN	NEW ZEALAND	COOPER	34
3	STIRLING MOSS	GREAT BRITAIN	COOPER, LOTUS	19
4	INNES IRELAND	GREAT BRITAIN	LOTUS	18
5	PHIL HILL	USA	FERRARI DINO	16
6	OLIVIER GENDEBIEN	BELGIUM	COOPER	10
	TAFFI VON TRIPS	GERMANY	FERRARI DINO, COOPER	10
8	JIMMY CLARK	GREAT BRITAIN	LOTUS	8
	RICHIE GINTHER	USA	FERRARI DINO, SCARAB	8
	JIM RATHMANN	USA	WATSON OFFENHAUSER	8

he made the transition from two wheels to four with Chapman's Team Lotus. Silverstone was Surtees's best finish of the year, with him coming in at second on only his second race. With a pole position in Portugal, he gave an immense performance, building up a 10-second lead over Brabham, before being forced out of the race with a split radiator. Yet again, Brabham profited from the misfortune of another and his second world title was assured.

A miserable year for the Italians

The Italian Grand Prix was marred by controversy; the British teams boycotted the event, protesting over the inclusion of the dangerous banked sections of the circuit. Ferrari was left to mop up the spoils on home territory with a win for Phil Hill. It had, however, been a dismal year for the Scuderia, who didn't enter the final round at the US circuit, Riverside. That victory went to Moss, back on form, but too late to be able to take the title.

Brabham has plenty to celebrate

ABOVE: Jack Brabham works on a VW engine, but Climax-engined cars dominated the 1960 championship, winning five of the top six places.

BELOW: Jack Brabham and Innes Ireland in conversation before the British Grand Prix at Silverstone. Both had reason to celebrate afterwards: Brabham achieving his fourth successive victory and Ireland finishing third in his Lotus.

OPPOSITE: Stirling Moss's (centre) season was blighted by injury but ended with a win in the US Grand Prix at Riverside. Graham Hill (right) had a disappointing year, managing to finish in only the Dutch Grand Prix in his BRM.

Brabham scores maximum points

RIGHT TOP: Jack Brabham's five consecutive wins, Zandvoort, Spa, Reims, Silverstone and Oporto, gave him maximum points in the championship, matching Ascari's achievement of 1952.

RIGHT MIDDLE: John Surtees was second behind Jack Brabham at Silverstone, giving him his first podium finish less than two months after his Formula 1 debut. He may have been a novice in Formula 1, but Surtees had won seven world motorcycling titles.

RIGHT BOTTOM: Ex-motorcyclist John Surtees made his F1 debut for Colin Chapman's Lotus team at the Monaco Grand Prix with four races remaining in the season.

BOTTOM LEFT: American Phil Hill, driving a Ferrari, won his first Grand Prix at Monza. However, the race had been boycotted by all of the British teams who considered the banked sections of the circuit to be dangerous.

OPPOSITE ABOVE CENTRE: Moss pictured at the Aintree 200 race. He had a very successful year in Formula 2 driving a Porsche, but he chose Lotus in the championship.

OPPOSITE ABOVE LEFT: Graham Hill is joined by his daughter Brigitte and wife Betty.

OPPOSITE ABOVE RIGHT AND OPPOSITE BELOW RIGHT: Sterling Moss is pictured at Battersea Heliport, on his way to Silverstone for the British Grand Prix, less than a month after breaking his legs in the Belgian Grand Prix. At Silverstone, Moss was to be the race starter, but he was back in the driver's seat for the Portuguese Grand Prix (below). His race ended in disqualification, while Brabham was confirmed champion.

OPPOSITE BOTTOM: Moss and Surtees. In 1960 Moss finished the Championship in third place, the sixth successive year that he had finished in the first three in the Drivers' Championship.

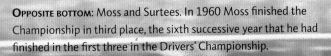

Surtees makes a spirited start

RIGHT: Despite his inexperience, Surtees finished in second place in the British Grand Prix and looked set to chalk up more points in Portugal, at the penultimate race of the season, but he was forced to retire because of a split radiator.

OPPOSITE ABOVE: Colin Chapman (right) chats to Jim Clark and John Surtees, both of whom were to win the Drivers' Championship. Jim Clark (left) was signed as a Formula 2 driver that year, but was promoted after the death of Alan Stacey.

BELOW: Wolfgang von Trips putting in a practice lap in his Ferrari before the British Grand Prix at Silverstone.

OPPOSITE BELOW LEFT: John Surtees tinkering with his Climax engine. His father owned a motorcycle shop and so Surtees was steeped in all things mechanical from an early age.

OPPOSITE BELOW RIGHT: Bruce McLaren displays the trophies received for winning the opening race of the 1960 season in Argentina. The championship finished with Brabham topping the table on 43 points. His Cooper team mate McLaren was runner-up, having acumulated 34 points.

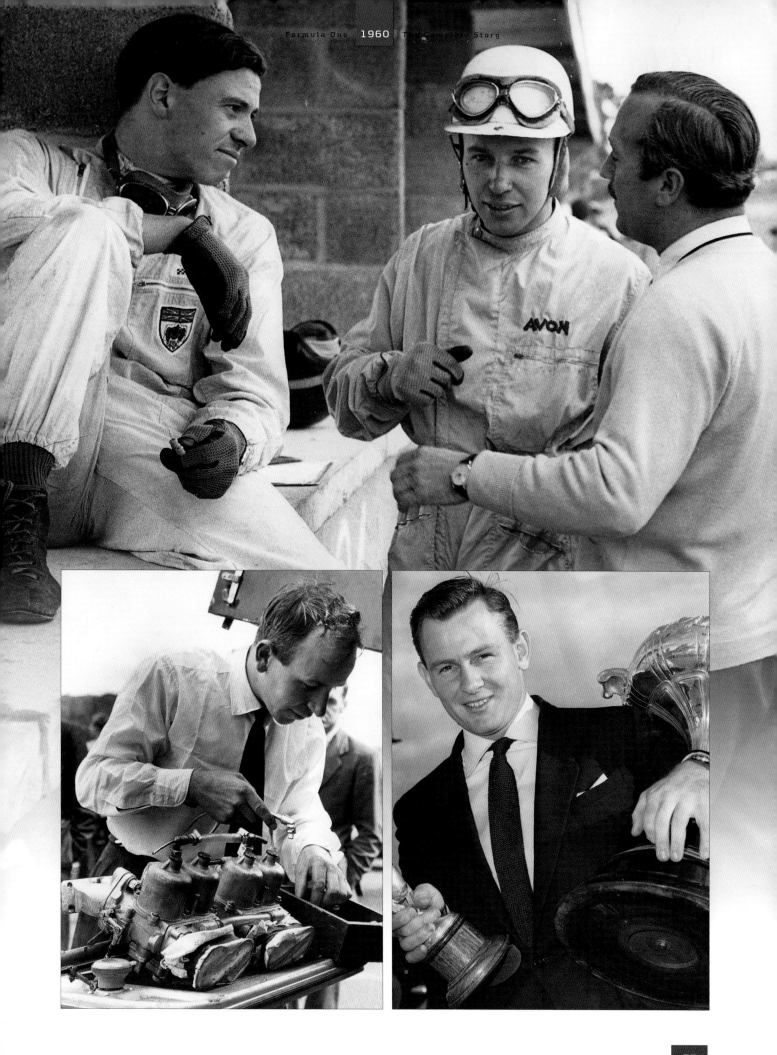

Ferrari fights back

1961 saw the introduction of 1.5-litre engines and Ferrari were able to take advantage of the changes. Well prepared, they introduced the new 'sharknose' V-6, equipped with a rear engine. The car proved to be more than a match for the British 4-cylinder units.

Moss outclasses the rest
American drivers Phil Hill and Ritchie Ginther were Ferrari's other main weapon. They were joined by the German ace Wolfgang 'Taffy' von Trips, but at the Monaco opener they were kept in second, third and fourth places by Moss. In fifth position was former Ferrari and BRM driver Dan Gurney, driving the new Porsche on its Formula One championship debut. Moss's performance was one of his finest. He was hampered by both his outdated Climax engine and his old square-shaped Lotus. Yet his handling skill on the tricky Monaco circuit ensured that he made up for the pace limitations of the Lotus, taking the flag just 3.6 seconds ahead of Ginther.

Hill versus von Trips
The rest of the season became a battle between Ferrari rivals Hill and von Trips. At Zandvoort von Trips finished just nine-tenths of a second ahead of Hill to give Germany its first Grand Prix winner for 22 years. He had led the race from the first, with Hill fighting off Jim Clark in the Lotus. Clark took third, while Moss scraped home ahead of Ginther. The race took its place in history as one of only two championship races in which every driver was to finish without incident. The other was the 2005 Italian Grand Prix.

Clean sweep for Ferrari
It was a clean sweep for Ferrari at Spa, the first four places belonging to Hill, followed by von Trips and Ginther, then Olivier Gendebien in fourth. Gendebien was a Belgian who had occasionally driven for the Scuderia during the year. That Ferrari's fourth driver was able to secure fourth place serves to illustrate their dominance at the time.

Baghetti makes history
In contrast to Zandvoort, there were retirements at Rheims. All three of Ferrari's top drivers – Hill, von Trips and Ginther – pulled up, leaving young Italian Giancarlo Baghetti the opportunity to win the race. Driving in a privately-entered Ferrari, Baghetti was making his Grand Prix debut, and in the process he made history, becoming the only man to win on his first outing. The wet British Grand Prix provided more success for the Ferrari team; this time von Trips finished ahead of Hill. At Nürburgring Moss managed to break Ferrari's run of success, using the same tactics that had worked so well at Monaco.

Championship leader killed
Heading into the penultimate event at Monza, von Trips was ahead on points, with a tally of 33 to Hill's 29. For Ferrari the title would be decided on home soil and the expectation was that the championship belonged to the German, but the race was to be marred by a terrible accident. Von Trips and Clark collided, both spinning off at Vedano Corner. Although Clark was unhurt, von Trips flew into the stand, killing 14 spectators as well as himself. Unaware of von Trips's death, Hill went on to win both the race and the title. The celebrations were short-lived and Ferrari pulled out of the final event out of respect for their lost comrade.

Brookes retires
At the United States Grand Prix at Watkins Glen, Moss and Brabham vied for the lead. However, when each driver was forced to retire, Innes Ireland took over and finished first in his Lotus. It was his first and only Grand Prix win. The race was also the last one for Tony Brooks, who retired after five years and six Grand Prix wins.

1961
THE DRIVERS' WORLD CHAMPIONSHIP

1	PHIL HILL	USA	FERRARI DINO	34
2	TAFFI VON TRIPS	GERMANY	FERRARI DINO	33
3	STIRLING MOSS	GT BRITAIN	LOTUS, FERGUSON	21
	DAN GURNEY	USA	PORSCHE	21
5	RICHIE GINTHER	USA	FERRARI DINO	16
6	INNES IRELAND	GT BRITAIN	LOTUS	12
7	JIMMY CLARK	GT BRITAIN	LOTUS	11
	BRUCE MCLAREN	NEW ZEALAND	COOPER	11
9	GIANCARLO BAGHETTI	ITALY	FERRARI DINO	9
10	TONY BROOKS	GT BRITAIN	BRM	6

Triumph and disaster for Ferrari

LEFT. American sports car ace Phil Hill, was one of four competitors driving Ferraris in 1961. Hill won the title following the death of team mate Wolfgang von Trips at Monza.

BELOW LEFT: Surtees drove Tony Vandervell's new rear-engined Vanwall for the recently introduced Inter-Continental Formula race at Silverstone. Vandervell offers Surtees some advice before the start.

BELOW RIGHT: Stirling Moss was the only driver of a British car to challenge Ferrari in 1961. In the championship Moss scored victories at Monaco and the Nürburgring, despite having to compete in the old Lotus 18. Here he is pictured during practice for the Gold Cup race at Oulton Park, which he won.

BELOW CENTRE: Graham Hill remained with BRM in 1961, joined by new team mate Tony Brooks. There was only one podium finish for BRM that season, third place for Tony Brooks at Watkins Glen.

BOTTOM: All the British teams struggled with the introduction of the new 1500cc formula. BRM worked to prepare its new V-8 car for Graham Hill. It was to make its first outing at Monza, the penultimate race of the season, but caught fire in practice. Hill was forced to end the season with the old 4-cylinder model.

OPPOSITE: Graham Hill with his wife Betty.

Brabham fails to score

LEFT: World champion in 1959 and 1960, Jack Brabham finished eleventh in 1961, scoring a total of four points after being forced to retire from six out of the eight races.

BELOW: Stirling Moss is set to start in the revolutionary 4-wheel-drive Ferguson at the Gold Cup race, Oulton Park.

OPPOSITE: Surtees finished in only three of the nine championship races in 1961 but his talent was not in doubt. Here he is pictured the wheel of the new Vanwall in the Daily Express Trophy Race, one of the new Inter-Continental Formula events. He recovered from a spin to finish in fifth place. Despite a good showing, the car never raced again.

Germany's racing ace dies at Monza

OPPOSITE BELOW: Racing idol Wolfgang von Trips was killed at Monza after a bid to clinch the world championship title. Eleven spectators were also killed and more than 25 injured following a horrific crash at 140mph. Thirty-three-year old von Trips edged into Jim Clark's path as the drivers braked for the bend in the Italian Grand Prix. After touching wheels von Trips' Ferrari crashed over the safety fence, while Clark's Lotus spun onto the trackside.

OPPOSITE TOP: Von Trips with Britain's Jim Clark and Stirling Moss before the race.

OPPOSITE CENTRE: This last picture of Von Trips shows him in his car before the start of the Italian Grand Prix on 10 September.

LEFT: New Zealander Bruce McLaren and Scotsman Jim Clark finished the season in joint seventh place with 11 points each.

BELOW: The Oulton Park Gold Trophy is filled with champagne for Graham Hill, who won the race in the new E-Type Jaguar. In the championship he drove an outdated car and scored just three points all season.

Graham Hill takes on Jim Clark

Ferrari's domination of the 1961 season would prove to be temporary; their cars would be completely outclassed by the technical advancements of the British manufacturers, with their new V-8 engines. In other respects too, 1962 was a year of change. It saw the end of Stirling Moss's career, following a bad crash at Goodwood before the Grand Prix season. Moss sustained such severe injuries that he was forced to take retirement, earning himself the soubriquet 'the best driver never to win a championship title'.

Hill's fortune changes

The year would also be remembered as being the one in which Graham Hill finally made his mark on the sport. He had endured frustration since 1958, first with unreliable cars at Lotus, then with more of the same at BRM. At the start of the 1962 season, the record books showed that Hill hadn't made it into the top six in any year. But that was all about to change.

Hill and BRM went to the Dutch Grand Prix in Zandvoort in buoyant mood. They had already notched up two non-championship Formula One wins that year. Hill took the lead early in the race and crossed the line first, giving BRM only their second-ever championship win. He started just as well at Monaco, gaining an early lead, only to be forced out with engine trouble. The race belonged to McLaren in his Cooper-Climax, and hot on his heels was Phil Hill, still with Ferrari. Hill loyally remained with the Italian marque until the end of the season, despite the internal unrest.

Clark challenges with the Lotus 25

Hill's main rival for the rest of the season was Jim Clark, who had also benefited from technological change; he too was driving a V-8 Climax unit, housed inside the Lotus 25. Colin Chapman's monocoque chassis was another revolutionary step that changed the face of the sport, yet in 1961 the Lotus was still a little unreliable. Clark had been forced to pull out of both Zandvoort and Monaco, but at Spa his luck turned and he notched up the first of an incredible 25 Grand Prix wins.

Hill celebrates back-to-back victories

At Aintree, Clark's run of success continued. He led from the off and won the race, taking the fastest lap into the bargain. He was now within one point of Hill and the fight for the title was on. Unfortunately, technical gremlins struck again: a stall on the line at Nürburgring effectively kept him back at fourth place and at Monza engine trouble forced a retirement. Instead, a jubilant Graham Hill took both victories. Although Clark managed to win at Watkins Glen, his points tally was nine short of his rival's.

Title decider

Technically, it was still possible for Clark to take the title, but only on condition that he win and Hill fail to take any points at all. If that were to be the case, Clark's greater number of victories would be taken into consideration. But there was to be no fairytale ending. Engine failure ended Clark's race and Graham Hill took the victory and his first championship title.

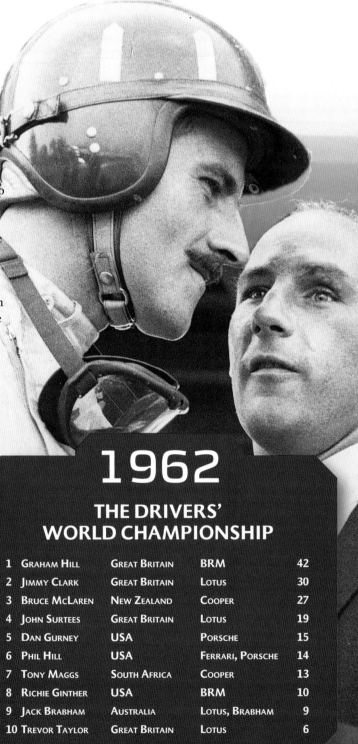

1962
THE DRIVERS' WORLD CHAMPIONSHIP

1	GRAHAM HILL	GREAT BRITAIN	BRM	42
2	JIMMY CLARK	GREAT BRITAIN	LOTUS	30
3	BRUCE MCLAREN	NEW ZEALAND	COOPER	27
4	JOHN SURTEES	GREAT BRITAIN	LOTUS	19
5	DAN GURNEY	USA	PORSCHE	15
6	PHIL HILL	USA	FERRARI, PORSCHE	14
7	TONY MAGGS	SOUTH AFRICA	COOPER	13
8	RICHIE GINTHER	USA	BRM	10
9	JACK BRABHAM	AUSTRALIA	LOTUS, BRABHAM	9
10	TREVOR TAYLOR	GREAT BRITAIN	LOTUS	6

Moss retires from racing

RIGHT TOP AND MIDDLE: On Easter Monday at Goodwood, Moss's car unaccountably left the track while he was attempting to overtake Graham Hill. Trapped in the wreckage of his car, Moss was conscious but severely injured. The cause of the accident remains a mystery.

OPPOSITE: Although Moss made a full recovery from his Goodwood crash, he was to retire from racing. Here he chats with fellow Britain Graham Hill. Wins in Holland, Germany, Italy and South Africa helped to give Hill victory in the title race with a margin of 12 points over Jim Clark.

BELOW: The Brabham team unveiled its own new Grand Prix car, the Brabham BT3, during the 1962 season. Here Brabham is pictured at the wheel of his stop-gap Lotus during practice for the British Grand Prix at Aintree, where he finished fifth.

BOTTOM LEFT: Phil Hill remained with the Ferrari team in 1962 but had an uncompetitive year with only three podium finishes. The new British V-8s were now more than a match for the V-6 Ferraris.

BOTTOM CENTRE AND BOTTOM RIGHT: Surtees finished in fourth place on 19 points in 1962, driving the new Lola for the Bowmaker-Yeoman team. He scored points in every race he finished, but was forced to retire in four out of the nine contests.

Clark shows his class

LEFT: Stirling Moss presents the garland and trophy to Jim Clark who won the Gold Cup race at Oulton Park. The mercurial Scot had his first championship wins in 1962 in Belgium, Britain and the US. However, four retirements hindered his chance of winning the title.

ABOVE: Clark led the British Grand Prix at Aintree from start to finish at an average speed of 90 miles per hour.

LEFT BELOW: Brabham's new car made its first appearance at the non-Championship Mexican Grand Prix in November 1962. The fact that Brabham was now using the knowledge and skills learned at Cooper in direct competition with his former team caused some degree of ill feeling.

OPPOSITE ABOVE LEFT: Surtees' team mate Roy Salvadori had a miserable year driving a Lola in the Drivers' Championship. Failing to finish a single race, he ended the season unplaced. He left Formula 1 at the end of the season, returning to sports and touring car racing.

OPPOSITE ABOVE RIGHT: A short time after the crash at Goodwood Stirling Moss is on his way to hospital again. This time he has to undergo an eye operation at St Thomas', London.

OPPOSITE BELOW: The world champion Graham Hill takes on a competitive opponent in to publicise the comedy film The Fast Lady.

Maximum points for Jim Clark

For Jim Clark and Lotus, 1962 had been a disappointment that they needed to wipe away. They did so in style: Clark won the first of his championship titles with an incredible haul of maximum points. The feat was all the more remarkable since the series consisted of ten races, with the best six scores counting; when Albert Ascari recorded his maximum in 1952, it was the best four finishes out of eight.

Manufacturers in turmoil

Since Hill's victory the previous year, the manufacturers were in turmoil. Both Porsche and Bowmaker-Yeoman had decided to withdraw, leaving prominent drivers looking for new outfits. Dan Gurney joined the Brabham team and John Surtees, who had been with Bowmaker-Yeoman, went to Ferrari. Ferarri themselves were struggling to fill the gap left by the departure of their engineer, Carlo Chiti, who had set up his own work team, ATS. Both Phil Hill and Giancarlo Baghetti left with him, a move they would sorely regret. Neither driver won a single point all season, and the team lasted for only one year.

Hill takes the opener

It was Graham Hill who took the honours in the opening race at Monaco; Jim Clark had been forced into ninth position, thanks to a seized gearbox. For Hill it was the first of a run of victories at Monaco during the next five years. However, Clark was to enjoy a series of victories within the championship itself, being the first to cross the line in the following four races. Of these, perhaps the Dutch race best epitomised the level of Clark's performance that year. He was fastest in practice, led the race from start to finish – lapping the entire field in the process – and became the first man to lap the Zandvoort circuit at over 100mph.

Clark reaps the points

Clark won a total of seven out of the ten races, meaning that he was able to choose his six best finishes, but following the Italian Grand Prix at Monza he had already secured the title. On the other two occasions where had Clark missed out he was simply unlucky. At Nürburgring he was hampered by a misfiring engine, yet still managed to come in second behind John Surtees. Clark's misfortune enabled Surtees to secure his first championship victory, and Ferrari's first success for two years. Clark's other 'failure' came at Watkins Glen, where he lost a lap and a half in the pits with battery trouble, yet still managed to finish third. Graham Hill won the race from his team mate Ritchie Ginther. The BRM pair would end the year on 29 points each, 25 behind Clark's maximum of 54 – with Hill awarded second place by dint of those two wins in Monte Carlo and the United States. Surtees had to content himself with fourth place in the championship, with 22 points.

Disappointment for Hill

For Graham Hill it was his turn to be sorely disappointed with a run of ill fortune. He had managed to finish in just six races, with two of those having been victories, at Monaco and Watkins Glen. BRM had emulated Lotus by introducing their own monocoque design, but the model handled poorly and Hill eventually returned to his original car. Both Surtees and Hill might well have proved to be more threatening to Clark in more reliable cars, but the Flying Scot's outstanding performance during the 1963 season ensured that he was fast becoming considered the greatest driver of his generation, and the man to beat.

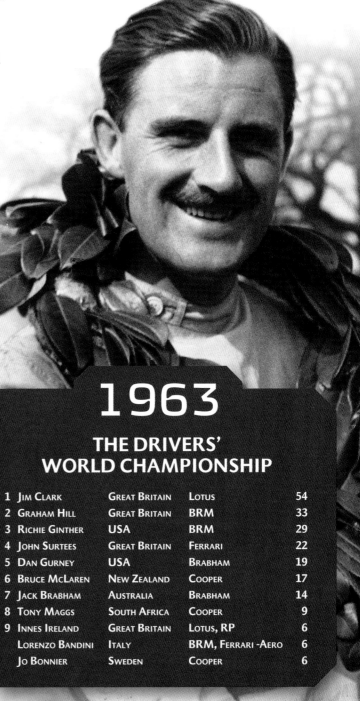

1963

THE DRIVERS' WORLD CHAMPIONSHIP

1	JIM CLARK	GREAT BRITAIN	LOTUS	54
2	GRAHAM HILL	GREAT BRITAIN	BRM	33
3	RICHIE GINTHER	USA	BRM	29
4	JOHN SURTEES	GREAT BRITAIN	FERRARI	22
5	DAN GURNEY	USA	BRABHAM	19
6	BRUCE MCLAREN	NEW ZEALAND	COOPER	17
7	JACK BRABHAM	AUSTRALIA	BRABHAM	14
8	TONY MAGGS	SOUTH AFRICA	COOPER	9
9	INNES IRELAND	GREAT BRITAIN	LOTUS, RP	6
	LORENZO BANDINI	ITALY	BRM, FERRARI -AERO	6
	JO BONNIER	SWEDEN	COOPER	6

Seven wins for Clark

BELOW: Jim Clark dominated the 1963 championship, with seven wins, a second and a third in the 10-race series. Here he is photographed paying for a ticket on a bus, having just become world champion.

RIGHT TOP: 1963 was a disappointing year for Jack Brabham with only one podium finish, in Mexico. He considered giving up racing to concentrate on team management.

RIGHT CENTRE: With his racing days over Stirling Moss is in great demand at celebrity events.

RIGHT BOTTOM: Surtees moved from Bowmaker-Yeoman to Ferrari. He finished fourth in the world championship, as he had the previous season, but notched up his first win, at the Nurburgring.

OPPOSITE: Graham Hill finished second in the 1963 championship, winning at Monaco and Watkins Glen. BRM introduced a monocoque car, but it wasn't a success and Hill was forced to revert to the older model.

Drivers with an agenda

BELOW: Members of the Grand Prix Drivers' Association pose for the camera before convening a meeting. Seated are current champion Graham Hill (left) and the Scot aiming to win the title, Jim Clark. Standing (left to right) are: Trevor Taylor, Bruce McLaren, Tony Maggs, Innes Ireland, Lorenzo Bandini, Jack Brabham, Jo Bonnier, Phil Hill, Tim Hall, Masten Gregory, Dan Gurney, Chris Amon, John Surtees, Ritchie Ginther.

RIGHT: John Surtees pictured at the British Grand Prix at Silverstone, where he finished second behind Clark. The following month their positions were reversed, when Surtees won the German Grand Prix and Clark came in behind him.

OPPOSITE ABOVE LEFT: Graham Hill with his children, Brigitte, 4, and 3-year-old Damon, at Silverstone before the Grand Prix. Hill came third in the race behind Jim Clark and John Surtees.

OPPOSITE RIGHT: Graham Hill goes for a spin with the US Air Force.

OPPOSITE BELOW: Some of Formula 1's top drivers are present at a publicity luncheon in Manchester. Pictured are (back row, left to right) Mike Hailwood, Bob Anderson, Graham Hill, Jim Clark, Ritchie Ginther. Front row (left to right) Rob Walker, Jo Bonnier, Innes Ireland. With three races still to go Clark is already out of sight in the championship.

Surtees takes his place in history

It was again Ferrari's turn to fight back. In 1964 they introduced their own new V-8 engine; in fact they were to try out three different engines during the season in their determination to win again. Their tactics paid off, but only thanks to the skill of their new star driver, Englishman John Surtees. Surtees already had seven motorcycling world titles to his name and now he was in with a chance of becoming the first man to take world crowns on both two wheels and four. There were, however, two other serious contenders for the crown, Clark and Hill, and yet again the title was to be hard fought.

The battle begins

Surtees wasn't the only motorcycling ace to impress behind the wheel of a car. At the Monaco opener, Mike Hailwood earned his first driver's point when he finished in sixth position. The race was won by Hill for BRM. Clark took the next two wins, at Zandvoort and then Spa. The Dutch victory was a blistering one: Clark lapped every driver except Surtees. At Spa, things were more open; both Hill and McLaren had led at points, but both had succumbed to fuel loss. Ironically, as Clark slowed down after the flag, he too was running on an empty tank.

Gurney won the French Grand Prix at Rouen, with Hill in second position, and Gurney's team boss, Jack Brabham, in third. Although Brabham was becoming more involved in the business side of Formula One, he still found himself competing from time to time. Brands Hatch was the venue for the British Grand Prix, its first time hosting the event. Clark won again, setting a new lap record in the process.

Surtees pulls back

Although he had suffered a disappointing start, Surtees was now beginning to put out more consistent performances, and collecting points as a result. The only event to let him down again would be the Austrian Grand Prix. At Brands Hatch he came in third for the first time and was now back in play for the title competition. At the halfway mark Clark led with 30 points, with Hill on 26. Surtees was still adrift on 10.

Austrian debut

By winning at Nürburgring, Surtees was now starting to challenge Clark and Hill. Although he retired early at the Zeltweg Airfield, Clark, Hill, McLaren and Gurney were also beset by mechanical problems and the first Austrian Grand Prix went to Ferrari's number two, Lorenzo Bandini. The race also saw the debut of a home-grown driver, Jochen Rindt, who would go on to to win the Championship posthumously in 1970.

Race for points

The penultimate European race, at Monza, saw a thrilling battle between Clark, McLaren and Surtees. Hill's race had ended before the event began as his jammed clutch kept him in the blocks. Clark retired early and first place went to Surtees. Hill edged into the lead on points, however, by winning at Watkins Glen in October. Surtees came in at second place and consequently brought himself up into second place in points too. It was to be a tense final round: Hill was on 39, Surtees on 34 and Clark stuck on 30, although a win in Mexico could still clinch it. Perhaps predictably, needing only a third-place finish, Hill was the favourite.

Surtees takes the crown

Typically, things were never going to be that simple. Hill collided with Bandini's Ferrari and both cars spun off. Clark, in first position, also succumbed to misfortune, in his case it was more bad luck than poor judgement: his engine let him down. Surtees was now in third, and when team mate Bandini let him through, he finished in second again, high enough to steal the crown from Hill by just one point. Despite the somewhat unsporting circumstances of his win, Surtees took his place in history with the remarkable achievement of winning both the driving and motorcycling championships.

1964

THE DRIVERS' WORLD CHAMPIONSHIP

1	JOHN SURTEES	GREAT BRITAIN	FERRARI	40
2	GRAHAM HILL	GREAT BRITAIN	BRM	39
3	JIM CLARK	GREAT BRITAIN	LOTUS	32
4	LORENZO BANDINI	ITALY	FERRARI - AERO	23
	RICHIE GINTHER	USA	BRM	23
6	DAN GURNEY	USA	BRABHAM	19
7	BRUCE MCLAREN	NEW ZEALAND	COOPER	13
8	JACK BRABHAM	AUSTRALIA	BRABHAM	11
	PETER ARUNDELL	GREAT BRITAIN	LOTUS	11
10	JO SIFFERT	SWITZERLAND	LOTUS, BRABHAM	7

Time for the family

Right: Young Garry Brabham is given a present by his father. On the track Jack was again outscored by his American team mate Dan Gurney.

Below left: Graham Hill and his family take a break after the Italian Grand prix.

Below right: Graham Hill at the Belgian Grand Prix in June, round 3 of the championship. With a victory and a fourth place already, Hill added to his points tally by finishing fifth in Belgium.

Bottom: Jim Clark shows off his new Lotus at an awards ceremony, held at London's Dorchester Hotel. Looking on (left to right) are Bruce McLaren, Mrs Hazel Chapman, Clark's girlfriend Sally Stokes, Graham Hill and Colin Chapman.

Opposite: John Surtees shows he still enjoys driving on two wheels.

RIGHT: Jim Clark chats with swimming stars Linda Ludgrove (left) and Stella Mitchell.

BELOW LEFT: Stirling Moss and Jim Clark attend a Variety Club luncheon in London. On Clark's right is holiday camp tycoon Sir Billy Butlin. Between the two is L. MacDonell.

BELOW RIGHT: Stirling Moss pictured on his wedding day.

BOTTOM RIGHT: John Surtees during practice for the British Grand Prix.

BOTTOM LEFT: Dan Gurney and Jim Clark are nose to nose in early stages of the British Grand Prix. Gurney's Brabham hit trouble and finished in 13th place; Clark led for the entire 80-lap race.

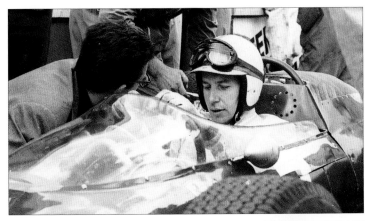

Surtees out in front

LEFT: Wins in Italy and Germany and podium finishes in Holland, Britain, Mexico and the US meant that Surtees became world champion in 1964.

LEFT CENTRE: Victory in the British Grand Prix in July had extended Jim Clark's lead over Graham Hill to four points with five races to go. Reliability problems meant that Clark's season fizzled out thereafter.

BELOW LEFT: Jim Clark and Graham Hill are out in front during the British Grand Prix.

BELOW RIGHT: Jackie Stewart and his wife Helen at London Airport.

BOTTOM: Jackie Stewart's achievements in Formula 2 and Formula 3 had attracted the attention of several teams. Stewart chose to join BRM's Formula 1 stable in 1965.

British rivals take first and second

RIGHT: Jim Clark takes the chequered flag at the British Grand Prix, finishing just 2.8 seconds in front of Graham Hill. Clark had started in pole position with Hill on the front row of the grid. The two great rivals finish the race in that order.

RIGHT BELOW: Jim Clark acknowledges the support of the crowd after winning the British Grand Prix. The dignitaries involved in the presentation ceremony include Earl Mountbatten (right).

BOTTOM: Graham Hill in his BRM.

OPPOSITE ABOVE: Jim Clark examines a photographer's camera. Following his success at the British Grand Prix, he was forced to retire from the German and Austrian events. However, he was back at Brands Hatch the day after the German race to win a Formula 2 event. Also pictured are Clark's girlfriend Sally Stokes, BRM driver Tony Maggs (second left), and representatives of BP and Esso.

OPPOSITE BELOW: Graham Hill's 4-year-old son Damon tries a miniature Lotus. The 20cc replica Lotus would be no match for his father's 1500cc, 200 bhp BRM which cost £10,000.

Formula 1 drivers on the road

Right above: Stars of Formula 1 leave London for the Austrian Grand Prix (left to right): Richie Ginther, Graham Hill, Phil Hill, Jim Clark and Bruce McLaren. All of the British contingent were beaten to the championship by John Surtees, who edged out Graham Hill by a single point.

Right below: Graham Hill and Jim Clark in New York for the upcoming Sebring races.

Opposite and bottom: The thrills and spills of Formula 1: Clark shrugs off the effects of a crash as he walks away from his wrecked Lotus.

Clark in ascendancy; Stewart rising

When Jim Clark finished the 1965 season with six wins from ten events, yet again the title was his. Despite disappointment the previous season, he was back on form – or rather, his cars were now more reliable and more powerful. His Lotus was fitted with a new 32-valve version of the Coventry-Climax engine. Man and machine were now unstoppable.

Jackie Stewart debuts

The first race of the season was held on the first day of the New Year, in Prince George, South Africa. Clark started on pole and set the fastest lap during a race that he totally dominated. Surtees and Hill came in at second and third respectively. In sixth place and claiming a debut first point was a young Jackie Stewart. The Scotsman had been proving himself at Formula Three and Formula Two events, impressing leading names such as McLaren and Chapman. He eventually chose to race with BRM alongside Graham Hill.

Clark wins Indie 500

The second event was Monaco, and with Clark away contesting the Indianapolis 500 for Lotus, the competition was open. Hill took his third successive win at the principality. Clark would return to Europe eager to contest the title with Hill. Although he had won the 500 in record time, it was no longer a championship event and there was no point advantage to be had.

One-two for Scotland

The Belgian Grand Prix saw Clark return in style with his fourth successive win at Spa. In horribly wet conditions Clark led all the way, while Stewart made it a one-two for Scotland. The two men repeated the performance at the French Grand Prix, held for the first time at Clermont-Ferrand. Stewart was clearly future champion material. Another driver destined to scale the heights, New Zealander Denny Hulme, also took his first points with fourth place. He followed this with fifth place at Zandvoort, immediately repaying the Brabham team for the faith they had shown in his potential.

Clark won Silverstone and Zandvoort. The Dutch race was comfortable enough, with Stewart following him in at second. The British Grand Prix was much closer. A dramatic loss of oil pressure threatened the victory, but the 'Prince of Speed' expertly nursed his Lotus home barely three seconds ahead of Hill.

Clark takes the championship

The title was settled in August at Nürburgring. Clark's sixth win of the season made his the fastest secured title in the championship so far. The race was a series of technical disasters for most of the other main drivers. For them the battle was now on to achieve the best rankings behind Jim Clark.

The final three rounds were marked by Jackie Stewart's fine win in Italy and the debut of Honda in the final round in Mexico. Stewart's victory came courtesy of a mistake by Hill in the penultimate lap, but it remained quite an achievement for a debut year; he had amassed 33 points to finish third, seven points behind Hill. The last year of the 1.5-litre Formula, 1965 was ultimately Clark's year. His second maximum haul of 54 points established him as the greatest driver of his generation. Like Fangio, Clark had an instinctive natural talent that set him apart, and his partnership with Colin Chapman and Lotus made him seem invincible.

1965
THE DRIVERS' WORLD CHAMPIONSHIP

1	JIM CLARK	GREAT BRITAIN	LOTUS	54
2	GRAHAM HILL	GREAT BRITAIN	BRM	40
3	JACKIE STEWART	GREAT BRITAIN	BRM	33
4	DAN GURNEY	USA	BRABHAM	25
5	JOHN SURTEES	GREAT BRITAIN	FERRARI	17
6	LORENZO BANDINI	ITALY	FERRARI	13
7	RICHIE GINTHER	USA	HONDA	11
8	BRUCE MCLAREN	NEW ZEALAND	COOPER	10
	MIKE SPENCE	GREAT BRITAIN	LOTUS	10
10	JACK BRABHAM	AUSTRALIA	BRABHAM	9

Fastest lap for Clark

OPPOSITE: Jim Clark photographed during practice for the Race of Champions at Brands Hatch in March. Clark took the champagne prize for lapping the circuit at more than 100 mph in practice but during the second heat he went off the track and the contest was won by Mike Spence in a Lotus.

LEFT: Graham Hill takes some time away from the track to appear with pop singer Adam Faith at a promotional event at the Mayfair Theatre, London.

BELOW RIGHT: 1965 was Austrian Jochen Rindt's first full season in Formula 1, driving for the Cooper team. He had made his Formula 1 debut at the Austrian Grand Prix the previous season, driving for the Rob Walker team.

BELOW LEFT: Graham Hill pictured before a Formula 2 race at Crystal Palace.

BOTTOM: Jack Brabham at Brands Hatch. Brabham and his team mate Gurney finished in eighth and sixth positions respectively in the 1965 season but a new engine deal was to transform the team's fortunes.

Hill is runner-up again

Opposite above: Graham Hill finished in second place in the championship for the third successive year, with wins at Monaco and and Watkins Glen and podium finishes in South Africa, Italy, Germany and the British Grand Prix at Silverstone.

Opposite below right: Jackie Stewart made his Formula 1 debut in 1965. A string of fine performances, including three podium finishes in the first four races, was crowned by a first championship win in the Italian Grand Prix at Monza.

Right: Jim Clark at the Race of Champions Ball, held at London's Park Lane Hotel.

Below and bottom: Reigning champion Surtees had just three podium finishes in his Ferrari in 1965, and finished fifth in the championship on 17 points.

Opposite below left: John Surtees arrives back in London three weeks after his crash at Mosport during practice for the non-championship Canadian Grand Prix. He suffered spinal injuries, a broken pelvis and a ruptured kidney.

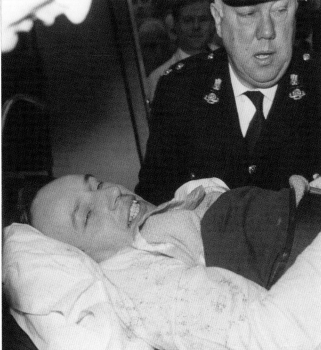

Clark secures the title in Germany

RIGHT: Jim Clark repeated his British Grand Prix victory over Graham Hill when he won the 192-mile Rouen Grand Prix in a Lotus Cosworth.

BOTTOM AND OPPOSITE BOTTOM: Jim Clark clinched his second world title by winning the German Grand Prix for the first time. It was Clark's sixth victory of the season, finishing 16 seconds ahead of this championship rival, Graham Hill. Before the race Clark talks to Lotus team boss Colin Chapman (opposite).

FAR RIGHT: Clark speaking at a ceremony at Silverstone where he is awarded the British Racing Drivers' Club Gold Star.

Taking some time off in Monaco

LEFT: Jackie and Helen Stewart are joined by the Mosses and Bruce McLaren on the beach at Monaco before the Grand Prix. The race was won by Graham Hill and Stewart, his BRM team mate, took third place.

LEFT BELOW: Clark hadn't competed in the Monaco race as Lotus had entered him in the Indy 500. At the British Grand Prix Clark crossed the line ahead of Graham Hill, giving him his fourth win in five races.

OPPOSITE CENTRE: Graham Hill and Jim Clark pictured with Donald Campbell, holder of several water and land speed records.

Brabham enjoys third success

The season saw the maximum engine capacity doubled to 3 litres, and along with Climax's decision to quit Formula One racing, there was more upheaval between marques and drivers. Surtees left Ferrari to join Cooper part way through the season and several drivers decided to branch out with their own teams, among them Dan Gurney, who left Brabham to head up Eagle, and Bruce McLaren, who ran a car under his own name for the first time at Monaco. Neither Gurney nor McLaren would see much success. However, Jack Brabham, who had been toying with racing his own Grand Prix cars since the early sixties, would finally reap the rewards in 1966.

Team Brabham best prepared
Although Gurney had won two Grands Prix in 1964 for Brabham, the following year had been less rewarding, mainly owing to lack of reliability. For the 1966 campaign, the team was better prepared for the 3-litre changes than most. The Brabham cars were powered by Australian V-8 Repco engines that proved to be models of reliability, whereas BRM and their H16 engine were not. Jim Clark's season started poorly since his Climax 2-litre engine simply could not compete, and despite the better performance offered by the H16 inside his Lotus, the year was not to be a repeat of the last.

Slow start to the season
The opener at Monaco turned out to be an inauspicious start for Brabham; he was forced to withdraw early with gearbox trouble. The win was taken by Jackie Stewart, still racing for BRM, and it was their fourth Monaco victory in a row. Gurney had already left Brabham to go it alone and his place had been filled by New Zealander Denny Hulme, who was forced to retire early.

The second race at Spa was held under stormy conditions and there was a high casualty count early on; fifteen was reduced to seven and Jackie Stewart was fortunate to escape one particular accident alive. The competition was between Surtees and Rindt, with the reigning champion taking the nine points at the flag. Brabham finished, but only at fourth. After this, the Australian enjoyed a spate of wins.

Run of victories
At Rheims, Brabham set a record by averaging over 136mph to win ahead of newcomer Mike Parkes, with team mate Hulme taking third place. At Brands Hatch, team Brabham went one better, taking first and second places, with Brabham finishing 1.6 seconds in front of his number two. The third win was at Zandvoort, where Graham Hill and Jim Clark were held to second and third. Jackie Stewart came in at fourth.

Jack Brabham had never won a Grand Prix in Germany but he put that right this time with a magnificent victory in the wet at the Nürburgring. Surtees followed him home, now driving the Cooper-Maserati. Simmering friction between Surtees and the Ferrari team boss Eugenio Dragoni had resulted in his departure, despite their sending out the very competitive new V-12. Surtees still managed to finish second in the championship, driving the less impressive Cooper.

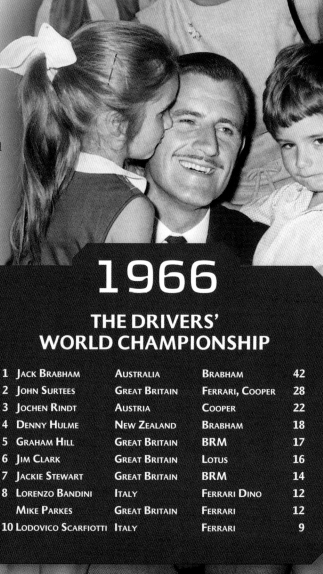

1966
THE DRIVERS' WORLD CHAMPIONSHIP

1	JACK BRABHAM	AUSTRALIA	BRABHAM	42
2	JOHN SURTEES	GREAT BRITAIN	FERRARI, COOPER	28
3	JOCHEN RINDT	AUSTRIA	COOPER	22
4	DENNY HULME	NEW ZEALAND	BRABHAM	18
5	GRAHAM HILL	GREAT BRITAIN	BRM	17
6	JIM CLARK	GREAT BRITAIN	LOTUS	16
7	JACKIE STEWART	GREAT BRITAIN	BRM	14
8	LORENZO BANDINI	ITALY	FERRARI DINO	12
	MIKE PARKES	GREAT BRITAIN	FERRARI	12
10	LODOVICO SCARFIOTTI	ITALY	FERRARI	9

Brabham collects honours

With the Italian Grand Prix next on the agenda, Brabham had the title within reach. Although he was forced out of the race by an oil leak, all the main contenders also fell by the wayside and Ludovico Scarfotti won on home soil for Ferrari. The main outcome of the race was that Brabham was confirmed as world champion for the third time.

The penultimate race at Watkins Glen saw another Brabham retirement and the victory went to Jim Clark, his only one of the season. Surtees took the final win of the year in Mexico, and with it he secured second place in the final points table. Brabham had won the championship for the third time at the age of 41, and the achievement brought him further honour as he was awarded both an OBE and then, later, the sport's first knighthood.

Rindt takes a step up at Cooper

ABOVE LEFT: Jochen Rindt took on the role of number one driver at Cooper for a while after Bruce McLaren left the team to set up his own outfit.

ABOVE: Many thought that John Surtees would never race again after the injuries he sustained in Canada but not only was he was back at the wheel at the start of the 1966 season but he won the second race of the championship at Spa.

BELOW LEFT: Graham Hill was one of many drivers involved in accidents on the opening lap at Spa. His car was undamaged, but Hill stopped to help his BRM team mate Jackie Stewart.

BELOW RIGHT: Mario Andretti first attracted the attention of Colin Chapman at the Indianapolis 500 in 1965.

OPPOSITE: Graham Hill is congratulated by his family after winning the Indianapolis 500.

Gurney replaced by Hulme

RIGHT AND OPPOSITE BELOW RIGHT: The departure of Dan Gurney from the Brabham team in 1966 gave New Zealander Denny Hulme, who had been a member of the team for several years, the opportunity to be promoted. In Hulme's first full season in Formula 1 he appeared on the podium in each of the four races he finished.

BELOW: Jack Brabham team's cars were powered by the excellent V-8 Repco engine.

BOTTOM: Denny Hulme drives in a sports car event at the Silverstone circuit.

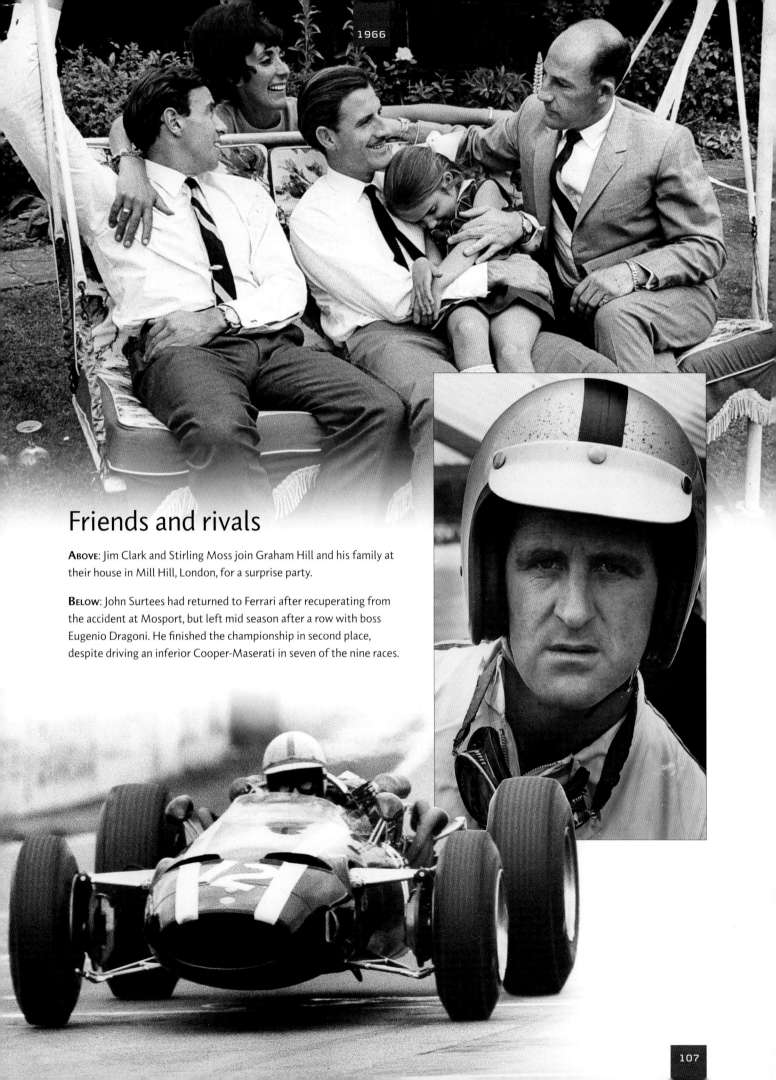

Friends and rivals

Above: Jim Clark and Stirling Moss join Graham Hill and his family at their house in Mill Hill, London, for a surprise party.

Below: John Surtees had returned to Ferrari after recuperating from the accident at Mosport, but left mid season after a row with boss Eugenio Dragoni. He finished the championship in second place, despite driving an inferior Cooper-Maserati in seven of the nine races.

Stewart crashes in treacherous conditions

RIGHT: Jackie Stewart, accompanied by his wife, is taken to hospital after an accident at Spa. In wet conditions Stewart's BRM left the track, one of a series of first-lap crashes. Stewart was luckly to survive, having been trapped in the car which was soaked in petrol.

BELOW LEFT: Helen Stewart visits Jackie in hospital.

RIGHT: Stewart leaves hospital less than two weeks after the crash at Spa. He returned to racing on 16 July at the British Grand Prix, having missed only one event.

OPPOSITE ABOVE: Jim Clark helps Graham Hill celebrate his victory in the Indianapolis 500. Clark, who was second in the race, missed out on the £55,000 prize money.

OPPOSITE BELOW: Denny Hulme at the wheel at Brands Hatch. Hulme took second place behind team mate and team boss Jack Brabham.

Brabham designs, builds and drives a winner

RIGHT: At the French Grand Prix at the beginning of July, Jack Brabham became the first man to design, build and drive a Formula 1 car to victory in a Grand Prix. His win at Brands Hatch in the British Grand Prix put him 10 points ahead of his rivals for the title.

BELOW RIGHT: Two things identify the driver in the racing car: the name embroidered on his overalls and the standard of his driving. Clark was at Brands Hatch where he put up the fourth fastest time of the day in his 2-litre works Lotus.

BELOW LEFT: Clark goes over last-minute details before going out onto the track at Goodwood during a practice session.

A lighter side...

Left: A light-hearted moment: words of advice from Jim Clark for Dutch racing driver Liana Engeman who hopes to compete in the Lombank Trophy saloon car race.

Below: Jack Brabham at the wheel of his Repco-engine car.

Bottom: Jack Brabham surrounded by members of his team at the British Grand Prix, the second of his four wins that year. He was now in the veteran class, having turned 40 at the start of the season.

Brabham first and second

Fortunately for Brabham the new Lotus 49 was still experiencing teething problems and the Repco was able to stay on top for one more year. Much of this was due to its reliability: it may not have been as fast on paper, but it was a light, compact and consistent performer and it enabled Denny Hulme to win the championship for the first time.

In 1966 Hulme had finished behind Brabham. This time Brabham came in second but he could still celebrate: it was the first 'team double' since Hill and von Trips in 1961. Jim Clark, on the other hand, was thwarted by the limitations of the Lotus and although he was the only serious title challenger he had to be content with third position.

Death at Monaco
The first round took place in South Africa, at the new Kyalami track. There were the usual changes in the line-up: Surtees was now with Honda, while Cooper were trying out Pedro Rodriguez. Hulme led the race for 60 laps, but a pit stop gave the lead to John Love in a Cooper-Climax. Love's own fuel stop lost him the winning position, which went instead to Rodriquez, the last driver to win a Grand Prix for Cooper.

Hulme beat Graham Hill to the flag in the Monaco street classic but the race was overshadowed by the horrific death of Lorenzo Bandini. His Ferrari had crashed into the barrier and burst into flames and he died in hospital three days later.

The Lotus 49 unveiled
The new Lotus 49 was unveiled at Zandvoort. Powered by a Ford Cosworth DFV V8 engine, it was immediately clear that the new car was something special. Hill had joined Lotus from BRM but was forced to retire with engine problems. It was up to Clark to take the honours for the car on its debut. The Lotus still had problems that needed to be addressed, and between them Hill and Clark were to finish only nine races out of 22 starts.

Dan Gurney wins in Belgium
Spa provided another example of Lotus's difficulties. Again Hill was out early and Clark was left with the task of racing for the team. An enforced pit stop put paid to any hopes for a second win and Gurney was the beneficiary. Both Brabham and Hulme had also retired early, so the Eagle-Westlake took its only Grand Prix win.

At the French Grand Prix, the Brabhams dominated, with the boss and Hulme taking first and second places and Jackie Stewart a whole lap behind in third. The British Grand Prix was next and Clark was able to take the win, the fifth time in six years that he had won at home. Typically, however, collecting points were Hulme and Brabham in second and fourth positions.

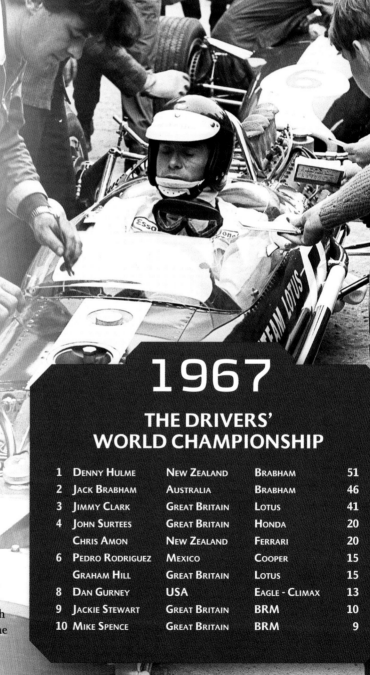

1967
THE DRIVERS' WORLD CHAMPIONSHIP

1	DENNY HULME	NEW ZEALAND	BRABHAM	51
2	JACK BRABHAM	AUSTRALIA	BRABHAM	46
3	JIMMY CLARK	GREAT BRITAIN	LOTUS	41
4	JOHN SURTEES	GREAT BRITAIN	HONDA	20
	CHRIS AMON	NEW ZEALAND	FERRARI	20
6	PEDRO RODRIGUEZ	MEXICO	COOPER	15
	GRAHAM HILL	GREAT BRITAIN	LOTUS	15
8	DAN GURNEY	USA	EAGLE - CLIMAX	13
9	JACKIE STEWART	GREAT BRITAIN	BRM	10
10	MIKE SPENCE	GREAT BRITAIN	BRM	9

Drama at Monza

The pattern remained the same for the rest of the season. In Germany Clark was out; Hulme and Brabham were first and second. Hulme was kept to second by Brabham at the Canadian Grand Prix; this time Hill finished, but in fourth behind Gurney. Monza proved to be the most dramatic race of the year and many would suggest it was Clark's finest, despite his coming only third. Typically the Lotus made the job difficult for the Scot, but to pull back from sixteenth position following a puncture he put in a remarkable performance, breaking the lap record repeatedly. His recovery took him into the lead, but he ran short of fuel on the final lap. The eventual battle for first place was between Surtees and Brabham and it was thrilling: Surtees took the win by just 0.2 seconds.

A third place at Watkins Glen, followed by a third in Mexico, was enough for the title to go to Hulme. He had amassed an impressive haul of 51 points, five ahead of Brabham who was second in the title race. Although he had only finished six races, Clark had won four of them. Hulme, who had finished first only twice, had deserved the glory, but Clark remained the star.

Reliability gives Brabham the edge

Opposite: Jim Clark is surrounded by Lotus mechanics at Silverstone. Clark was the only serious rival to the Brabham team in 1967, but his car lacked the reliability of the Brabham-Repco.

Left: Graham Hill pictured at the London School of Flying, Elstree, where he studied to gain his pilot's licence. On Hill's right is model Joanna Lumley.

Below left: Graham Hill pilots a plane.

Below right: Denny Hulme in his Brabham-Repco on his way to second place behind Jim Clark at Silverstone. Hulme won only two races, Monaco and Germany, but consistent performances meant he amassed 51 points and could take the title from his team mate Brabham.

Brabhams dominate

RIGHT: The Brabham-Repco dominated the championship again in 1967.

BELOW: Graham Hill left BRM for Lotus, allowing Jackie Stewart to be promoted to BRM's number one driver in 1967. Stewart would soon want a change too, because the BRMs proved to be unreliable.

BOTTOM: John Surtees had high hopes for Grand Prix success in the V-12 Honda but continued to drive a Lola-Ford in Formula 2 races.

Hill misses out in Monte Carlo

LEFT: Graham and Betty Hill pictured before the Monaco Grand Prix. He finished in second place in Monte Carlo, but a succession of mechanical failures during the rest of the season forced him to retire in eight out of the 11 races.

BELOW: Surtees took joint-fouth place in the championship with 20 points, driving for the Honda team. The V-12 Honda had great potential but needed much development work.

Tragic death of Jim Clark

The 1968 season will always be remembered as the year in which the great Jim Clark died. He was killed when his Lotus 48 left the track at Hockenheim in a Formula Two race in the April. He had already won the opening round of the Formula One championship, the Grand Prix at Kyalami. The victory, his twenty-fifth in just 72 Grands Prix, took him one ahead of the great Fangio and assured him of his rightful place in the history books. The year was marred further by the deaths of drivers Mike Spence and Ludovico Scarfiotto in other non-championship events.

The year was also the first with unlimited sponsorship, leading to quite a visual change on the circuit. Lotus cars no longer sported the famous green and yellow livery; now the Gold Leaf Team Lotus car was bedecked in red, white and gold. In addition to this, wings were used for the first time in the championship, with more sophisticated designs appearing as the season went on.

Lotus in contention

Lotus had lost not only their finest driver but also their exclusive rights to the DMV engine and all of the cars were now faster and more powerful. With Graham Hill as their lead driver, now supported by Jackie Oliver, hopes were high that Lotus could still take the title. Hill's main rival, Stewart, would be absent for several races owing to a pre-race accident, losing vital ground that was to prove crucial later.

Hill endures bad luck

Hill further enhanced his reputation as the 'King of Monte Carlo' by winning at Monaco. He won again at the Spanish Grand Prix but then a spate of bad luck saw him fail to finish in the next four races. The first of these was Spa, when Stewart returned to the fray. The Scot looked certain to give new team Matra their first win when, with just two laps left and leading McLaren, he ran out of fuel. McLaren won in the car that bore his name for its debut victory.

Stewart handles the rain

Stewart drove brilliantly in the wet at Zandvoort, lapping the entire field, except for Beltoise, on his way to victory. It was wet again at Rouen, and when Jo Schlesser's Honda crashed out of the race in flames the year saw another tragic death. The win was taken by Ickx in the Ferrari who led for 59 of the 60 laps. It was the last win for a non-Ford-powered car for two years.

Brands Hatch saw the first championship victory for privateer Jo Siffert. In the Rob Walker Lotus 49B, he had held off Ferrari's Chris Amon in a tense race. Stewart was desperate for points, but the circuit put too much strain on an injured wrist and he was placed sixth. The torrential rain

and fog of the German Grand Prix seemed to work for Stewart, who had fitted Dunlop rain tyres to his car. Despite his wrist, he took the flag four minutes ahead of Hill. He was now within four points of Hill.

Monza saw both Stewart and Hill succumb to technical problems and at the Canadian Grand Prix Hill's better placing – fourth to Stewart's sixth – saw him edge further ahead on points. Reigning champion Denny Hulme scored back-to-back wins in both races, a late surge that would help him to finish third overall this time round.

At Watkins Glen, home-grown star Mario Andretti made an immediate impact, setting the fastest lap in practice. He led in the early part of the race, but was overhauled by Stewart. In what was set to be a nail-biting decider, three drivers – Hill, Stewart and Hulme – could have taken the crown in Mexico, yet the finish was an anti-climax. Both Stewart and Hulme retired and Hill drove impeccably to take the race and his second world crown, which, fittingly, he dedicated to his lost friend, Jim Clark.

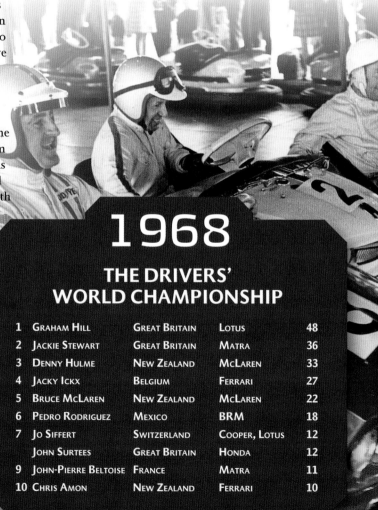

1968
THE DRIVERS' WORLD CHAMPIONSHIP

1	Graham Hill	Great Britain	Lotus	48
2	Jackie Stewart	Great Britain	Matra	36
3	Denny Hulme	New Zealand	McLaren	33
4	Jacky Ickx	Belgium	Ferrari	27
5	Bruce McLaren	New Zealand	McLaren	22
6	Pedro Rodriguez	Mexico	BRM	18
7	Jo Siffert	Switzerland	Cooper, Lotus	12
	John Surtees	Great Britain	Honda	12
9	John-Pierre Beltoise	France	Matra	11
10	Chris Amon	New Zealand	Ferrari	10

Honda calls a halt

LEFT TOP: Surtees remained with Honda in 1968 after an unsatisfactory series in 1967, believing it was only a matter of time before the car was a success. However, Honda pulled out of racing at the end of 1968.

LEFT CENTRE: Graham Hill pours a glass of champagne at the beginning of what was to be a very successful season.

LEFT BELOW: In Formula 1 Jochen Rindt struggled in the Brabham-Repco, only finishing in South Africa and Germany. Here is is pictured winning a Formula 2 race at Crystal Palace, one of many successes in the category in 1968.

OPPOSITE: Formula 1 competitors engage in some off-track racing at Battersea in London.

BELOW AND BOTTOM: Denny Hulme joined McLaren in 1968, despite winning the previous year's world title with Brabham. He had already teamed up with fellow New Zealander Bruce McLaren for the 1967 Can-Am series. The McLaren car, which brought Hulme and team boss McLaren considerable success in 1968, was designed by Robin Herd.

Clark dies at Hockenheim

BELOW: Grim-faced spectators look for parts of the wreckage of Jim Clark's Formula 2 Lotus which was torn to pieces in an accident during the German Trophy. Alone on an almost straight stretch of road and at a speed of about 170mph, he zig-zagged across the circuit, somersaulted several times and crashed broadside into trees beside the track.

LEFT: The top British racing drivers were close friends, and everyone involved with motor sport mourned the popular and talented Jim Clark. In this light-hearted moment earlier in the year Graham Hill (right) and Jim Clark (centre) show themselves to be good sports in a send-up of The Beatles.

Siffert takes the chequered flag

LEFT: Siffert crosses the line at in the British Grand Prix at Brands Hatch, his first Grand Prix victory. This season saw several teams experiment with 'wings' to generate extra downforce.

LEFT BELOW: Jo Siffert pictured with his wife Nina after his victory in the British Grand Prix.

BOTTOM: Siffert takes the applause of the crowd after his victory.

A 'Nice Time' at the fair

THIS PAGE: Former top British drivers John Surtees and Stirling Moss go head to head at Battersea fun fair while filming the TV programme 'Nice Time'.

Stewart makes a good start with Tyrrell

LEFT: In 1968 Jackie Stewart left the struggling BRM, joining up with Ken Tyrrell's Matra team, and notched up 36 points to take second place in the championship.

BELOW LEFT: McLaren began the season with the BRM-powered M5A. This was soon replaced by the Robin Herd-designed M7A, powered by the Ford V-8 engine. Both Hulme and McLaren performed well in the new car.

BOTTOM: The Lotuses of Graham Hill and Jackie Oliver occupy the front row as the British Grand Prix gets under way. Neither finished the race, which was won by Jo Siffert.

OPPOSITE ABOVE LEFT AND OPPOSITE BELOW RIGHT: Denny Hulme with the Chevrolet-powered M8A, which he drove in the 1968 Can-Am races. He beat team boss Bruce McLaren into second place in the prestigious six-race series.

OPPOSITE ABOVE RIGHT: Earl Mountbatten drinks from the winner's trophy at Brands Hatch.

OPPOSITE BELOW LEFT: Brabham struggled with the unreliable new Repco engine. Jack Brabham himself only managed to complete one of the 12 championship races, while his team mate Jochen Rindt finished in just two.

OPPOSITE BOTTOM: Graham Hill won the championship in his Lotus, with victories in Spain, Mexico and Monaco.

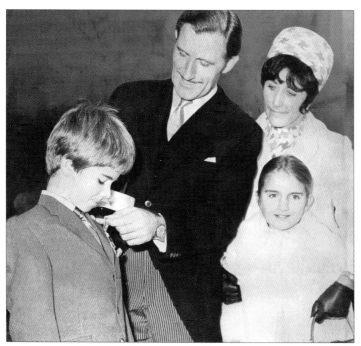

Graham Hill receives an honour

Opposite and left: Graham Hill is honoured with an OBE after winning his second world title. His proud wife Betty and children Brigitte and Damon accompany Graham to Buckingham Palace for the investiture.

Below left and right: Piers Courage in his state-of-the-art £13,000 Brabham car. Although the old Etonian was heir to the Courage brewing fortune, he had to make his own way in motor racing. His best performance was in 1968, a fourth-place finish in the Italian Grand Prix.

The flying Scot

The 1969 season was full of promise for Jackie Stewart, who started the season driving the new Ford-powered Matra MS80. All the problems from the previous model had been ironed out, and since he had still secured the runner-up spot despite injury in 1968, Stewart had every reason to be optimistic. The year saw the usual departures. This time Matra withdrew its works team, leaving its Formula One involvement in the hands of Ken Tyrrell. Three other teams also departed: Honda, Cooper and Eagle.

Stewart finishes two laps ahead

The first race, at Kyalami was dominated by Stewart. His closest challenge came from Mario Andretti, who was continuing his occasional flirtation with Grand Prix racing when other commitments allowed. On this occasion, he was contesting the lead with Stewart before his Lotus gave out with transmission trouble.

Stewart's win in Barcelona was marked by the fact that he finished two laps ahead of the first runner-up, Bruce McLaren, a feat only achieved once since, in 1995. The race was held on the narrow Montjuic circuit and the particularly bad accidents suffered by the Lotus cars saw the massive wings that were held to blame banned for the next event, Monaco.

Hill takes final Grand Prix win

At the start of the Monte Carlo race, Stewart was set to take another fine victory. However ,problems with his halfshaft caused an early retirement and Graham Hill was able to score another Monaco win. It would be Hill's only win of the year and a brief respite for Lotus, who were destined to endure a disappointing season. Privateers fared well at Monaco: Piers Courage, driving a Frank Williams-entered Brabham-Ford, was second and Jo Siffert, in a Walker-Durlacher, third.

Wing controversy

Disagreements over the implementation of safety measures at Spa led to the cancellation of the Belgian Grand Prix. Next instead was Zandvoort, where Rindt took pole position. He led the race until driveshaft failure put him out, and Stewart claimed a third win. Smaller, less controversial wings had sprouted again: the aerofoil was back to stay. Stewart won again in France, then took a fifth victory at Silverstone just two weeks later. His British success was taken on the back of Rindt's problems with his wing, which had come loose, forcing a costly pit stop.

Wings were not the only innovation making headline: both Lotus and McLaren were responding to the previous season's wet-weather challenges by turning out new four-wheel drives. It was to be a brief flirtation with the 4WD, since they were generally unsuccessful.

1969

THE DRIVERS' WORLD CHAMPIONSHIP

1	JACKIE STEWART	GREAT BRITAIN	MATRA	63
2	JACKY ICKX	BELGIUM	BRABHAM	37
3	BRUCE MCLAREN	NEW ZEALAND	MCLAREN	26
4	JOCHEN RINDT	AUSTRIA	LOTUS	22
5	JEAN-PIERRE BELTOISE	FRANCE	MATRA	21
6	DENNY HULME	NEW ZEALAND	MCLAREN	20
7	GRAHAM HILL	GREAT BRITAIN	LOTUS	19
8	PIERS COURAGE	GREAT BRITAIN	BRABHAM	16
9	JO SIFFERT	SWITZERLAND	LOTUS	15
10	JACK BRABHAM	AUSTRALIA	BRABHAM	14

Jacky Ickx drives for Brabham

Gearbox trouble put Stewart into the runner-up position at the Nürburgring; instead young Belgian Jacky Ickx with the Brabham team took the prize.

Jack Brabham himself had an unremarkable year but his new signing, Ickx, was impressive and was now lying second in the championship with 22 points. Stewart's haul of 51 made him virtually untouchable, and with the Italian Grand Prix finishing yet again in his favour, the title was confirmed. On his return to Dumbarton, the Flying Scot received a hero's welcome.

The final three races were all about the runners-up places in the championship table. In Canada, Ickx took the crown – Stewart had already retired. With Stewart finishing early at Watkins Glen, it was Rindt who took the opportunity to score up a Grand Prix win. Graham Hill suffered a bad injury after he experienced a blown tyre and although he raced again during the next season, his Grand Prix career was effectively ended. The final event was won by Danny Hulme for McLaren, but predictably it was Jackie Stewart as Driver Champion and Matra as Constructor Champion who were celebrating at the close.

Stewart celebrates

RIGHT ABOVE AND RIGHT BELOW: Jackie Stewart won six of the 11 championship races in 1969. He was 26 points clear of his nearest rival at the end of the season, clinching the title with three races still to go. Here he celebrates after winning the Race of Champions at Brands Hatch in March.

LEFT: Brazilian Emerson Fittipaldi was a Formula 3 champion in 1969, and had already attracted the attention of several Formula 1 teams.

BOTTOM: Ex-team mates Stewart and Hill stop for a friendly word in the pits. Hill won the Monaco race but only managed one other podium finish during the 1969 season.

OPPOSITE: Jackie Stewart and his wife Helen pictured shortly before the British Grand Prix at Silverstone.

Aerofoil 'wings' cause controversy

BELOW: Flimsy high aerofoils were the subject of much controversy in 1969 after they caused the crashes which put Jochen Rindt and Graham Hill out of the Spanish Grand Prix in Barcelona.

RIGHT: Graham Hill pours his wife Betty a glass of champagne from one of 100 bottles he won after setting the fastest lap during practice for the Race of Champions at Brands Hatch.

OPPOSITE TOP: Jackie Stewart in the new Ford-Cosworth powered Matra MS80.

OPPOSITE CENTRE LEFT AND RIGHT: Helen and Jackie Stewart. Having known Jackie since childhood, she had considerable experience of the stresses of racing.

OPPOSITE BELOW: For Jochen Rindt it was generally an unsuccessful season. He chalked up his first Grand Prix victory, winning at Watkins Glen, but only managed to finished in four races out of the ten in which he started. Here he wins a Formula 2 race at Thruxton.

A new car fit for a champion

BELOW: Jackie Stewart is photographed trying the new March 701 for size. Stewart agreed to drive the March after a dispute caused a split from Matra.

RIGHT: Graham Hill shakes hands with Prime Minister Harold Wilson at a Sportsmen and Sportswomen's lunch.

OPPOSITE ABOVE: Less than two months after his crash at Watkins Glen, Graham Hill jokes with the new champion Jackie Stewart at the Savoy hotel in London.

OPPOSITE BELOW: Jochen Rindt in a Lotus Ford at Oulten Park. The Austrian finished fourth in the world championship. He could have finished higher but he crashed out in Barcelona when well placed and his injuries forced him to sit out of the Monaco race.

Rindt is posthumous champion

Lotus had endured a frustrating season in 1969 but more technical innovation proved useful and in 1970 they unleased the Lotus 72, with its wedge shape, torsion bar suspension and high rear-mounted wing. Colin Chapman's outfit also had a new lead driver, Jochen Rindt, who replaced Graham Hill as number one. On the back of his own disappointing season, Rindt was determined to emulate the kind of success that Stewart and Ickx had enjoyed – in 1970 he did, but fate was cruel to the young Austrian.

In the traditional South African opener, Rindt took a hefty bump from Jack Brabham early in the race and was later then forced to retire with engine trouble. Veteran Brabham, now in his twenty-third year of racing, enjoyed the win with his new Brabham-Ford BT33. Graham Hill, back following an impressive recovery from the accident at Watkins Glen the previous year, finished a creditable sixth.

Bruce McLaren killed

Jackie Stewart was now racing in the new March 701, the car owned by Ken Tyrrell, who had parted ways with Matra. It was an impressive start; the reigning champion won the Spanish Grand Prix, ahead of Bruce McLaren and Mario Andretti. Typically, the new Lotus had teething trouble, and Rindt had retired from the race with ignition problems.

It was the final race for Bruce McLaren, who failed to finish. Just five days before the Belgian Grand Prix, the driver designer was killed while testing his new Can Am car at Goodwood. He was 32 years old.

As a mark of respect, the McLaren team were absent at Spa, but BRM had returned, now sponsored by Yardley, and won the race with Pedro Rodriguez behind the wheel. At Zandvoort, Rindt was back in the Lotus 72, and the modifications were proved a success; he won the race in convincing style. The death of driver friend Piers Courage early in the race had led Rindt to consider retiring, but instead he determined to finish the season.

Three in a row for Rindt

The Austrian went on to win the next three races, extending his lead in the points table. The first of these was in France, where he profited after Ickx's Ferrari and Beltoise's Matra both hit trouble. At Brands Hatch Brabham challenged Rindt for much of the race but ran out of fuel on the final lap. Rindt crossed the line an unlikely winner. A protest regarding the Lotus's aerofoil would have resulted in Brabham being declared the winner, but Rindt was reinstated after a brief period of indecision.

Ickx challenges for the title

The German Grand Prix moved to Hockenheim, and Rindt again came out on top with a narrow victory over Ickx. Together with team mate Regazzoni, Ickx celebrated a one-two in Austria, and with it he became a real threat to Rindt title chances. The Austrian needed a win at Monza.

It was in a high-speed practice run for the Italian Grand Prix that Rindt was killed, his Lotus having smashed into the crash barrier. He was 28. Lotus withdrew from the main race, which was won by Regazzoni in his first season in Formula One.

Trophy awared posthumously

The championship could still have been won by Ickx, who was in a position to better the 45 points that had been amassed by Jochen Rindt; he needed to win all of the final three rounds. Although he finished first in Canada and Mexico, the US Grand Prix eluded him, and he came in fourth at Watkins Glen. Rindt became the only driver to be awarded the championship title after death; his widow collected the trophy.

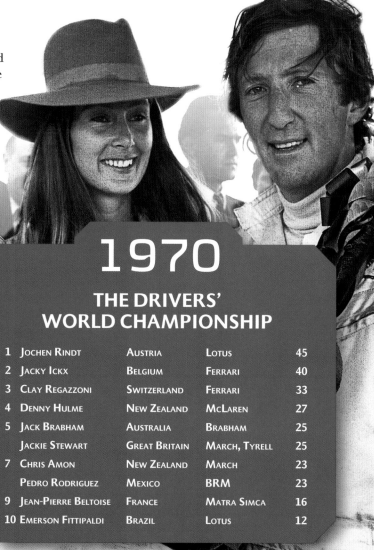

1970
THE DRIVERS' WORLD CHAMPIONSHIP

1	Jochen Rindt	Austria	Lotus	45
2	Jacky Ickx	Belgium	Ferrari	40
3	Clay Regazzoni	Switzerland	Ferrari	33
4	Denny Hulme	New Zealand	McLaren	27
5	Jack Brabham	Australia	Brabham	25
	Jackie Stewart	Great Britain	March, Tyrell	25
7	Chris Amon	New Zealand	March	23
	Pedro Rodriguez	Mexico	BRM	23
9	Jean-Pierre Beltoise	France	Matra Simca	16
10	Emerson Fittipaldi	Brazil	Lotus	12

Hill back at the wheel

LEFT AND FAR LEFT: Graham Hill and family en route to South Africa for the start of the season. It was Hill's first Formula 1 race since his accident at Watkins Glen the previous season; he finished sixth.

BELOW LEFT: Hill and wife Betty at Kyalami

BELOW RIGHT: Ken Tyrrell and Jackie Stewart discuss tactics. The 1970 season was their first as boss and number one driver of the new Tyrrell Racing Organisation.

BOTTOM: Forty-three-year-old Jack Brabham at the wheel of the Brabham-Ford BT33.

OPPOSITE: Jochen Rindt and his wife Nina celebrate his win at Brands Hatch. Rindt had chosen to remain with Lotus despite a poor run during the previous season.

Stewart takes the honours at Jarama

RIGHT: Jackie Stewart winning the Spanish Grand Prix; the victory gave the fledgling Tyrrell team a success in the second race of the season.

BELOW AND OPPOSITE CENTRE LEFT: Jackie Stewart receives the trophy and is congratulated by Graham Hill (below) after winning the Race of Champions.

OPPOSITE TOP: Jack Brabham may have been a veteran but he was still capable of winning the South African event.

OPPOSITE CENTRE RIGHT: MacLaren's number two driver, Denny Hulme, was second at Kyalami and fourth at Monaco but he suffered bad burns when his car caught fire during practice for Indianapolis and was forced to miss the Dutch Grand Prix. He finished the season in fourth position.

OPPOSITE BOTTOM: Hulme driving the new McLaren M14A.

Winners and losers

TOP: Rindt celebrates his success at the French Grand Prix. It was the first of three consecutive wins for the Austrian.

MIDDLE: Graham Hill's departure from Lotus had given Rindt the top driver spot. He is seen here with Colin Chapman (left).

BOTTOM: Hill behind the wheel of the Lotus 49c. Hill had joined Rob Walker's team and was driving an outdated model.

OPPOSITE ABOVE: A Ferrari mechanic shows that it helps to be a contortionist as he works on Jacky Ickx's car at Brands Hatch. It was to no avail: the Belgian failed to finish.

OPPOSITE RIGHT: American Mario Andretti in the March Ford. He failed to make an impact during the 1970 season and would move to Ferrari the following year.

OPPOSITE BOTTOM: Jack Brabham in action at Brands Hatch.

Rindt victorious at Brands Hatch

RIGHT: Jackie Stewart with Nina Rindt.

CENTRE RIGHT: Bruce McLaren had an inauspicious start to the year. He managed to finish only once in the first three races. He was killed just days before the fourth event at Spa.

BELOW: Rindt leads the way with Brabham behind in the British Grand Prix at Brands Hatch.

BOTTOM: Although Brabham finished in second place at Brands Hatch, he did so on an empty tank, having run out of fuel on the last lap.

Bruce McLaren dies at Goodwood

LEFT: Tyre marks on the track at Goodwood show where Bruce McLaren lost his life. The driver-designer had been testing his new Can-Am car when he lost control at high speed.

BELOW: The new Lotus 72, driven by Jochen Rindt. Teething problems forced Rindt to revert to the outdated 49c model at Monaco but he still managed to wrest victory from Jack Brabham, who was leading the race in the last lap.

BOTTOM: Ferrari and Jacky Ickx came to dominate the latter part of the season, winning the Austrian, Canadian and Mexican events and eventually finishing second in the Drivers' Championship.

Rindt becomes posthumous champion

MAIN PICTURE: Rindt behind the wheel of his Lotus. His fatal accident occurred during the final practice for the Italian Grand Prix at Monza when his car hit the crash barrier.

BELOW LEFT: Jacky Ickx was in contention to take the title following Rindt's death if he could win all three final races. However, Ickx's fourth-place finish at Watkins Glen wasn't enough and the title was posthumously won by Rindt.

BELOW RIGHT: The wreckage of Rindt's Lotus is dragged from the circuit. The Austrian was only 28 years old when he died.

Tyrrell takes the title

Despite their success the previous year, the Lotus team were to find the 1971 season disappointing again. Losing Rindt meant that they would have to rely heavily on young and less experienced drivers such as Emerson Fittipaldi, and their continued drive to try out new technologies, such as gas turbines, meant that they finished without a single win. In contrast, 1970 had been a poor year for Jackie Stewart, who had been behind the wheel of the inferior March. But Ken Tyrrell was planning ahead. There was a new car under development, and Stewart had driven it in the final three rounds of the 1970 series. Although he failed to finish on each occasion, the car looked promising. For the 1971 season the car had been further refined, and with its Ford Cosworth engine, it proved to be more powerful and reliable than its rivals.

The main threat to the new Ford-powered cars came from Ferrari. Their new flat-12 engine had shown promise at the end of 1970, and it began 1971 in the same vein. Andretti won the opening Grand Prix, at Kyalami, some 20 seconds ahead of Stewart. It was the first championship success for the worshipper of Alberto Ascari. Twelve-year-old Andretti had been at Monza in 1952 to see Ascari claim his sixth win and his first world title. Signing for Ferrari, the team his hero had driven for, seemed poetic and his South African victory appeared to herald a dream season. However, Andretti would come back to earth with a bump.

Stewart dominates

Instead it was Jackie Stewart who began to steamroller his way to the title. He won the Spanish Grand Prix from Jacky Ickx's Ferrari, finishing 3.4 seconds ahead of the Belgian.

At Monaco he dominated the race from start to finish. In second place was young Swede Ronnie Peterson who impressed as he battled his way past Siffert and Ickx to finish 25 seconds behind the winner in his works March-Ford 711.

The Dutch Grand Prix was marred by bad weather and Stewart's Tyrrell suffered engine problems during practice. During the main event he was forced to go through the motions and trailed home eleventh. Ickx, by contrast, gave a masterclass in wet-weather

driving and came out on top after a race-long battle with another expert in such conditions, Pedro Rodriguez, in the BRM. They finished a lap ahead of the field.

Rodriguez killed

After a further Grand Prix win for Stewart at the new Paul Ricard circuit, near Marseilles, the circus headed towards Silverstone. Sadly, before their arrival, Pedro Rodriguez was killed in a minor sports car event in Germany. Clay Regazzoni, the greatest talent to emerge in 1970, took pole at Silverstone, and led early on. Stewart then took over, and typically, dominated to the finish, followed in by Peterson.

1971

THE DRIVERS' WORLD CHAMPIONSHIP

1	JACKIE STEWART	GREAT BRITAIN	TYRRELL	62
2	RONNIE PETERSON	SWEDEN	MARCH	33
3	FRANCOIS CEVERT	FRANCE	TYRELL	26
4	JACKY ICKX	BELGIUM	FERRARI	19
5	JO SIFFERT	SWITZERLAND	BRM	19
6	EMERSON FITTIPALDI	BRAZIL	LOTUS – TURBINE	16
7	CLAY REGAZZONI	SWITZERLAND	FERRARI	13
8	MARIO ANDRETTI	USA	FERRARI	12
9	CHRIS AMON	NEW ZEALAND	MATRA-SIMCA	9
	PETER GETHIN	GREAT BRITAIN	MCLAREN	9
	DENNY HULME	NEW ZEALAND	MCLAREN	9
	PEDRO RODRIGUEZ	MEXICO	BRM	9
	REINE WISELL	SWEDEN	LOTUS – TURBINE	9

The Tyrrell team enjoyed a further top two finishes at the Nürburgring, with Stewart heading Francois Cevert home, closely challenged in third and fourth by the two Ferrari drivers, Regazzoni and Andretti. Stewart crashed out of the Austrian Grand Prix, but Ickx, who was challenging on points, also failed to finish. Ironically, Stewart was able to assure his world title, despite not finishing. The race was won by Jo Siffert for BRM, his second win since 1968.

There were two Austrians making their Formula One debut that day: Helmut Marko, who finished eleventh and failing to finish in a borrowed March-Ford, Niki Lauda.

Tyrrell and Stewart

Stewart was absent from the tight finish at Monza, where BRM's Peter Gethin stole the line from the pack. With the title in the bag, Stewart's season seemed to be fizzling out, although he did win in Canada, beating Peterson. Watkins Glen provided a fine finish for Tyrrell, with Francois Cevert taking the spoils. The team won the constructors title with eleven victories; Stewart had amassed 62 points in the March. But there was another sad death before the year's end: Jo Siffert was killed in an accident at Brands Hatch.

Lotus and Ferrari prepare their challenge

OPPOSITE: Emerson Fittipaldi with team Lotus. The young Brazilian replaced Rindt as the number one driver in Colin Chapman's outfit.

TOP: Fittipaldi took third place in the British Grand Prix at Brands Hatch.

CENTRE: Fittipaldi drove both the Lotus 72 and the experimental 56B gas turbine car in the 1971 season.

BOTTOM: Jacky Ickx remained at Ferrari for 1971, but the Ford-powered Tyrrell would prove too good for the Scuderia.

Stewart aims for second title

OPPOSITE: Jackie Stewart enjoys a round of golf. The 1971 season started well with Stewart notching up 24 points in the first three races, only one short of his total for the whole of the previous season. With four more wins, he finished the year on 62 points, almost twice the tally of his nearest rival Ronnie Peterson.

RIGHT: Brazilian driver Emerson Fittipaldi.

BELOW: Fittipaldi with his wife Maria Helena.

Young Fittipaldi takes crown

The young Emerson Fittipaldi had shown some early potential, but 1971 had been a disappointing season for the Lotus number one. When Lotus, still under the sponsorship of Imperial Tobacco, unveiled its new-look John Player Special motor, with its black and gold livery and type 72 chassis, they were laying down the gauntlet to Tyrrell. The season was set for an exciting battle between the Scot and the Brazilian.

Jackie Stewart won the opening race in Argentina, but for the remainder of the year he was beset by a stomach ulcer. Fittipaldi had retired early with suspension trouble, but in South Africa he took second behind Denny Hulme. Hulme himself had already notched up second place behind Stewart in Argentina. He was still driving for McLaren, who had been all but absent for three years, concentrating instead on racing in the United States and Canada. Under Yardley's sponsorship, they were back in Formula One and keen to make an impression.

Fittipaldi and Stewart battle for points
Fittipaldi scored the next victory at Jarama besting Jacky Ickx into second. Monaco followed, where appalling weather conditions led to some spectacular retirements. The man who mastered the wet conditions best on the day was Jean-Pierre Beltoise in his BRM. It was the British marque's final Grand Prix success. Fittipaldi heroically managed third, despite poor visibility on the winding circuit. Stewart's Tyrrell was less fortunate and came in at fourth. Another win for the Brazilian came in the Belgian Grand Prix at the new Nivelles circuit; Stewart's ulcer kept him absent. He was back in time for the race at Clermont-Ferrand though, and won with Fittipaldi second. The two were now engaged in a serious battle for points. Fittipaldi beat Stewart to second at Brands Hatch and now led with 43 points to Stewart's 27.

Ickx wins final Grand Prix
The German Grand Prix was just as exciting, although the final line-up did provide a change. Fittipaldi had been chasing the Ferrari of Jacky Ickx when his engine caught fire, enabling Ickx to take his eighth and last Grand Prix victory. Team mate Clay Regazzoni was second, giving Ferrari a much-needed one-two. Unlucky Stewart failed to finish, giving Fittipaldi a clear points lead. His win in Austria extended this. He had kept both Stewart and Denny Hulme at bay and eventually Stewart was relegated to seventh place. The playboy Revlon heir, Peter Revson, finished third, his best finish of the year.

Going into the Italian Grand Prix, Fittipaldi led Stewart by 52 points to 27. Although there were some concerns in the Chapman camp about returning to Monza in the wake of Rindt's death, Fittipaldi took the win to confirm the title. The Ferraris of Ickx and Regazzoni had both retired and the Brazilian easily crossed the line 14 seconds clear of Hailwood. Still racing was Graham Hill, who finished the race that day in fifth position.

Although Stewart won two convincing final wins at Canada and then Watkins Glen, he had to be content with second place in the title line up. Fittipaldi finished 15 points ahead of the Scot and entered the record books as the youngest holder of the championship at just 25 years and 273 days.

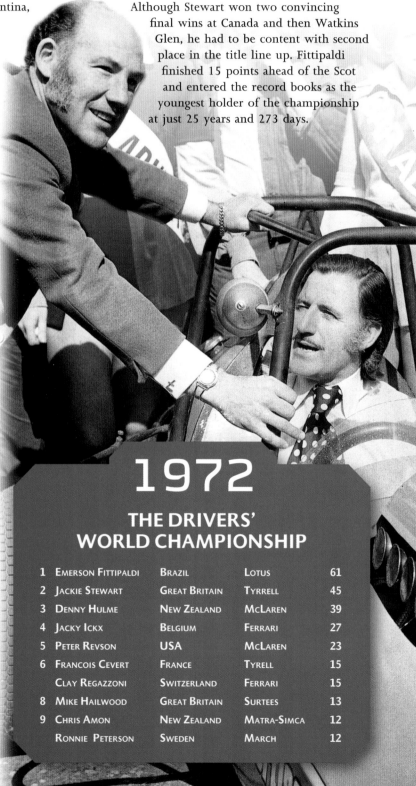

1972
THE DRIVERS' WORLD CHAMPIONSHIP

1	EMERSON FITTIPALDI	BRAZIL	LOTUS	61
2	JACKIE STEWART	GREAT BRITAIN	TYRRELL	45
3	DENNY HULME	NEW ZEALAND	MCLAREN	39
4	JACKY ICKX	BELGIUM	FERRARI	27
5	PETER REVSON	USA	MCLAREN	23
6	FRANCOIS CEVERT	FRANCE	TYRELL	15
	CLAY REGAZZONI	SWITZERLAND	FERRARI	15
8	MIKE HAILWOOD	GREAT BRITAIN	SURTEES	13
9	CHRIS AMON	NEW ZEALAND	MATRA-SIMCA	12
	RONNIE PETERSON	SWEDEN	MARCH	12

Jackie Stewart honoured

OPPOSITE: Graham Hill with Stirling Moss. This was Hill's second championship season with Brabham; he scored just four points but it was an improvement on the previous season's total of two.

LEFT: Jackie Stewart, accompanied by his wife Helen, displays his OBE.

BELOW LEFT: Denny Hulme's victory at Kyalami was his and McLaren's first success since 1969. He is seen here celebrating his fastest lap at the Race of Champions.

BELOW RIGHT: John Surtees during his final season. A champion on two wheels and four, he had accumulated six Formula 1 wins and one world title.

Fittipaldi steals the title

BELOW LEFT AND RIGHT: Fittipaldi wearing victor's laurels. He took five championship wins in 1972 to steal the championship title from favourite Jackie Stewart.

RIGHT: Jackie Stewart was a a popular figure both on and off the track. Here he is in discussion with film director Roman Polanski.

OPPOSITE: Ronnie Peterson (centre) and Niki Lauda (right) were the main drivers for the March team. It was Lauda's first Formula 1 season, but by the end of the year both men would be frustrated by their drives and keen to move on.

Stewart wins final championship

When the competition began again in 1973, it was the same line-up as the previous year. Lotus were fielding Fittipaldi supported by Peterson; Tyrrell had Stewart with Cevert. Both Peterson and Cevert had endured relatively disappointing seasons up to now, Peterson had felt particularly held back by the limitations of the March, so he had joined Lotus.

Lotus took the first two victories of the season with Fittipaldi but Stewart had to wait until South Africa before he could celebrate his own win. He was already considering retirement and was keen to finish his career at the very top. In second place at Kylami was Peter Revson, who was driving the old M19, whereas team mate Hulme, who had been given the new McLaren M23, could only manage fifth. Both drivers would race the new machine from now on.

Fittipaldi won his third victory in Spain, with Francois Cevert a distant second. Both Stewart and Peterson failed to finish: Stewart with brake problems, the Swede with gearbox trouble, having already led and set the fastest lap. Stewart then had back-to-back victories in Belgium and Monaco.

James Hunt debuts
The top six finishers at Monaco mirrored exactly the final championship table. Stewart won narrowly from Fittipaldi. Peterson finally had some luck and finished third, ahead of Cevert. Revson and Hulme in the new McLarens came fifth and sixth – they were clearly the strongest of the other contenders. Making a debut for Hesketh Racing in a March 731 was a new British hope, James Hunt. He finished in ninth position.

First Swedish Grand Prix
Sweden hosted its first Grand Prix event next and the winner in Anderstorp was Denny Hulme. It was his only his second win in four years. Second place went to Peterson, who had been so desperate to celebrate on home soil that he had taken pole and led for all but the final two laps, until a puncture ended his hopes.

Accidents and tragedy
It all came right for Peterson at the French Grand Prix, when he capitalised on the misfortune of others, in this case, Jody Scheckter. The South African crashed out, having led to the three-quarter mark. Scheckter was going to become a force to be reckoned with, but he was still impulsive and hot-headed. At Silverstone he crashed out in the first lap, taking 13 other cars with him. Revson eventually won, with Peterson in second. James Hunt had made fourth. The Silverstone pile-up was relatively harmless, but an accident at Zandvoort saw Roger Williamson's March hit the barriers in flames. The race continued as the car burned, and although David Purley stopped to save Williamson, he was unable to do so alone. Williamson died in the wreck and was left on the side of the track until after the race had ended. It was a muted podium celebration for Stewart, Cevert and Hunt, who finished in first, second and third respectively.

Tyrrell took the one-two with Stewart and Cevert again in the German Grand Prix. Fittipaldi and Peterson looked about to finish the same way in Austria until the Brazilian was put out and Peterson won. As ever, the decider was Monza. Peterson, leading Fittipaldi, failed to let his number one through and he cost him the championship. Peterson would win again in the final round at Watkins Glen, finishing three points behind Fittipaldi on the final table, but it wasn't enough and he left to join McLaren at the end of the season.

Stewart retires after tragedy
Revson won in Canada. It was Stewart's 99th race and he finished fifth. But on what would have been his 100th and final race, tragic circumstances led to his withdrawal. Team mate Francois Cevert was killed in practice and a distraught Jackie Stewart never raced again. His five wins that year made a total of 27, putting him two ahead of Jim Clark on the all-time list. It was a record that would stand for fourteen years.

1973
THE DRIVERS' WORLD CHAMPIONSHIP

1	Jackie Stewart	Great Britain	Tyrrell	71
2	Emerson Fittipaldi	Brazil	JPS/Lotus	55
3	Ronnie Peterson	Sweden	JPS/Lotus	52
4	Francois Cevert	France	Tyrell	47
5	Peter Revson	USA	McLaren	38
6	Denny Hulme	New Zealand	McLaren	26
7	Carlos Reutemann	Argentina	Brabham	16
8	James Hunt	Great Britain	March	14
9	Jacky Ickx	Belgium	Ferrari, McLaren Iso	
			Williams/Marlboro	12
10	Jean-Pierre Beltoise	France	BRM	9

Stewart celebrates on the road to victory

OPPOSITE: Stewart celebrates his victory at the German Grand Prix, one of five wins that season that helped bring him his third title. The death of his team mate Francois Cevert in practice before the US Grand Prix influenced his decision to make this his final season in Formula 1.

LEFT: Ronnie Peterson (left) with Jacky Ickx.

BELOW LEFT: Emersen Fittipaldi, flanked by Helen Stewart (left) and his wife Maria (right).

BELOW RIGHT: Ronnie Peterson, one of the best drivers never to win the championship. He spent much of the 1972 season contending with team mate Fittipaldi, enabling Stewart, supported by Cevert, to secure the title.

Reigning champion defeated

RIGHT: Calm before the storm. Fittipaldi is able to relax having won three events from the first four of the season. However, after a flying start, he failed to win another race and was forced to retire on four occasions.

BELOW: Fittipaldi's expression shows the pressure of defending the world title. When Lotus put its support behind Peterson, the Brazilian's hopes were dashed further.

OPPOSITE LEFT: Denny Hulme at the Nürburgring in his sixth season at McLaren. Hulme finished the year in sixth place, having notched up 26 points.

OPPOSITE RIGHT: Helen Stewart, the dutiful racing wife.

Fittipaldi wins again

The 1974 turned out to be a dramatically close race for the title with no fewer than seven different drivers taking the top spot on the podium and three men still in with a chance of winning the championship going into the final race. McLaren were now backed by Texaco and Marlboro and had brought Fittipaldi onto the team alongside Denny Hulme, who was now in his seventh year with the team. Lotus replaced Fittipaldi with Ickx who raced alongside Ronnie Peterson. Ferrari, keen to bounce back, welcomed on board Clay Regazzoni, who had been with BRM the previous season. Alongside him came Niki Lauda, also from BRM.

Hulme took the opening honours in Argentina, in what was to be his final year. Although local hero Carlos Reutemann had led virtually all the way in the impressive Gordon Murray-designed Brabham BT44, he had run out of fuel two laps from the finish and Hulme came first. In Brazil it was Fittipaldi who prevailed. Like his team mate Hulme, he had a piece of luck when his rival, Peterson, suffered a puncture. McLaren had enjoyed back-to-back wins

Death of Peter Revson

The race at Kyalami was overshadowed by the death of Peter Revson in practice. Carlos Reutemann claimed the victory and it was his maiden Grand Prix. It was Ferrari's turn to be jubilant at the Spanish Grand Prix when Lauda and Regazzoni scored a one-two respectively; but the team mates were to become rivals as the season progressed. At the Belgian Grand Prix, Regazzoni initially led but it was Fittipaldi who won a fraction of a second ahead of Lauda, with Regazzoni back in fourth.

Ronnie Peterson became the fifth winner in six races when he came out on top at Monaco. The victory coincided with Lotus's decision to bring back the ageing but competitive 72 model following the disappointment of the 76. Scheckter took second in Monaco, while Regazzoni continued his impressively consistent form by finishing fourth.

Ferrari failed to finish in Sweden, but Scheckter came in first in front of fellow Tyrrell driver Patrick Depailler. The Scuderia bounced back in Holland however, when Lauda and Regazzoni made it a one-two.

Lauda is quickest driver

At the French Grand Prix it was all about Lauda and Peterson. Although Lauda had pole position, it was Peterson who dominated the race and won. At Brands Hatch, Lauda fared better, leading for 69 of the 75 laps, but a puncture cut him short and Scheckter profited. Lauda's reputation was growing; he was fast becoming the quickest driver of the year,

taking pole position nine times out of 15 championship races. But he was inexperienced and apt to make mistakes, such as his early exit from the Nürburgring when he had failed to warm up his tyres. The German Grand Prix went to Regazzoni.

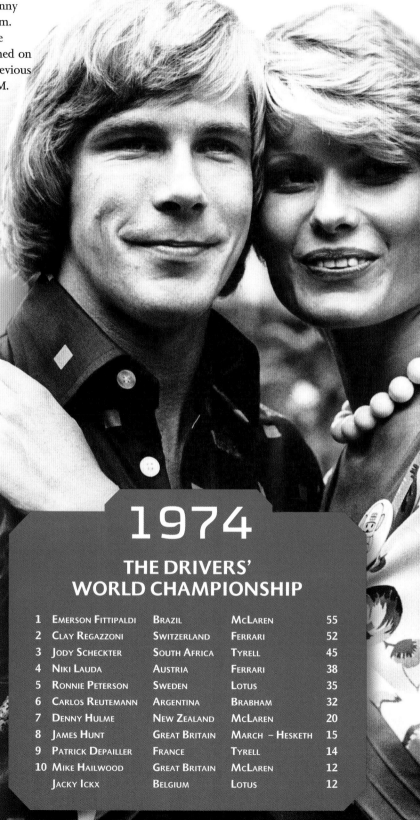

1974

THE DRIVERS' WORLD CHAMPIONSHIP

1	EMERSON FITTIPALDI	BRAZIL	MCLAREN	55
2	CLAY REGAZZONI	SWITZERLAND	FERRARI	52
3	JODY SCHECKTER	SOUTH AFRICA	TYRELL	45
4	NIKI LAUDA	AUSTRIA	FERRARI	38
5	RONNIE PETERSON	SWEDEN	LOTUS	35
6	CARLOS REUTEMANN	ARGENTINA	BRABHAM	32
7	DENNY HULME	NEW ZEALAND	MCLAREN	20
8	JAMES HUNT	GREAT BRITAIN	MARCH – HESKETH	15
9	PATRICK DEPAILLER	FRANCE	TYRELL	14
10	MIKE HAILWOOD	GREAT BRITAIN	MCLAREN	12
	JACKY ICKX	BELGIUM	LOTUS	12

Eleven races had run and Regazzoni led the table with 44 points: six ahead of Lauda. Yet Ferrari failed to instruct Lauda to give Regazzoni the support to win. Instead the team mates went head to head at Monza, and they were both forced to retire their shattered engines as a result. Peterson, Fittipaldi and Scheckter took the race in that order and now suddenly everyone was in the mix.

Fittipaldi wins thrilling climax

At the penultimate race in Canada, Lauda made another costly mistake, skidding out to let Fittipaldi win. Again

Regazzoni had reason to criticise Lauda: his actions had brought Fittipaldi up level with him on points. The US Grand Prix was the traditional finale venue and it was a head to head between Fittipaldi and Regazzoni. Although Jody Scheckter had a slender chance of taking the title, he failed to finish. Regazzoni experienced terrible handling problems. He only needed to finish ahead of Fittipaldi, and despite Lauda's sportsmanlike efforts to hold up the rest of the pack, he failed to do so, handing the Brazilian another title.

Hunt emerges as British number one

OPPOSITE: James Hunt with fiancée Susie Miller. Hunt was the natural successor to Jackie Stewart, who had retired at the end of the 1973 season, as Britain's top driver.

LEFT: James Hunt showing he is as competent on two wheels as on four.

BELOW: Niki Lauda had joined Ferrari and had quickly established himself as the fastest driver of the year in the 312B3. Lauda was first home at Jarama in Spain, the first of his 25 Grand Prix victories.

McLaren team takes the double

OPPOSITE ABOVE LEFT : Emerson Fittipaldi driving the McLaren M23. The year would see the outfit win both the drivers' and the constructors' championships.

OPPOSITE ABOVE RIGHT: Lauda started in pole position in nine of the 15 events of the season.

OPPOSITE BELOW: Niki Lauda is forced into the pits at Brands Hatch by a puncture.

LEFT: James Hunt poses for the cameras. His Hesketh 308 was inspired by the March cars, and despite the team's underdog status, with Hunt behind the wheel it soon began to perform.

JAMES HUNT

GOODƒ

Celebrations on and off the track

RIGHT: Jacky Ickx in contemplative mood before the start of the British Grand Prix.

BELOW RIGHT: The British Grand Prix is won by Jody Scheckter, his second victory of the season, having already won the Swedish event in June.

BELOW LEFT: Jackie Stewart gives his wife Helen some tips about handling a gun. Stewart had excelled at shooting before becoming involved in motor racing, only just missing inclusion in the British Olympic team in 1960.

OPPOSITE: Grand Prix racing and glamour were closely entwined: James and Susie Hunt on their wedding day.

Scheckter loses out on title

OPPOSITE ABOVE: Jody Scheckter (left) and Denny Hulme (right) seen with Helen Stewart at the annual charity cricket match between the drivers and the Lord's Taverners. Perhaps unsurprisingly, the drivers lost.

OPPOSITE BELOW: Scheckter drives the Ford-powered Tyrrell 007. Scheckter still had a chance of winning the championship in the final round at Watkins Glen but his retirement from the race left Fittipaldi free to take the title.

LEFT: Jacky Ickx made the move from Ferrari to Lotus, but his decision was to prove disappointing. He could only manage third places in Brazil and at Brands Hatch, failing to finish in nine of the season's 15 races.

BELOW: Team mates Ronnie Peterson and Jacky Ickx. Peterson finished fifth in the title race on 35 points, while Ickx ended the season with 12 points.

Ferrari back on form

Ferrari held on to Lauda and Regazzoni for 1975, but now it was clear that Regazzoni was the number two driver. Lauda was now a year older and wiser, and he was determined to learn from the mistakes of the previous year and to win the world crown. It wouldn't be easy; Fittipaldi won the opener in Argentina and then again in Brazil. But Ferrari had a new 312T model ready to debut. Designed by Mauro Forghieri, the new car had a transverse gearbox, which improved weight distribution. They unveiled the car at Kyalami and their fortunes were immediately reversed.

Controversy at Barcelona

Although the Ferrari didn't win in South Africa – that honour went to Jody Scheckter – initial teething problems were ironed out and Lauda, who finished fifth, was enthusiastic. There was no victory in Spain either; this time a shunt from Mario Andretti put Lauda out and Regazzoni got caught up in the ensuing chaos. The race was ended after just 29 laps. A terrible crash involving Rolf Stommelen resulted in the death of four spectators when the barrier was breached. The Drivers Association had already protested about the safety of the barriers and threatened to withdraw; concerns over barrier safety had been rising since the deaths of drivers such as Francois Cevert and Helmut Koinigg. Jochen Mass had been leading, from Ickx and Reutemann and all received half points. The race also saw the first ladies point awarded, to Lella Lombardi who came sixth.

In Monaco, Lauda's charge began. He beat Fittipaldi at Monte Carlo by three seconds, then in Belgium it was Scheckter who came second. Following a third win in Sweden he was forced to accept the runner-up position at Zandvoort, behind James Hunt in the Hesketh. The Hesketh team were running without sponsorship, now a financial necessity and they were forced to quit at the end of the year. In France, Lauda took revenge on Hunt, having led for the majority of the race. Like Barcelona, the British Grand Prix was curtailed, but this time because of heavy rain, which had made the track impossibly slippery. Fittipaldi had been leading when the red flag was waved.

At the German Grand Prix, Jacques Laffite picked up a much needed second place for the Williams team, which had been involved in Formula One since their partnership with de Tomaso in 1969. By the mid seventies, Frank Williams was struggling with sponsorship and the attention brought by Laffite's success would save the outfit. Lauda had been pulled up with a puncture and so finished in third, the win had gone to Reutemann.

Bad weather dogged the Austrian Grand Prix. A fatality in the practice, that of Mark Donohue of the Penske team, overshadowed the race. It was won by Vittorio Brambilla, although he too crashed over the line in his works March. Half points were again awarded for the curtailed event. Regazzoni beat Lauda for only the third time in the season at Monza, the penultimate race. Yet Lauda's third place put him out of sight on points. His fifth position in the final round at Watkins Glen put him 19.5 points clear of Fittipaldi.

The title belonged to Lauda and Ferrari: for Lauda it was thanks to the investment of the team and the car itself; to everyone else, Lauda's sheer determination was an inspiration.

The season again ended on a sad note, with the premature death of Graham Hill. Hill had been running the Embassy Racing team for two years and was retiring from racing to concentrate on management. When the light aircraft he was piloting crashed in fog, both he and several members of the team, including driver Tony Brise, lost their lives. It was a sad loss; Hill had become a popular ambassador for racing. He left behind a wife and three children.

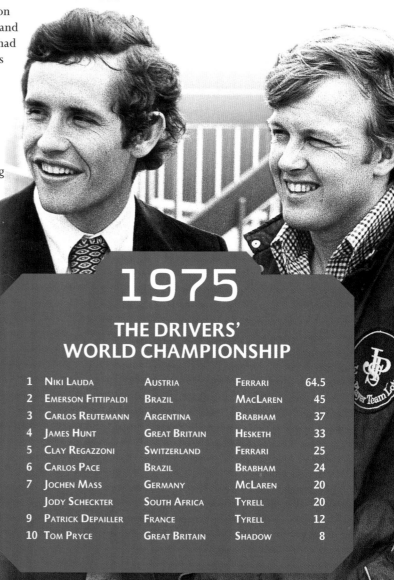

1975

THE DRIVERS' WORLD CHAMPIONSHIP

1	NIKI LAUDA	AUSTRIA	FERRARI	64.5
2	EMERSON FITTIPALDI	BRAZIL	MACLAREN	45
3	CARLOS REUTEMANN	ARGENTINA	BRABHAM	37
4	JAMES HUNT	GREAT BRITAIN	HESKETH	33
5	CLAY REGAZZONI	SWITZERLAND	FERRARI	25
6	CARLOS PACE	BRAZIL	BRABHAM	24
7	JOCHEN MASS	GERMANY	MCLAREN	20
	JODY SCHECKTER	SOUTH AFRICA	TYRELL	20
9	PATRICK DEPAILLER	FRANCE	TYRELL	12
10	TOM PRYCE	GREAT BRITAIN	SHADOW	8

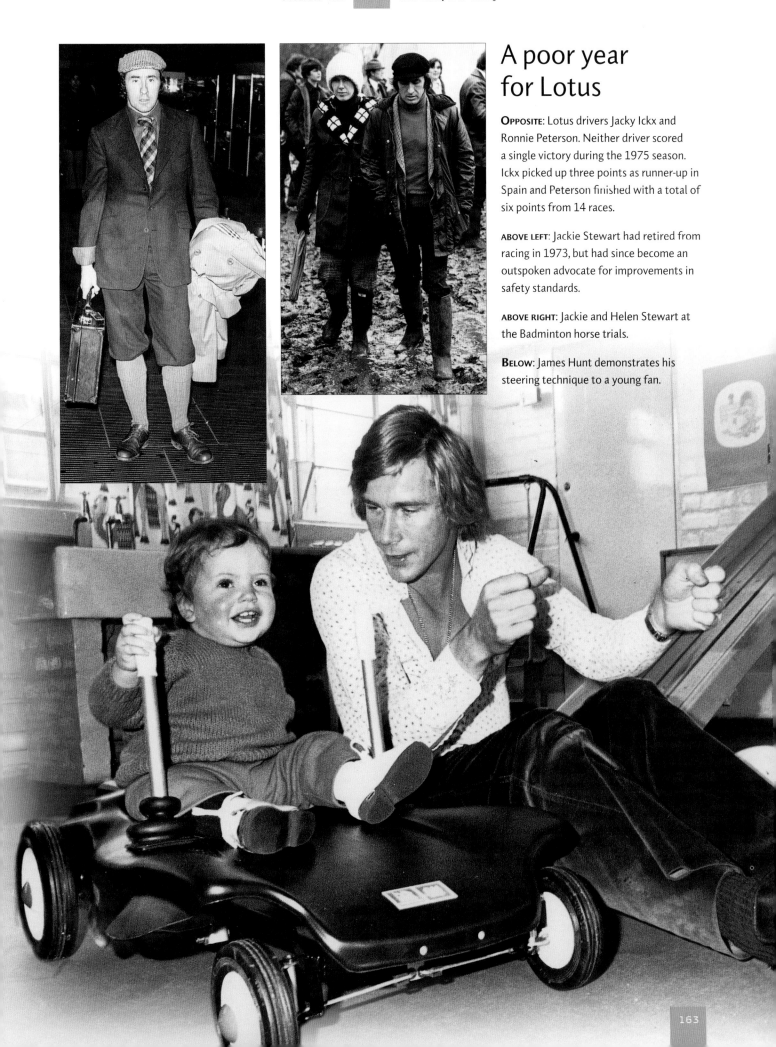

A poor year for Lotus

OPPOSITE: Lotus drivers Jacky Ickx and Ronnie Peterson. Neither driver scored a single victory during the 1975 season. Ickx picked up three points as runner-up in Spain and Peterson finished with a total of six points from 14 races.

ABOVE LEFT: Jackie Stewart had retired from racing in 1973, but had since become an outspoken advocate for improvements in safety standards.

ABOVE RIGHT: Jackie and Helen Stewart at the Badminton horse trials.

BELOW: James Hunt demonstrates his steering technique to a young fan.

Scheckter wins in South Africa

BOTTOM LEFT AND RIGHT: Jody Scheckter enjoyed the glory of a home win at Kyalami, but the victory in South Africa was unmatched for the rest of the season.

BELOW: Hunt was victorious in only one race during 1975, but he still managed a creditable fourth position in the final standings.

LEFT: Former Tyrrell champion Jackie Stewart (right) pictured with Tyrrell's number one driver Jody Scheckter (left).

FAR LEFT: James and Susie Hunt at a charity event for the Anglo-American Sporting Club.

Loss of a former champion

OPPOSITE: The wreckage of the Piper Aztec light aircraft which had crashed in thick fog just three miles from Elstree airfield. Pilot Graham Hill was killed along with five others from his Embassy Hill team.

RIGHT: Hunt poses for the cameras.

BELOW: 1975 was a spectacular season for Nikki Lauda, pictured here with his girlfriend Micki de Rauch. Victories in Monaco, Belgium, Sweden, France and the USA, as well as three other podium finishes, ensured that he won the championship with a huge margin over his nearest rival, Emerson Fittipaldi.

Drama and near-death

1976 was a year packed with drama. The championship was closely contested by Niki Lauda, who dominated the first part of the season, and James Hunt, who reigned in the second half. Appeals and disputes peppered the season, and Lauda's crash at the Nürburgring in August almost cost the Austrian his life.

Lauda began with an excellent run, winning the first two races in Brazil and South Africa and then taking second place behind team mate Regazzoni at Long Beach in the US. Hunt, on the other hand, was having less luck. He had moved to McLaren following Hesketh's withdrawal at the end of the 1975 season but had so far only finished once, at Kyalami where he came in second.

Appeal at Spanish Grand Prix

The first drama was at the Spanish Grand Prix in Jarama. The race itself was won by Hunt, who had overtaken Lauda halfway through and had held onto to his lead. Afterwards, Hunt was sensationally disqualified for having driven in a car that was considered too wide; Lauda was then awarded first place. McLaren put in an appeal that would take several weeks to resolve and eventually the decision was reversed and Lauda's points were consequently reduced.

Tyrrell unveil six-wheel car

In Belgium Lauda finished well again; he and Rigazzoni took the one-two for Ferrari in their new 312T2 cars. Tyrrell, meanwhile, had unveiled their latest creation, the six-wheeled P34, which took points for Scheckter, who came in fourth. The car would go on to win at Sweden, its only Grand Prix win. The six-wheel concept was later abandoned.

At Monaco Lauda beat off the threat posed by both Scheckter and Depailler in the six-wheelers to win the race, ahead of both Tyrrells. He was now well ahead in the title race, with a haul of 47 points in only six races. There were, however, ten more Grands Prix left to run and Lauda's fortune was about to turn.

In France it was James Hunt's turn to wear the winner's laurels; he had benefited from the early retirement of Lauda owing to engine trouble. Salt was rubbed further into Lauda's wound when the news of the decision following the Spanish appeal came in. The point margin between the two had closed and suddenly Hunt was threatening.

There was further controversy at Brands Hatch. A collision at the start had led to a restart, but during the time before the race could begin again, Hunt had illegally swapped to a spare car. Hunt went on to win the race ahead of Lauda, but Ferrari contested and a second inquiry took place. Hunt was disqualified and the Austrian was awarded the maximum points.

The British Grand Prix was followed by the German Grand Prix, that is primarily remembered for the crash which disfigured Niki Lauda. His car had gone into a spin on only the second lap. As it bounced off the bank it burst into flames and was then hit by two cars. Lauda was trapped inside and sustained terrible burns; the inhalation of toxic gases put him into a coma from which it was feared he would never recover. Yet just five weeks after the crash, Lauda was back behind the wheel of his Ferrari at Monza, where he took fourth place.

Hunt won the restarted German race and later took fourth at Osterreichring and won at Zandvoort. His back-to-back wins at Canada and Watkins Glen meant that he had caught up on points. Therefore the final race, the debut Grand Prix for Japan, was a tense decider. Lauda was three points ahead, but poor visibility and a wet track meant that it was all down to risk. Perhaps unsurprisingly, Lauda decided to withdraw after just two laps and the title went to Hunt, who by finishing in third place took just one point more than Lauda for the championship.

1976
THE DRIVERS' WORLD CHAMPIONSHIP

1	JAMES HUNT	GREAT BRITAIN	MCLAREN	69
2	NIKI LAUDA	AUSTRIA	FERRARI	68
3	JODY SCHECKTER	SOUTH AFRICA	TYRELL	49
4	PATRICK DEPAILLER	FRANCE	TYRELL	39
5	CLAY REGAZZONI	SWITZERLAND	FERRARI	31
6	MARIO ANDRETTI	USA	LOTUS, PARNELL	22
7	JACQUES LAFFITE	FRANCE	LIGIER	20
	JOHN WATSON	GREAT BRITAIN	PENSKE	20
9	JOCHEN MASS	GERMANY	MCLAREN	19
10	GUNNAR NILSSON	SWEDEN	LOTUS	11

Car designs spark controversy

LEFT ABOVE: Race officials check the aerofoils on Niki Lauda's Ferrari as the driver looks on.

LEFT BELOW: The technical inventiveness of designers meant that officials needed to be even more vigilant in their search for possible infringements of the rules.

BOTTOM: Reggazoni's Ferrari can be seen facing in the wrong direction following a shunt; the McLaren of James Hunt is caught up in the aftermath.

OPPOSITE: Hunt had moved to McLaren for the start of the 1976 season, but initial successes were thin on the ground, Hunt retiring from four of the first six events. He is seen here celebrating his record fastest lap at the Race of Champions.

RIGHT: Niki Lauda enjoys a brief spell as a race marshall.

BELOW RIGHT: The Penske is being driving by Ulsterman John Watson. Watson began racing in 1973, entering only two events that year. The following season he notched up 6 points, but it wasn't until 1976 that he stood on the podium, taking third place in the French Grand Prix. His first Formula 1 victory came in the same season, at the Austrian event in August. It was the Penske team's only win.

BOTTOM: The Brabham team of Carlos Reutemann and Carlos Pace were now driving with Alfa Romeo engines, but 1976 was a disappointing season for both drivers.

OPPOSITE ABOVE AND BELOW: James Hunt pictured among the spectators.

the danger, says
only cloud in my

Near disaster at the Nurburgring

LEFT: Niki Lauda made a remarkable recovery from his terrible accident at the Nurburgring when his car spun off the track and burst into flames. He was unconscious when he was finally rescued and for several days it was not certain that he would survive the ordeal. However, he managed to rejoin the competition a few weeks later, although many felt that his return was too soon.

BELOW LEFT: Fifteen-year-old Damon Hill shows early signs of following in his father's footsteps.

BELOW RIGHT: James Hunt and new girlfriend in a domestic pose.

OPPOSITE ABOVE: By the last event of the season, in Fuji, Japan, both Hunt and Lauda were within reach of the title. Rain and fog made driving dangerous and after two laps Lauda withdrew from the race. Hunt pressed on and managed to hang on to third place, taking the World Championship title by just one point.

OPPOSITE BELOW: Hunt poses with the new McLaren M26.

Lauda takes second title

Niki Lauda's relationship with Ferrari suffered after the events in Japan in 1976 and although the Italian outfit kept him on board, he was now effectively the number two driver to Argentinean Carlos Reutemann. Before the year was out Lauda would leave Ferrari, but only once his championship title had been confirmed. The year also saw the debut of a new team: Wolf, which had been formed following the demise of Hesketh. With Jody Scheckter on board, Wolf managed to win their debut outing, at the opening Grand Prix at Argentina.

Tragedy at Kyalami

Reutemann won the next event at Interlagos, Brazil. He led with a comfortable 10-second cushion over Hunt, with Lauda coming in at third. At Kyalami, Lauda took the spoils in his first Grand Prix victory since the crash in Germany. Yet there was tragedy in South Africa that day when Tom Pryce accidentally hit a marshal, who was crossing the track; both men were instantly killed. Another loss to the sport came just before the next round at Long Beach when Brabham's key driver, Brazilian Carlos Pace, was killed in a plane crash.

Long Beach was the setting for a victory by Mario Andretti, the first of four wins for the Lotus driver that year. He was now driving a Lotus 78, which made use of sidepods on either side of the cockpit in order to create downforce.

When Niki Lauda missed the Spanish Grand Prix for no apparent reason, many put the blame on his souring relations with Ferrari. Andretti took a convincing win; his Lotus had led for the majority of the race. Ferrari had to be content with second place, thanks to Reutemann. At Monaco it was Scheckter's turn, giving Wolf its second win of the season and the Cosworth DFV engine its 100th Grand Prix win. Lauda was second once again, and his steady, consistent performances were earning him valuable points.

Gunnar Nilsson took his only Grand Prix win at Zolder, driving for Lotus; his career was cut short by cancer in 1978. Lotus were less fortunate at the Swedish Grand Prix, when Andretti, who had both led and set the fastest lap, was overtaken by five cars at the end, the first of which belonged to Jacques Laffite in the Ligier. But typically, fortune turned full circle by the next race, and Andretti was able to capitalize on the misfortune of John Watson in order to win the French event.

Return of Renault

Meanwhile, the reigning champion had been enduring a poor season, with too many retirements and low finishes. On home soil, Silverstone, Hunt was involved in a close tussle with Watson for two-thirds of the race, until the Ulsterman's Brabham developed a fuel injection problem. Hunt finally won and Lauda came in at second, but for the Englishman it was too late to contend the championship. The race was also significant for Renault's return to racing, after an absence of almost 70 years – despite teething trouble, their turbo-charged car was the thing of the future.

By the time the circus arrived at Canada, the championship was already in the bag for Lauda. Although he had had only three wins, one fewer than Andretti, his consistent collection of points had secured him a second. After waving goodbye to Ferrari, Lauda signed for Bernie Ecclestone's Brabham team.

1977

THE DRIVERS' WORLD CHAMPIONSHIP

1	Niki Lauda	Austria	Ferrari	72
2	Jody Scheckter	South Africa	Wolf	55
3	Mario Andretti	USA	Lotus	47
4	Carlos Reutemann	Argentina	Ferrari	42
5	James Hunt	Great Britain	McLaren	40
6	Jochen Mass	Germany	McLaren	25
7	Alan Jones	Australia	Shadow	22
8	Gunnar Nilsson	Sweden	Lotus	20
	Patrick Depailler	France	Tyrell	20
10	Jacques Laffite	France	Ligier	18

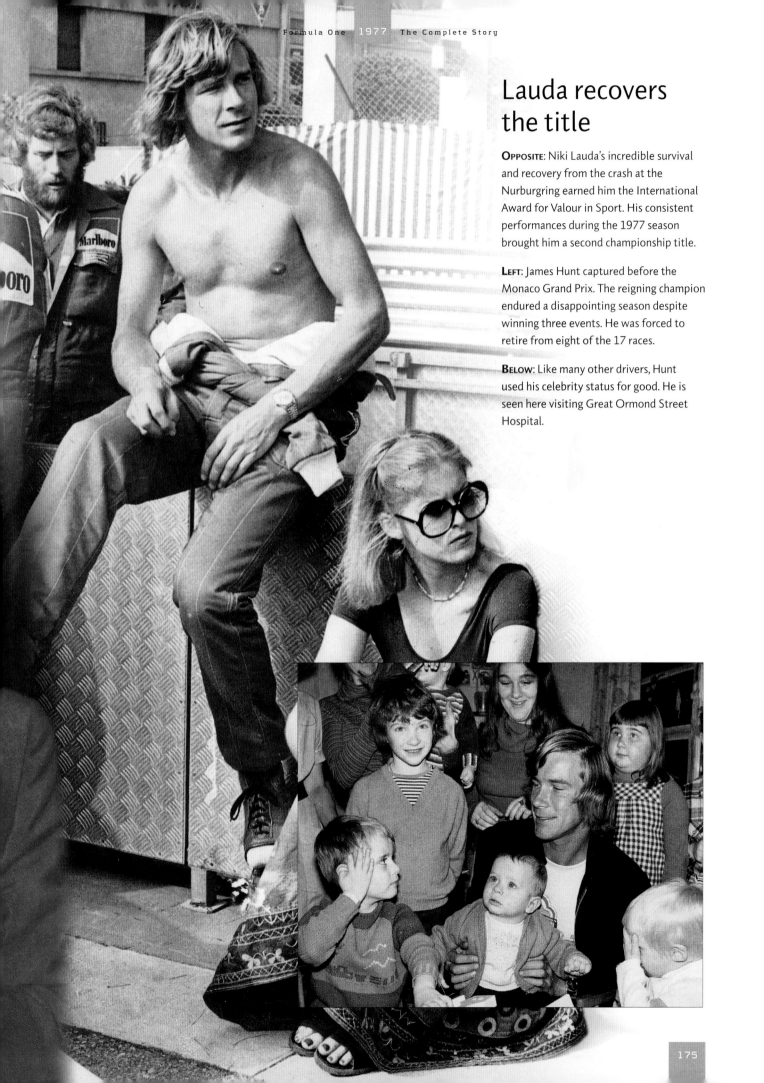

Lauda recovers the title

Opposite: Niki Lauda's incredible survival and recovery from the crash at the Nurburgring earned him the International Award for Valour in Sport. His consistent performances during the 1977 season brought him a second championship title.

Left: James Hunt captured before the Monaco Grand Prix. The reigning champion endured a disappointing season despite winning three events. He was forced to retire from eight of the 17 races.

Below: Like many other drivers, Hunt used his celebrity status for good. He is seen here visiting Great Ormond Street Hospital.

Opposite above left: Jody Scheckter pictured with his wife. The South African joined the new Wolf team and finished the season in an impressive second position.

Opposite above right: Hunt celebrates his first victory of the year at Silverstone.

Opposite below left: Despite winning four races, one more than Lauda, Mario Andretti came third in the title race.

Opposite below right: Niki Lauda prepares for the British Grand Prix at Silverstone, a race in which he came in second. With the rest of the pack evenly competing for points, Lauda was steadily accruing an unassailable total.

This Page: Hunt attracted as much attention off the track as on it. Here he is pictured with girlfriend Jane Birbeck. The couple were the focus of much media speculation, but rumours of marriage were denied – Hunt had still not divorced Susie, despite her 'marriage' to Richard Burton.

Ickx preparing to bow out

RIGHT AND FAR RIGHT: Jacky Ickx never really recovered from a crash at Watkins Glen during the previous season and by 1977 his career was clearly on the wane. He made just one appearance for Ensign, at Monaco where he finished tenth, although he did have a third successive win at Le Mans that year.

CENTRE: Ulsterman John Watson had joined Brabham but he reached the podium only once in 1977, a second place at Dijon.

BOTTOM: Carlos Reutemann at Silverstone. Despite being Ferrari's number one driver, the Argentinian was overshadowed by team mate Lauda.

OPPOSITE: Lauda pictured with motorcycle ace Barry Sheen: both men were headed towards championship titles.

OPPOSITE BELOW: Ronnie Peterson raced with Tyrrell and was chosen to drive their revolutionary, but ultimately unsuccessful, six-wheeler.

Lotus outdo Ferrari

There was the usual shuffle of drivers in advance of the 1978 season. Niki Lauda's move to Brabham left space at Ferrari for some new blood and Carlos Reutemann was joined by French-Canadian Gilles Villeneuve. At Lotus, the loss of Gunnar Nilsson to Arrow made space for Ronnie Peterson to return. Although he would now be playing second fiddle to Andretti, the move was a positive one for the Swede, who had had three poor seasons. Three teams would dominate the running in 1978: Ferrari and Lotus, were still caught in their seemingly eternal struggle, and Brabham, now run by entrepreneur and champion of constructors everywhere, Bernie Ecclestone.

Lotus and Ferrari fight it out

Lotus had continued the development of their cars. This year they made even more use of the ground effect concept and the new Lotus 79 gave Andretti the edge. He won the opening round in Argentina, ahead of Lauda in Brabham's Alfa Romeo. It was Ferrari who took the spoils next, with Reutemann winning at Jacarepagua, Brazil. The see-saw continued, with Lotus and Ronnie Peterson winning at Kyalami, then Reutemann again at Long Beach. The next race, at Monaco, was the only one in the entire series in which neither Ferrari nor Lotus registered a single point. Peterson and Villeneuve retired, while Reutemann and Andretti finished out of the points. Patrick Depailler, the nearly man on so many occasions, took advantage of the fact and eased home ahead of Lauda.

Brabham run the 'fan car'

Andretti duly won in Belgium, with Peterson following him home in the old 78 model. They followed this up with another one-two in Spain, with both drivers in 79s. Brabham were also keen to create downforce; their creation was the brainchild of Gordon Murray who had mounted a large fan on the rear of the car that would draw the air from underneath, creating a vacuum effect, thus keeping the car on the track. When Lauda was victorious with Anderstorp, rival teams complained and the innovation was subsequently banned by the FIA.

It was businnes as usual for Andretti and Peterson at Paul Ricard, as the Lotus duo made it a one-two finish. Although Peterson was often quicker, he was a great support to Andretti, always respecting the terms of his contract. Reutemann won at Brands Hatch, but he was helped by the fact that neither Andretti nor Peterson finished the race. But in Austria, Peterson was rewarded with a win; Andretti had crashed out and the race was his for the taking.

Peterson dies at Monza

Andretti was back on form at Zandvoort, so Peterson duly reverted to his usual role of second-place man. Monza started badly for Peterson. His 79 was wrecked in a practice accident, and although the Swede was unhurt, he was forced back into the old 78. Then a multiple pile-up at the beginning of the main race forced Peterson into the barrier, where his car caught fire. When he was pulled out by Hunt, Depailler and Regazzoni, his injuries weren't considered life threatening, but he later died in hospital. The laurels from Monza went to Lauda, who benefited from the disqualification of Andretti and Villeneuve.

It was the culmination of a 10 year dream when Andretti was confirmed as champion, but the moment lost its lustre in the wake of his friend's death. Peterson, the quickest driver of his era, had fulfilled his contract and finished posthumous runner-up.

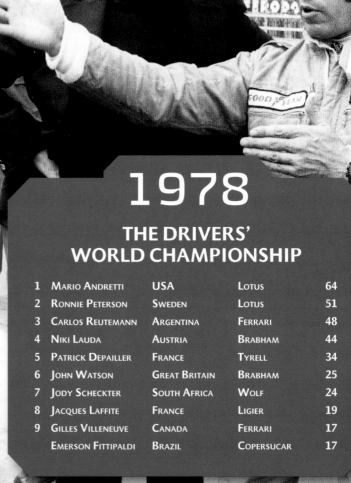

1978
THE DRIVERS' WORLD CHAMPIONSHIP

1	MARIO ANDRETTI	USA	LOTUS	64
2	RONNIE PETERSON	SWEDEN	LOTUS	51
3	CARLOS REUTEMANN	ARGENTINA	FERRARI	48
4	NIKI LAUDA	AUSTRIA	BRABHAM	44
5	PATRICK DEPAILLER	FRANCE	TYRELL	34
6	JOHN WATSON	GREAT BRITAIN	BRABHAM	25
7	JODY SCHECKTER	SOUTH AFRICA	WOLF	24
8	JACQUES LAFFITE	FRANCE	LIGIER	19
9	GILLES VILLENEUVE	CANADA	FERRARI	17
	EMERSON FITTIPALDI	BRAZIL	COPERSUCAR	17

Innovation and design secure success

TOP: The Williams FW06, designed by Patrick Head, with Alan Jones behind the wheel at the Brazilian Grand Prix.

CENTRE LEFT: Alan Jones had already been racing in Formula 1 for three years when he joined the fledgling Williams team in 1977, and won them their first victory at Austria.

CENTRE RIGHT: James Hunt pictured with Jane Birbeck. The season was the beginning of the end for Hunt. He and the McLaren team struggled to score points and Hunt ended the season in thirteenth place.

BELOW LEFT: Lauda moved to Brabham following a fractious relationship with Ferrari. He struggled, however, with the temperamental Lotus cars.

BELOW RIGHT: Brabham designer Gordon Murray (centre). Murray was responsible for the infamous 'fan car' which Lauda had raced to such incredible effect in Sweden. Deemed as 'not in the spirit of the sport', it never raced again.

BOTTOM: The McLaren M26 lacked the 'ground effect' design of its competitors and was consequently outclassed.

OPPOSITE: Mario Andretti in consultation with Lotus boss Colin Chapman. The year was a glorious one for the two who took both the Drivers' and the Constructors' titles.

Andretti fulfils his dream

OPPOSITE PAGE: After ten years in Formula 1, Andretti's winning of the championship was the culmination of a lifelong dream; he had longed to emulate his hero Alberto Ascari. However, Andretti's six victories were notched up over 16 races, while Ascari won six consecutive races in 1952.

RIGHT: With Brabham in decline, Niki Lauda could only finish fourth at the end of the season.

BELOW LEFT: Emerson Fittipaldi had left McLaren to join his elder brother Wilson's Fittipaldi team. The 1978 season was the outfit's best one to date and Fittipaldi scored 17 points.

BOTTOM: Jody Scheckter in the Wolf Ford. Sheckter ended the year in seventh place on 24 points, a significant drop on the tally of 55 that had earned him the runner-up spot in 1977. He would depart for Ferrari at the end of the year.

Tragedy at Monza

BELOW AND OPPOSITE BOTTOM LEFT: Ronnie Peterson was performing well for Lotus during the season, although he failed to finish at the British Grand Prix; his car is seen here being pushed off the circuit because of a fractured fuel pump.

OPPOSITE ABOVE LEFT: Peterson's career is cut tragically short by his death following a crash at Monza. At his funeral his comrades acted as pallbearers (left, front to back: Ake Strandberg, Emerson Fittipaldi, James Hunt and right, front to back: Jody Scheckter, Niki Lauda, Tim Shenken).

OPPOSITE ABOVE RIGHT AND BELOW RIGHT: 1978 was Argentinian Carlos Reuteman most successful season with wins at the British Grand Prix and the two races staged in the USA. However, the success wasn't enough to get him beyond third in the race for the title. His contract with Ferrari came to an end that year.

RIGHT: Jacky Ickx behind the wheel of his Ensign-Ford. He would retire the following season.

Scheckter and Villeneuve prevail

Ferrari, frustrated by their lack of success against the superior Lotus, showed Carlos Reutemann the door, claiming that his erratic, hot-headed driving style had cost the outfit the title. In return, they welcomed Jody Scheckter onto the team to partner Villeneuve. Reutemann, meanwhile, moved across to Lotus, teaming up with Andretti in what he hoped was a golden opportunity for him since the Lotus 79 had clearly been the best drive of the 1978 season. Yet there had been even more technical innovation as the marques strove to outdo one another, particularly focusing on 'ground effect'. Ligier and Ferrari both imitated Lotus and introduced wing cars, to good effect – the 79 was no longer dominant.

The season got off to a very disappointing start for Ferrari. Scheckter had an accident in Argentina and managed only sixth in Brazil. Villeneuve fared little better in South America; with just two points for finishing ahead of his team-mate at Interlagos. The winning team instead was Ligier, with Jacques Laffite winning both South American Grands Prix and team mate Patrick Depailler coming second in Brazil.

Williams chase Ferrari

Kyalami and Long Beach were a better indication of the season's overall pattern. The Ferraris took one-two in both, with supporting driver Villeneuve taking the top honours. Ferrari's new car, the 312-T4, was introduced at Kyalami, and its teething troubles were gradually ironed out as the season progressed. As the early challenge from Ligier faded, strong opposition was provided by Williams and the turbo-powered Renault.

Lotus plagued by problems

Depailler took the laurels in Spain, leading from start to finish. But it was also a rare good day for Reutemann and Andretti, who came in at second and third. The Lotus 80, the successor to the all-conquering 79, was plagued by problems and Reutemann was finding out the hard way that Lotus had already peaked. The 80 was eventually dropped but it would be three long years before Lotus would win another race.

Hunt bows out

In Belgium and Monaco it was Jody Schecker who was celebrating, as were Ferrari who had been about to swing their efforts behind Villeneuve's bid for the title. Monaco was the final outing for James Hunt; he had endured six retirements in seven races in the Wolf and had decided enough was enough. There was also some suggestion that he had lost motivation following the death of Ronnie Peterson, about which he remained publicly very angry.

Challenges to Ferrari

Belgium was the venue for the debut of Williams's FW07, the team's first 'ground effect' car. Raced by

Alan Jones and Clay Regazzoni, it performed well, although neither car finished. Williams, now backed by Saudi Arabian money, was firmly on the march.

The other looming threat to Ferrari appeared at Dijon-Prenois, when Renault's Jean-Pierre Jabouille crossed the line first in the turbo-charged RS10. His team mate Rene Arnoux just lost out to Villeneuve for second place.

Regazzoni came home first at Silverstone, bringing Williams its maiden victory. His team mate Alan Jones began to build on that success by taking three wins in a row: the German, Austrian and Dutch Grands Prix. Despite Jones's domination, Scheckter was in the points for each race which would prove vital in terms of the championship.

1979
THE DRIVERS' WORLD CHAMPIONSHIP

1	JODY SCHECKTER	SOUTH AFRICA	FERRARI	51
2	GILLES VILLENEUVE	CANADA	FERRARI	47
3	ALAN JONES	AUSTRALIA	WILLIAMS	40
4	JACQUES LAFFITE	FRANCE	LIGIER	36
5	CLAY REGAZZONI	SWITZERLAND	WILLIAMS	29
6	CARLOS REUTEMANN	ARGENTINA	LOTUS	20
	PATRICK DEPAILLER	FRANCE	LIGIER	20
8	RENE ARNOUX	FRANCE	RENAULT	17
9	JOHN WATSON	GREAT BRITAIN	McLAREN	15
10	MARIO ANDRETTI	USA	LOTUS	14

There was now more finesse to Scheckter's driving; he was still quick, but his performances were consistent and measured.

Ferrari wins one–two

Ultimately, Jones's superb run wasn't going to be enough to bring him the title. As Monza loomed, only Scheckter or Villeneuve could take the crown. Team orders were issued and Villeneuve duly followed them and protected race leader Scheckter. The South African won the race and with it the championship.

Scheckter later admitted that the technological refinements in the Formula One car were now making it more difficult than ever for a driver to compete in a car that was off the mark. His comment was to prove accurate in the coming years.

James Hunt and Lauda retire

Opposite: Niki Lauda failed to complete the season for Brabham, walking out at Montreal.

Above left: James Hunt and Jane Birbeck depart for Spain.

Above centre: In 1979 Hunt had signed for Wolf, but following six retirements in seven races, Hunt decided to withdraw from Formula 1 after the Monaco Grand Prix.

Above right: Celebrity status brings James Hunt plenty of admirers; seen here at the launch of a London club.

Left and centre: Hunt in relaxed pose. With his racing career over, the media star was ready to embark upon a career in commentating.

Scheckter on the way to winning the title

RIGHT AND BELOW RIGHT: Jody Scheckter winning the Italian Grand Prix at Monza. It was the fiftieth Formula 1 race and a fitting win for the Ferrari driver.

BELOW LEFT: Emerson Fittipaldi struggled to regain his former status while driving for his brother, scoring only one point in the 15 races.

OPPOSITE TOP: John Watson (centre) joined McLaren for the 1979 season and remained with them for the rest of his career.

OPPOSITE CENTRE AND BELOW: Jacques Villeneuve celebrates his win at the Race of Champions at Brands Hatch. The Canadian was now partnered at Ferrari by Scheckter, and the two would dominate the season, finishing in first and second places in the championship.

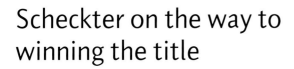

The rise of Williams

There were a number of fresh faces making an impact in 1980. Brabham elevated their second driver, the Brazilian Nelson Piquet, following the departure of Lauda. Piquet had only completed one full Formula One season, but he had shown promise, and now that Brabham had switched to the more reliable Ford engines, their hopes were high. Also new this season was Keke Rosberg, who had signed for Fittipaldi the previous year and Didier Pironi, who, having risen through the French government-sponsored driving academy, made his debut in Belgium. Perhaps the most significant debut this year was that of Alain Prost, who had joined McLaren on the back of his success at Formula Three. Although still young and inexperienced, by the end of the decade Prost would be a household name.

Regazzoni's final race

The Williams team had kept Alan Jones at the forefront of their campaign to take the title and he won the opener ahead of Piquet. Rosberg was in third position. The next two events were won by another new French talent, Rene Arnoux, who was driving the new Renault RE20, but it would be another two years before he would taste victory again. It was Piquet's turn to win next, at Long Beach, where he led all the way, setting the fastest laptime in the process. That race saw the end of a distinguished career, when Clay Regazzoni was involved in a horrible accident which left him confined to a wheelchair. Ferrari's Jody Scheckter could only manage fifth at Long Beach and the two points he earned were the last of his season; it was a terrible reversal of fortune for the driver and the team. Ferrari's Villeneuve didn't fare much better; he only accrued six points in 1980.

Reutemann, for Williams, had his first success for two years at Monaco, although it was Pironi who had led for the first 50 laps; a crash put him out. The early years of the 1980s were also dominated by political infighting between FISA and FOCA. A casualty of their warring was the Spanish Grand Prix and Alan Jones, who had won the race which was subsequently declared void. However, Jones went on to win the French and British Grands Prix. He now had three victories to his name. Williams, who had taken the honours in three consecutive races, was certainly performing well, but with half of the season still to go Ligier, Renault and Brabham were still threatening.

At the German Grand Prix, Jones was unlucky. He suffered a puncture while leading the race, allowing Laffite to come through in the later stages and give Ligier their second success of the season. Reutemann took second, while Jones had to content himself with third. Piquet's fourth place on the day continued a fine run of consistency; of the nine races so far he had been in the points seven times. There was also tragedy at Hockenheim when Patrick Depailler, who had only recently recovered from a serious hang-gliding accident, was killed after a high-speed crash in his Alfa Romeo.

Tense decider at Montreal

By the start of the Dutch Grand Prix, Jones had a healthy 11-point lead. Arnoux took pole but Jones took the lead. When he was forced into the pits, he found himself out of the points; the race was Piquet's, bringing him within two points of Jones. The slender advantage became a one-point deficit after Monza, where Piquet led from lap 4 to the end. The penultimate race at Montreal was the decider, but when Piquet's engine blew on the 24th lap, Jones was relieved. He followed Pironi home, but the Frenchman had received a 60-second penalty for jumping the start and so Jones took maximum points. He won again at Watkins Glen and the title was his. Williams had become the latest team to celebrate a clean sweep of the honours. The task now was to avoid the rapid decline in fortunes that had befallen Ferrari and Lotus.

1980

THE DRIVERS' WORLD CHAMPIONSHIP

1	ALAN JONES	AUSTRALIA	WILLIAMS	67
2	NELSON PIQUET	BRAZIL	BRABHAM	54
3	CARLOS REUTEMANN	ARGENTINA	WILLIAMS	42
4	JACQUES LAFFITE	FRANCE	LIGIER	34
5	DIDIER PIRONI	FRANCE	LIGIER	32
6	RENE ARNOUX	FRANCE	RENAULT	29
7	ELIO DE ANGELIS	ITALY	LOTUS	13
8	JEAN-PIERRE JABOUILLE	FRANCE	RENAULT	9
9	RICCARDO PATRESE	ITALY	ARROWS	7
10	DEREK DALY	IRELAND	TYRELL	6

Hunt era ends as Hill begins to race

OPPOSITE: Arrows driver Riccardo Patrese celebrates his victory at the Race of Champions at Brands Hatch. It was not to be repeated in any of the Championship events; the Italian would win only 7 points.

BELOW: Rumour was that James Hunt had asked for $1m from Marlboro in order to stage a comeback. The McLaren sponsors would only stretch to $400,000 and so the season was set to continue without the former champion.

BOTTOM: Rene Arnoux began to establish a name for himself during 1980; he is pictured here setting the fastest lap at the practice for the German Grand Prix.

RIGHT: Damon Hill, aged 19. Hill spent most of the decade making a name for himself as a motorcycle ace; his first major competitive win came in 1984 with the 350cc Clubman's Cup held at Brands Hatch. He made the move to Formula 3 racing in 1986.

First championship for Williams

RIGHT: Riccardo Patrese at Brands Hatch. Although he started an impressive 256 times during his career, Patrese won just six championship races.

BELOW: Alan Jones in the superb FW07B. Designed by Patrick Head, it was Williams' first ground effect car and it would earn the team it first constructors' title and ensure that Jones became their first champion driver. The Australian was the first of seven drivers to win the championship with Williams.

OPPOSITE BELOW: Jones won five races during the 1980 season and he is seen here being presented with the trophy at Silverstone, his third victory. On his left is Mrs Hermans, the wife of the managing director of Philip Rothman, and on his right is Lady Rothermere.

OPPOSITE ABOVE LEFT AND RIGHT: Alan Jones during the practice for the British Grand Prix. Having started his F1 career in 1976 with John Surtees' team, Jones had initially met with little success.

Brabham edge out Williams pair

It looked as if 1981 could be a repeat of the previous season, with the same top four drivers vying for the season's title. But the competition was even tighter, and the outcome was decidedly different. Williams still had Jones and Reutemann; Brabham had Nelson Piquet, and Jacques Laffite was still number one at Ligier. McLaren also made a greater impact during 1981, thanks in part to Alain Prost, but also as a result of their MP4 with its new carbon-fibre chassis.

The disputes between FISA and FOCA continued during 1981, their focus shifting towards some the innovations that had taken place during the past few seasons, particularly the skirts on the 'ground effect' cars. FISA was particularly critical, preferring to champion instead the manufacturers of turbo engines. One casualty of the quarrelling was Lotus, which was forced to withdraw the new Lotus 88; had it run the Lotus would have beaten the McLaren MP4 as the first carbon-fibre car.

Reutemann and Jones become rivals

The opening race was eventually held in March at Long Beach, USA, and it was won by Alan Jones, with Reutemann coming in second to make it a one-two repeat of Watkins Glen at the end of the previous season. The result in the next round – Brazil, was the opposite. This time Reutemann disregarded an order to let Jones through and led him to the finish. The consequences of this were a souring in relations both between Reutemann and Williams and between the two drivers.

Both the Argentina and San Marino races were won by Piquet, but it was at Zolder where the tension between Jones and Reutemann could really be seen to take its toll; Jones had been pressing his team mate too hard and he came off the track. The rain shortened the race, which Reutemann eventually won, followed by Laffite. Third was Nigel Mansell's Lotus, giving him his first podium finish in his first full Formula One season. Jones lost out to a fuel problem in Monaco and Villeneuve gave Ferrari their first win for two years. He repeated the performance in Spain.

McLaren begin their rise

Dijon was the fitting location for Alain Prost's first victory, his first of three in this season and of a career total of 51. The Frenchman came home two seconds ahead of Watson's McLaren, but Watson overturned any disappointment by winning on home soil at Silverstone. It was a key win for the MP4 and the first of many stunning successes throughout the 1980s for McLaren. Reutemann's second place at Silverstone gave him a 17-point lead in the championship, but he only managed to win two of the following three races and, despite nine years of trying, he lost out on the championship yet again. Piquet won his third race of the year in Germany while Laffite became the seventh different winner of the year when he took first place in Austria. Piquet's second place behind Prost at Zandvoort gave him 19 points for the three races. He was now ahead of Reutemann on points.

Piquet by a single point

Prost led all the way at Monza, with Jones and Reutemann finishing behind him, whereas Piquet picked up just one point in sixth place. Montreal belonged to Laffite, and as they went into the final decider, in the car park of Caesar's Palace in Las Vegas, Reutemann led on points yet again. Piquet, however, was only one point behind, and Laffite in contention too with 43. Reutemann was superb in practice and took pole, but his race was disappointing and he could only finish in eighth position. Piquet's fifth place proved decisive; it was enough to give him his first championship by a single point from a disappointed Reutemann.

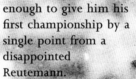

1981
THE DRIVERS' WORLD CHAMPIONSHIP

1	NELSON PIQUET	BRAZIL	BRABHAM	50
2	CARLOS REUTEMANN	ARGENTINA	WILLIAMS	49
3	ALAN JONES	AUSTRALIA	WILLIAMS	46
4	JACQUES LAFFITE	FRANCE	TALBOT-LIGIER	44
5	ALAIN PROST	FRANCE	RENAULT	43
6	JOHN WATSON	GREAT BRITAIN	McLAREN	27
7	GILLES VILLENEUVE	CANADA	FERRARI, ARROWS	25
8	ELIO DE ANGELIS	ITALY	LOTUS	14
9	RENE ARNOUX	FRANCE	RENAULT	11
	HECTOR REBAQUE	MEXICO	BRABHAM BT49C	11

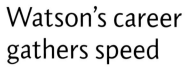

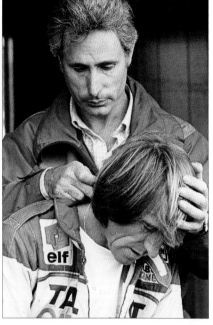

Watson's career gathers speed

OPPOSITE: John Watson celebrates his victory in the British Grand Prix in the customary manner. Carlos Reutemann was second and Jacques Laffite third.

FAR LEFT: Watson's win at Silverstone was only his second Grand Prix victory. He had won the Austrian event five years earlier but it was his move to McLaren in 1979 that helped to lift his racing career, earning him four more Grand Prix wins.

LEFT TOP AND LEFT CENTRE: Frenchman Jacques Laffite receives a neck massage following a race. Physiotherapists had already become a common sight at the track, particularly dealing with neck and back problems .

BOTTOM LEFT: Rene Arnoux, in the car, shakes hands with Alain Prost at the Austrian Grand Prix. The race was eventually won by their compatriot, Jacques Laffite.

BELOW: Despite being first on the grid at the British Grand Prix, Arnoux was unable to finish in the points thanks to engine trouble. Renault's experiments with the turbo engine during this period often resulted in unfinished races and earned their cars the nickname 'little yellow teapots'.

Lauda makes a comeback

RIGHT: Nelson Piquet won his first championship by a single point when he managed to finish in fifth place at Caesar's Palace. His main rival for the title, Carlos Reutemann had been forced into eighth position by a faulty gearbox.

BELOW: Ron Dennis (left) pictured with his drivers for the 1982 season, John Watson (right) and Niki Lauda (centre). Lauda had been persuaded out of retirement by the McLaren boss, while Watson was about to begin his fourth season with the team.

OPPOSITE ABOVE: Watson drives the new MP4, which would make its full debut in the coming season.

OPPOSITE BELOW: Watson and Lauda in publicity shots for the new car. Although joining McLaren had been profitable for Watson, he had parted from the outfit by the time their period of domination really began. Watson was eventually replaced by Alain Prost.

Rosberg wins with consistent effort

The 1982 season was another difficult one, the disputes between FISA and FOCA reached a climax with the San Marino event, when the FOCA teams boycotted the race. However, matters were finally resolved this year, in the wake of accidents involving Didier Pironi and Gilles Villeneuve. Villeneuve's crash was fatal, and the sport also lost Riccardo Paletti in a smash and Lotus boss Colin Chapman to a heart attack. Before the season had even begun there was controversy as returning champion Niki Lauda staged a drivers' strike, although this was swiftly resolved. Lauda's first win came at Long Beach, where he had led convincing for the final 60 laps.

Despite being part of the team of the moment, Williams' drivers Jones and Reutemann both decided to quit. Jones went before the season began and Reutemann after a disappointing second place at the opener in South Africa. In their place, Williams signed Finnish driver Keke Rosberg, whose relationship with the Fittipaldi team had become difficult. His first outing for Williams, the South African Grand Prix, saw him take fifth place. The winner was Prost, despite having suffered a puncture in the early stages. Prost also won in the second round in Brazil, but won no more Grands Prix that year.

Tension at Ferrari

There was also considerable tension within the Ferrari camp between top drivers Villeneuve and Pironi. At San Marino, with so many drivers missing because of the FOCA withdrawal, Villeneuve and Pironi were in contention for the lead with Arnoux in the Renault. When Arnoux retired, Villeneuve looked set to come in first until his team mate passed him to steal the win. Villeneuve was incensed and their relationship was irrevocably soured. Matters worsened when Villeneuve was killed during a high-speed practice for the Belgian Grand Prix just two weeks later. Many claimed that the Canadian had been adversely affected by the row with Pironi, leading him to make a rash and ultimately costly error. Ferrari withdrew from the main race and Watson won for McLaren.

Riccardo Patrese claimed his first Formula One win in Monaco, a race in which the lead changed hands four times in the last three laps, from Prost to Patrese, to Pironi and then back to Patrese again. The Frenchman gave Brabham their first win of the season.

1982

THE DRIVERS' WORLD CHAMPIONSHIP

1	KEKE ROSBERG	FINLAND	WILLIAMS	44
2	DIDIER PIRONI	FRANCE	FERRARI	39
	JOHN WATSON	GREAT BRITAIN	MCLAREN	39
4	ALAIN PROST	FRANCE	RENAULT	34
5	NIKI LAUDA	AUSTRIA	MCLAREN	30
6	RENE ARNOUX	FRANCE	RENAULT	28
7	PATRICK TAMBAY	FRANCE	ARROWS, FERRARI	25
	MICHELE ALBORETO	ITALY	TYRELL	25
9	ELIO DE ANGELIS	ITALY	LOTUS	23
10	RICCARDO PATRESE	ITALY	BRABHAM	21

Watson won again at Detroit, and then another tragedy occurred at Montreal when Riccardo Paletti's Osella smashed into Pironi's Ferrari during a start-line collision; he was killed instantly.

Pironi's career ends

Pironi may have had a good racing season, but his involvement in the deaths of two drivers must have affected him. Following his win at the Dutch Grand Prix, he took second at Brands Hatch behind Lauda. With third position in France, he now led on 39 points, 9 clear of his nearest rival. But at a wet Hockenheim, Pironi crashed in practice, in a manner which eerily echoed Villeneuve's

fatal accident. Pironi broke both legs and his racing career was over. As the season continued, his lead melted away.

After a string of finishes in the points, Rosberg finally scored a victory in the Swiss Grand Prix; on the last lap he passed Prost, who was struggling with gearbox trouble. Although Rosberg finished out of the points at Monza, he went into the final round at Caesar's Palace with 42 points from his nine finishes. Watson, on 33, needed a win to have a chance of snatching the title, but could only manage second. Rosberg finished fifth anyway, to take the crown by five points. Despite having won only once, his consistent run of 10 finishes in the points was decisive and Watson was denied.

Rosberg wins for Williams

LEFT AND BELOW RIGHT: Keke Rosberg at Brands Hatch. The Finn had joined Williams following the departures of both Alan Jones and Carlos Reutemann. Despite taking only one victory, consistency and 10 finishes delivered him his first championship.

BELOW: Former champion Niki Lauda finished an impressive fourth at Kyalami, his first race on returning to Formula 1.

OPPOSITE: Lady Rothermere presents Niki Lauda with the trophy after he won the British Grand Prix. Lauda went on to finish the season in fifth place, but only 14 points behind the champion.

Gilles Villeneuve killed at Zolder

LEFT: Only 32 when he died, Canadian Gilles Villenueve was a much loved figure in Formula 1, his aggressive driving style and spirited attitude making him popular with fans. He was killed when he struck the rear of Jochen Mass's March during the practice run at Zolder in Belgium.

Left: Keke Rosberg was the first successful driver to emerge from Finland, but certainly not the last. He retired in 1986 following the death of friend Elio de Angelis, but went on to manage. Mika Häkkinen and his own son, Nico, were among his clients.

Below: In his comeback year Niki Lauda took first place at both Long Beach and Brands Hatch. His two victories were one more than Rosberg's single win at Dijon, but Lauda's performance was less consistent than the Finn's.

Piquet and Prost go head to head

1983 year saw the rise in the domination of the turbo-powered car. With turbo-boost technology requiring less highly explosive fuel on board, many felt that these were the safer means of obtaining incredible rates of acceleration. The famous Ford-Cosworth engine was finally forced into retirement. The Brabham team, who in 1982 had fielded both turbo cars and normally aspirated cars, now turned to turbo; this proved an advantageous move for Patrese and, more importantly, Piquet. The 1981 champion had had a disappointing season in 1982 and was keen to reassert himself in 1983. He did so in style at the opening race, which was on his home territory. Rosberg was second in Brazil, but he was subsequently disqualified for a push start in the pits.

Rosberg wins in Monaco

Watson led Lauda home in a one-two for McLaren at Long Beach; but it was a rare moment of glory for them that year. In France, it was Prost who took the home victory, his sixth victory with Renault. When he came second in the next race, it began to look as if he would be in with a chance of the championship. Also in the title run was Keke Rosberg, who took a fantastic victory over Piquet and Prost in Monaco. His win was all the more sweet for having been made with a Cosworth engine, which had to push all the way to beat the turbo-charged competition. The Cosworth would achieve one more victory, at Detroit with Michele Alboreto, before it became obsolete; 155 Formula One races had been won by the famous engine.

Spa was the venue for Prost's second win of the season. Then Rene Arnoux scored his first win with Ferrari at Montreal. Nigel Mansell finally got into the Renault turbo car at Silverstone. He was immediately competitive, finishing fourth, some 40 seconds behind race-winner Prost.

Ferrari began a good run at Hockenheim, where Rene Arnoux came first. Then in Austria he came in second behind Prost. It was then a one-two for Ferrari at Zandvoort, where Arnoux and then Tambay took advantage of the retirements of both Piquet and Prost. Prost's four wins gave him an eight-point advantage over Arnoux, with Piquet and Tambay a further six points behind. Yet Monza was disastrous for Prost. His turbo blew halfway round, enabling Piquet, Arnoux and Tambay to finish first, second and fourth respectively.

Prost loses out in showdown

Prost came second in the European Grand Prix, at Brands Hatch, but Piquet had dominated the race, crossing the line seven seconds ahead of the Frenchman. Neither Ferrari was in the points, so it was a straight fight between Prost and Piquet in the final round, and there were only two points in it, with Prost having the advantage.

Tambay was on pole with Piquet on the front row. The Brazilian got the better start and led for the first 59 laps of the 77-lap race. Prost could only qualify fifth and his race ended with a turbo failure on the 35th lap. He now had to hope that Piquet finished no better than fifth. Although the Brazilian did relinquish the lead, to both Patrese and de Cesaris, his third place was enough to give him his second title. While Piquet celebrated, Prost was generally criticised in his home press for letting the championship slip from his grasp. It was a sour end to the year, and marked the parting of the ways between him and Renault.

1983

THE DRIVERS' WORLD CHAMPIONSHIP

	Driver	Country	Team	Points
1	NELSON PIQUET	BRAZIL	BRABHAM	59
2	ALAIN PROST	FRANCE	RENAULT	57
3	RENE ARNOUX	FRANCE	FERRARI	49
4	PATRICK TAMBAY	FRANCE	FERRARI	40
5	KEKE ROSBERG	FINLAND	WILLIAMS	27
6	JOHN WATSON	GREAT BRITAIN	McLAREN	22
	EDDIE CHEEVER	USA	RENAULT	22
8	ANDREA DE CESARIS	ITALY	ALFA ROMEO	15
9	RICCARDO PATRESE	ITALY	BRABHAM	13
10	NIKI LAUDA	AUSTRIA	McLAREN AUSTRIA	12

Champions of the future

OPPOSITE: A new young talent came out of Brazil when Ayrton Senna grabbed the attention of a number of Formula 1 teams because of his success at Formula 3. He would eventually choose to drive with Toleman for the 1984 season.

TOP: Damon Hill began to race in Formula Ford 2000 in 1983. Despite his father's fame, he had to claw his way into motor racing.

CENTRE: Williams were still running normally aspirated engines but Rosberg gave the Ford Cosworth a fine send-off with an excellent win at Monaco.

BELOW LEFT: Reigning champion Rosberg took 27 points to finish in fifth position, without the benefit of turbo power.

BELOW RIGHT: Nigel Mansell made his Formula 1 debut in the Austrian Grand Prix in 1980 driving for Lotus. His best performance of the year in 1983 came at Brands Hatch in the European Grand Prix, where he finished in third behind Piquet and Prost. He finished the season on 10 points, his highest total thus far.

BOTTOM: John Watson puts McLaren's new turbo unit through its paces.

The rise of the turbo

OPPOSITE: Keke Rosberg won the final non-championship event, the Race of Champions at Brands Hatch, but could only win one Formula 1 Grand Prix event, at Monaco. The turbo-powered opposition were simply too good.

RIGHT: Despite outscoring team mate Niki Lauda, John Watson (left) was replaced at McLaren by Alain Prost.

RIGHT BELOW: McLaren introduced their turbo-powered MP4 with its TAG Porsche engine during the 1983 season. The following three seasons were won by McLaren drivers Prost and Lauda in the car.

BOTTOM: Smoke belches from the Lotus of Elio de Angelis during practice for the European Grand Prix at Brands Hatch. The Roman would be killed during another practice race at the Paul Ricard circuit in 1986.

Piquet pips Prost to take a second title

RIGHT: Nelson Piquet poses in the driving seat of a London cab. Piquet scored consistently throughout the season, failing to add to his points total in only five of the 15 events. However, Alain Prost had also consistently accumulated points and the title was not decided until the last race of the season in South Africa. When Prost was forced to retire from the race, Piquet held onto third place, scoring four points to bring his tally to 59 compared with Prost's 57.

BELOW LEFT: Niki Lauda looks on as with interest as a McLaren mechanic makes some adjustments to the new TAG engine.

BELOW RIGHT: John Watson proudly presents his MBE.

OPPOSITE ABOVE: Ayrton Senna's climb to the top continued with victory over Martin Brundle in the Formula 3 championship.

OPPOSITE BELOW: Rosberg in his TAG Williams Ford Cosworth V8, seen here at the European Grand Prix.

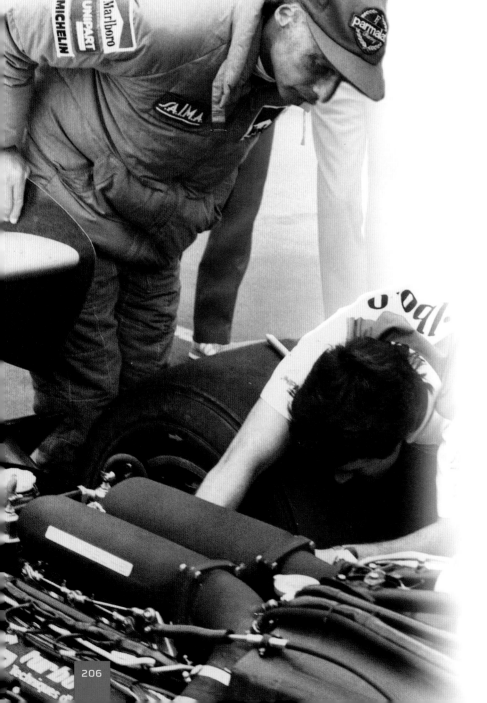

Lauda wins third in turbo McLaren

In the last races of the 1983 season McLaren had been giving a quiet debut to their new TAG Porsche engine. Despite several retirements, the car showed promise. Lauda stayed on for 1984 and was joined by Prost, who had finally had enough of the criticism at Renault. McLaren now had everything in place: an impressive new turbo unit fitted into a superb carbon-fibre MP4, and two top-flight drivers. The results were dramatic.

Prost won at the opener in Brazil; Lauda's McLaren had succumbed to an electrical fault and in the subsequent fight with Renault's Derek Warwick, it was the Frenchman who was victorious. It was the first in an avalanche of McLaren successes.

Senna wins first championship points
The power of the McLarens quickly became apparent; despite qualifying in only fifth and eighth places, Prost and Lauda scored a comfortable one-two success at Kyalami. A first championship point was earned by Ayrton Senna in the same race. The young Brazilian was racing for the relatively small Toleman team and came home in sixth position.

Prost and Lauda failed to win points in only two races all season and Zolder was the first of these. Neither McLaren completed the race; the victory went instead to Alboreto, who enjoyed a start-to-finish victory. Reigning champion Piquet was having a wretched start to the season; he failed to finish in three races and at Imola his turbo failed 12 laps from the line when he was running second. Prost won, having led for the entire 60-lap distance. Piquet finally had more luck at Montreal, where he relegated the McLarens to the minor placings, repeating the feat at Detroit, in a race that was restarted after a first-lap shunt involving the Brazilian and both McLarens. Lauda's engine blew in the early stages at San Marino but he came back to win the French at Dijon. In the same race Nigel Mansell finished third, a stoic performance since he had just been given the news of his mother's death.

Scorcher in Dallas
The next race in Monaco was almost won by Mansell. He had taken the lead from Prost in torrential rain, but lost grip and slid into the Armco. The race was stopped shortly afterwards and Prost was declared the winner. Senna had also performed brilliantly, battling from an initial ninth position to within eight seconds of Prost when the race was halted. In Dallas, Mansell and de Angelis occupied the front row, the first time Lotus had had that distinction for six years. Baking conditions cracked the surface, and some hastily added cement didn't set. Mansell led to halfway but Rosberg passed him in the Williams-Honda. The Finn went on to win, whereas Mansell had transmission failure

on the last lap. He finished sixth by pushing his car to the line, the heat causing him to faint in the process.

Lauda and Prost battle for title
McLaren took another victory at Brands Hatch. This time it was Lauda who won, inheriting the lead from Prost, who had to retire halfway round with gearbox trouble.

Fortunes were typically reversed at Hockenheim, where it was the Frenchman's turn to benefit from misfortune when De Angelis and Piquet both retired. Lauda won again in Austria, crossing the line ahead of Piquet; Prost had spun off and failed to score. Zandvoort was the venue for a third McLaren one-two of the year, with Prost taking the flag 10 seconds ahead of Lauda. The two McLaren drivers were now vying with each other for the title. Lauda went on to win Monza, Prost the European at the new Nürburgring circuit.

1984
THE DRIVERS' WORLD CHAMPIONSHIP

1	NIKI LAUDA	AUSTRIA	McLAREN	72
2	ALAIN PROST	FRANCE	McLAREN	71.5
3	ELIO DE ANGELIS	ITALY	LOTUS	34
4	MICHELE ALBORETO	ITALY	FERRARI	30.5
5	NELSON PIQUET	BRAZIL	BRABHAM	29
6	RENE ARNOUX	FRANCE	FERRARI	27
7	DEREK WARWICK	GREAT BRITAIN	RENAULT	23
8	KEKE ROSBERG	FINLAND	WILLIAMS	20.5
9	NIGEL MANSELL	GREAT BRITAIN	LOTUS	13
	AYRTON SENNA	BRAZIL	TOLEMAN	13

By the decider at Estoril, Lauda led on points. Prost took the lead from Rosberg and held on to win, but the wily Lauda drove cannily and finished in second place. Again, Prost had won more races, seven to Lauda's five, but the Austrian had secured a wafer-thin half-point advantage. Alongside Fangio, Brabham and Stewart, Lauda had now won three championships.

Lauda wins by a half-point.

OPPOSITE: Niki Lauda claims the trophy at the British Grand Prix. He would score a stunning win over his team mate Prost to secure the title for a third time, despite taking one fewer victory than Prost.

FAR LEFT: Having been sacked by McLaren, John Watson retired from motor racing and headed for a career in commentating.

LEFT: Alain Prost celebrates setting the fastest lap at the British Grand Prix. Competing against his team mate cost him the title, but he would eventually go on to beat Fangio's record haul.

BELOW: Nelson Piquet at the European event. Although the Brazilian had secured Brabham two world titles, the team had begun its steady decline.

BOTTOM: Philippe Alliot's RAM and Jo Gartner's Osella make contact at Brands Hatch.

Senna makes his debut

RIGHT: Ayrton Senna made his Formula 1 debut with Toleman in 1984. He scored just 13 points, finishing ninth in the championship. The Brazilian was soon keen to find a more competitive team.

BELOW TOP, CENTRE AND BOTTOM: A shunt between Gartner and Alliot leads to dramatic rescue scenes. Safety had improved considerably over the years, but the incredible speeds combined with a certain degree of risk-taking often led to spectacular accidents.

OPPOSITE: Lauda's celebrations at Brands Hatch brought his GP career points total to a record 367.5. Jackie Stewart may only have managed a haul of 360 points but the Scot was still ahead on outright victories: 27, to Lauda's 22.

Vindication for Prost

Coming second in the championship for two years running was a bitter disappointment for Alain Prost, particularly since he had performed so well in both 1983 and 1984. The 1985 season, however, was the year in which he would make no mistakes, although there was fierce competition to be had; Senna would prove himself a formidable opponent and the Williams team headed by Mansell and Rosberg were also threatening. But it was Prost who made the first impact, winning the opener in Brazil despite being sixth on the grid, behind Alboreto and Rosberg.

Senna moves to Lotus

The winner at Estoril was Ayrton Senna, who was now driving for Lotus. Despite atrocious conditions Senna led all the way to finish more than a minute clear of Michele Alboreto. He could have made it two in a row in San Marino, had he not run out of fuel. Senna had been in the lead for the first 56 laps, yet six drivers passed him in the final four laps. Prost was also out of luck. His McLaren crossed the line first, only to be disqualified for being underweight. Instead Elio de Angelis was announced the winner.

Nigel Mansell was another driver keen to prove his mettle during this season; he had finally left Lotus, who were unconvinced of his talent, and moved to Williams. Like Rosberg, Mansell retired in Brazil, but he was in the points at Estoril. Despite starting from the pit lane, he recovered to finish fifth.

It was Senna who was quickest in Monaco, and he was leading until his engine gave out on lap 13. The win went instead to Prost, who beat Alboreto back into second. Alboreto finally managed to win after a 17-race gap, and with Stefan Johansson in second it was a one-two for Ferrari in Monaco. By Detroit, however, they were behind Keke Rosberg on the podium. The former champion, and his team mate Mansell had been experiencing handling problems with the Williams-Honda, but the Honda engine had now arrived and matters had improved considerably. Although Mansell crashed out in practice for Paul Ricard, Rosberg kept the side up by taking pole position. However, he lost out to Piquet at the end and had to settle for second.

Alboreto takes lead on points

Although Prost won a third victory at Silverstone and Rosberg set a record fasted lap of 160 mph during the same race, the main contender for the title as they reached the halfway stage appeared to be Alboreto. When he won at the Nürburgring, it was only his second win, but he had been on the podium seven times in seven finishes. He now led the championship on 46 points, five ahead of Prost. This was about to change. Prost won in Austria, bringing himself level on points, with Alboreto coming third. Prost went on to come second in Holland, then first at Monza. At the same time Alboreto's season began to dry up; he endured a string of retirements and in the second half of the season could only amass further seven points.

Lauda hangs up his helmet

Niki Lauda had struggled to repeat his form of the previous season. He had eight retirements in ten races and was considering hanging up his helmet for good. His win at Zandvoort was his twenty-fifth Grand Prix victory and the last of his career.

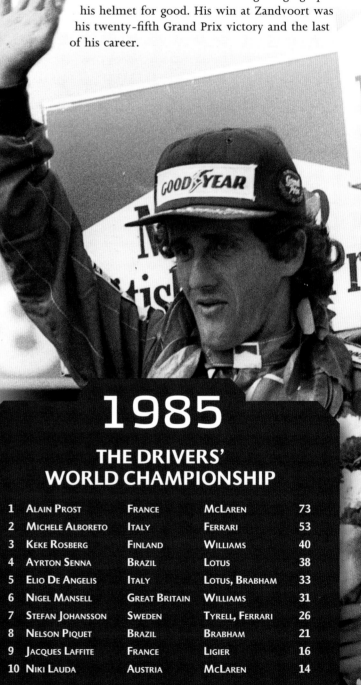

1985
THE DRIVERS' WORLD CHAMPIONSHIP

1	ALAIN PROST	FRANCE	MCLAREN	73
2	MICHELE ALBORETO	ITALY	FERRARI	53
3	KEKE ROSBERG	FINLAND	WILLIAMS	40
4	AYRTON SENNA	BRAZIL	LOTUS	38
5	ELIO DE ANGELIS	ITALY	LOTUS, BRABHAM	33
6	NIGEL MANSELL	GREAT BRITAIN	WILLIAMS	31
7	STEFAN JOHANSSON	SWEDEN	TYRELL, FERRARI	26
8	NELSON PIQUET	BRAZIL	BRABHAM	21
9	JACQUES LAFFITE	FRANCE	LIGIER	16
10	NIKI LAUDA	AUSTRIA	MCLAREN	14

At Spa, the moment belonged to Senna yet again, it was his second win in Belgium and his fifth podium finish of the season. Mansell and Rosberg were faring better in the new Williams-Honda, and came in second and fourth respectively. Significantly it was Prost in third place, racking up points on the way to the title.

First victory for Mansell
Nigel Mansell finally tasted victory at home in the European Grand Prix at Brands Hatch, he then scored an immediate second win at Kyalami. But Prost's three points for fourth place at Brands Hatch gave him a total of 72 points and he became the first Frenchman to win the title.

Prost takes centre stage

OPPOSITE: Alain Prost following his victory at the British Grand Prix. At this stage in the championship he was behind Italy's Michele Alboreto by five points.

LEFT: Sons of illustrious fathers. Gary Brabham and Damon Hill pose for the cameras.

LEFT BELOW: Nigel Mansell scored his first victory during the 1985 season in the European at Brands Hatch, proving his detractors wrong. Mansell had been replaced at Lotus by Senna, but his move to Williams had proved fortuitous for both team and driver.

BOTTOM: Ayrton Senna pictured before the British Grand Prix at Silverstone. He was out of luck that day, but his move to Lotus in 1985 brought immediate results: seven poles and a debut victory at Estoril.

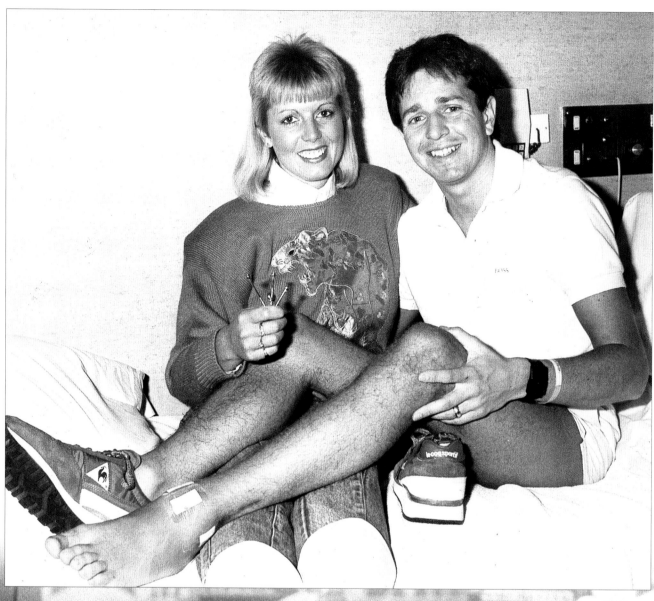

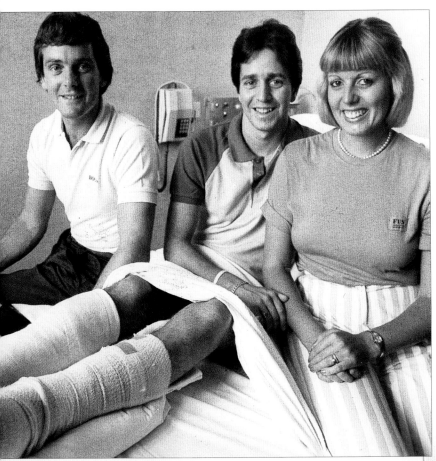

The agony and the ecstasy

LEFT AND OPPOSITE ABOVE: Martin Brundle is visited by his wife and rival Jonathan Palmer as he recovers from a crash during practice for the 1984 Dallas Grand Prix in which both his ankles were broken. The Norfolk, born driver had spent most of his career coming in behind Senna, both at Formula 3 and now again at Formula 1, where he had joined Tyrrell.

OPPOSITE BELOW: Frenchman Patrick Tambay in his Renault crashes out of the British Grand Prix on the first lap.

BELOW: Alain Prost receives the winner's trophy at Brands Hatch. He eventually won the championship by a comfortable 20 points from Ferrari's Michele Alboreto.

Farewell to the turbos

1986 was dominated by four men: Mansell, Piquet, Prost and Senna. Between them they won every race except one, and by the end of the year there was a gulf of more than 30 points between them and the fifth-placed driver, Stefan Johansson. Three of them remained with their teams, but Piquet, who had been with Brabham for eight years, joined Mansell at Williams. Rosberg had left the marque at the start of the season, joining McLaren instead, but it proved to be an unwise move; Williams were on the up.

The season was a watershed in the history of Formula One; FISA had had enough of the turbo-charged engines and their ever-increasing power. After all the disputes in the early years of the decade the decision was taken to outlaw the turbo and the sport returned to normally aspirated power.

Champions in waiting

The Brazilian opener was won by Piquet, who held off second-placed Senna. Prost had to retire and Mansell had withdrawn after an accident. In the next race, in Spain, Mansell looked threatening, but Senna, having started from pole for the second time, squeaked the win. Senna would hold pole in eight out of the 16 races and although only two were converted into victories, he was demonstrating just what a talent he was. The Williams and McLaren cars were superior, but the Brazilian was a champion in the making.

Prost scored his first win of the year at Imola, followed home by Piquet, the only other man to complete the 60-lap distance. It was two in a row for the Frenchman at Monaco and Rosberg finishing in second place made it a one-two for McLaren.

Nigel Mansell's season had a mixed beginning with only two finishes, but his form improved and he began to win. Belgium, Canada and France were comfortable victories; Brands Hatch was a battle with Piquet but he still finished ahead of the Brazilian. He too was looking like a champion of the future.

There was a new venue that season – Hungary's Hungaroring circuit. It was the first time Formula One had penetrated the Iron Curtain, and over 200,000 fans converged on Budapest to witness an unforgettable battle between Piquet and Senna. The two traded the lead on the narrow, winding circuit, and the Hungaroring was later voted Course of the Year. With the move to Austria, a fistful of retirements gave some of the other drivers a chance to contend for the laurels, although the win belonged to Prost.

Monza was the venue for another one-two for Williams, this time it was Piquet beating Mansell to the flag by 10 seconds. The see-sawing continued when Mansell hit back at Estoril, taking his fifth win of the season. Both Mansell

and Piquet were desperate to win the championship for themselves, and their driving against one another rather than forming a tactical partnership was ultimately the undoing of Williams. They split valuable points, so that in the end neither man could win. In Mexico in the penultimate round the win belonged to Gerhard Berger, who was driving for newcomers Benetton. The Italian clothing manufacturer had been a sponsor of the Toleman team, but had taken over to become a team in their own right. Austrian Berger had given them an early reward. In the final race at Adelaide, it was Mansell who looked favourite to win the title, he only needed a third-place finish irrespective of what his rivals did. But when his tyre blew on the sixty-third lap his race was over and the crown lost. Instead, Prost came through to take the race and a successive championship win, the first since Jack Brabham in 1959–60. Prost's victorious campaign added to his reputation for being the most complete driver of his era, but he had certainly benefited also from Mansell and Piquet's rivalry.

1986

THE DRIVERS' WORLD CHAMPIONSHIP

1	ALAIN PROST	FRANCE	MCLAREN	72
2	NIGEL MANSELL	GREAT BRITAIN	WILLIAMS	70
3	NELSON PIQUET	BRAZIL	WILLIAMS	69
4	AYRTON SENNA	BRAZIL	JPS/LOTUS	55
5	STEFAN JOHANSSON	SWEDEN	FERRARI	23
6	KEKE ROSBERG	FINLAND	MCLAREN	22
7	GERHARD BERGER	AUSTRIA	BENETTON	17
8	JACQUES LAFFITE	FRANCE	LIGIER	14
	RENE ARNOUX	FRANCE	LIGIER	14
	MICHELE ALBORETO	ITALY	FERRARI	14

Williams and McLaren vie for points

LEFT: Nigel Mansell in contemplative mood before the start of the British Grand Prix, which turned out to be his fourth win of the season.

LEFT BELOW: Reigning champion Alain Prost. There was no single dominant force in the 1986 season. While Prost and Piquet had each chalked up four victories by the end of the year, Mansell was on five. Of the remaining three races, two were won by Senna and the other by Gerhard Berger.

BELOW AND BOTTOM: Thierry Boutsen's Arrows smashes into the crash barrier then bounces back across the track, causing a multiple collision at Brands Hatch.

OPPOSITE: Senna in the Lotus is ahead of Mansell's Williams in the great road race, Monaco. It was Prost who took the flag first, however.

The aftermath at Brands Hatch

MAIN PICTURE: Boutsen's crash ended both the race and the career of Jacques Laffite, who suffered appalling leg injuries. The consequent restart enabled Mansell to switch cars and go on to win the race. His first car had been carrying a broken driveshaft.

BELOW: Mansell had beaten his team mate Piquet to win the British Grand Prix. Mansell was favourite to win the title by the last event of the season in Australia. However, a burst tyre meant that he was forced to withdraw from the race and had to make do with second place in the championship.

Piquet is fastest, but title belongs to Prost

LEFT: Nelson Piquet is spotted aboard a classic two-wheeler.

BELOW RIGHT: The son of a Brazilian government minister, Nelson Piquet had been forced to adopt his mother's maiden name when he first started racing in order to hide his identity. His championship wins put to an end any notion of a quiet life.

OPPOSITE ABOVE: Piquet is rewarded for setting the fastest lap during practice at Brands Hatch.

OPPOSITE BELOW: The podium finish at the Spanish Grand Prix. Senna crossed the line just 0.014 seconds ahead of a clearly disappointed Mansell, the closest finish for 15 years. Prost was a distant third. Ultimately a win here would have won the championship for Mansell. Prost was consistent throughout the year. His victorious campaign merely added to his reputation for being the most complete driver of his era.

Piquet edges out Mansell

The main drama of 1987 starred the same four characters as 1986: Prost, Senna, Piquet and Mansell. The season was almost a perfect rerun of the year before in that these four shared the first 14 races, then Gerhard Berger stepped in with a victory in the penultimate round. It was the final race which provided the surprise ending.

In preparation for the transition to non-turbo 3.5-litre engines in 1989, FIA introduced two new awards for both drivers and constructors. It was the Tyrrell outfit who were best prepared for the change and consequently they dominated the category. They won the constructors' Colin Chapman Cup and their driver, Jonathan Palmer, won the Jim Clark Cup.

Prost equals Stewart's record

In the main competition, Prost started well, winning two of the first three races, despite driving a new and therefore potentially unreliable car. The Williams pair were still in their turbo Hondas and were quickest in practice for Brazil, but the wet weather enabled Prost to win from Piquet with clever tactics. Piquet profited from a temperamental shunt involving Mansell and Senna in Belgium, but the race was eventually won by Prost, when Piquet too was forced to retire early. For Prost the win brought him equal to Jackie Stewart's record of 27 Grand Prix wins.

Senna enjoys Mansell's misfortune

Mansell had managed a win at Imola, his rivals having been eliminated from the race, Prost with a failed alternator and Picquet following a pre-race accident. Mansell did have the pleasure of beating Senna, however. In response, Senna won the next two races, Monaco and Detroit, and in both of them he benefited from Mansell's early retirements. At this stage, Mansell was behind on points, having only scored two in three races, but in France he began to make progress, winning the maximum for beating Piquet to the flag. The pair repeated their one-two finish at Silverstone, Mansell having sneaked the win from Piquet by dramatically passing him on the sixty-third lap.

McLaren had been dealing with technical problems during the previous races, but at Hockenheim they appeared to have ironed these out. Prost was cruising to victory when just five laps from the end his alternator failed and Piquet took his first win of the season. Senna was third, and the competitive Brazilian finally decided that Lotus wasn't strong enough, so he began negotiations with McLaren. Both Senna and Piquet were preparing to move at the end of the season and now the two fought for top spot in Hungary. Piquet won, Senna was second, Prost third. It was Mansell's turn to win in Austria in a race that was restarted twice. Again, he was fortunate that both Senna and Prost had pulled up. The table now stood with Senna four points ahead of Mansell, but in the lead was Piquet, eleven points in front with 54.

Piquet wins championship again

It was a lead he extended by winning at Monza and then taking third position at Estoril, behind Prost's win. Prost's main contender for the title became Mansell after he won back-to-back victories in Spain and Mexico and Prost and Senna failed to finish, leaving them well adrift and out of the running. But the championship was decided in the practice for the penultimate race at Suzuka. Mansell went off at 120 mph and was ruled out of the race. He was bitterly disappointed that winning more races than his rivals was once again not enough to bring him the coveted title. Whatever happened in the final two rounds was immaterial, as the championship belonged to Piquet. Both of the final races were won by Gerhard Berger for Ferrari.

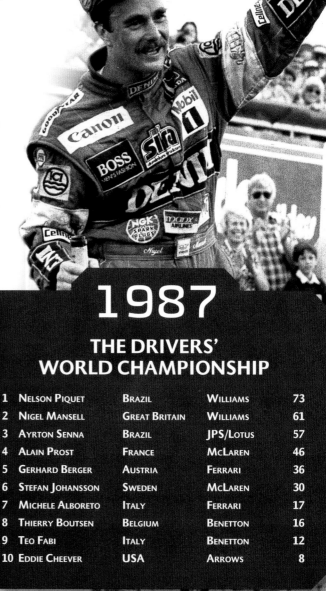

1987

THE DRIVERS' WORLD CHAMPIONSHIP

1	NELSON PIQUET	BRAZIL	WILLIAMS	73
2	NIGEL MANSELL	GREAT BRITAIN	WILLIAMS	61
3	AYRTON SENNA	BRAZIL	JPS/LOTUS	57
4	ALAIN PROST	FRANCE	MCLAREN	46
5	GERHARD BERGER	AUSTRIA	FERRARI	36
6	STEFAN JOHANSSON	SWEDEN	MCLAREN	30
7	MICHELE ALBORETO	ITALY	FERRARI	17
8	THIERRY BOUTSEN	BELGIUM	BENETTON	16
9	TEO FABI	ITALY	BENETTON	12
10	EDDIE CHEEVER	USA	ARROWS	8

A promising start for Prost

FAR LEFT: Alain Prost got off to a good start by winning in the curtain-raiser in Brazil and the Belgian Grand Prix the following month.

LEFT: John Watson makes a ciruit of Silverstone which underwent some changes during 1987, the bridge corner being slightly re-routed.

BELOW: Senna puts the new Lotus 99T through its paces. The car featured an innovative active suspension system.

BOTTOM: Silverstone's tricky Woodcote Corner gets the better of Nigel Mansell during practice for the British Grand Prix.

OPPOSITE: Nigel Mansell salutes the crowd after his Silverstone victory, while Ayrton Senna, who finished third, prepares for the traditional celebration.

Victory at home for Mansell

THIS PAGE: Mansell's victory at Silverstone had been the culmination of a hard-fought battle between him and Piquet (below left). His famous 'two step' move on the Hangar straight had edged him ahead of the Brazilian.

OPPOSITE ABOVE: Piquet had struggled to defeat Mansell early in the season and had finished in second place in each of the first six races finished. His first victory came in the German Grand Prix in June, when Mansell retired with engine trouble.

OPPOSITE BELOW: Prost is ahead of the two Williams cars going into the first bend at Silverstone. The Frenchman failed to finish, while Williams scored one of their four one-two successes of the season.

Consistency secures the title for Piquet

RIGHT AND BELOW LEFT: Nelson Piquet had only three victories to Mansell's six in 1987. Yet again, consistency and reliability were key to the Brazilian gaining his third world crown. Piquet claimed the title at Suzuka, after Mansell was forced to withdraw through injury.

BELOW RIGHT: The McLaren team fine-tune the new MP4/3 for Prost. It turned into a disappointing season for the reigning champion who finished in fourth place.

BOTTOM RIGHT: Barbro Peterson, widow of Ronnie, committed suicide in November, 1987. She is seen here with her then partner, John Watson.

OPPOSITE: Ayrton Senna prepares to race during his third, and last, season at Lotus. Senna's fearless style of driving excited Formula 1 fans but many were uneasy about the risks he took.

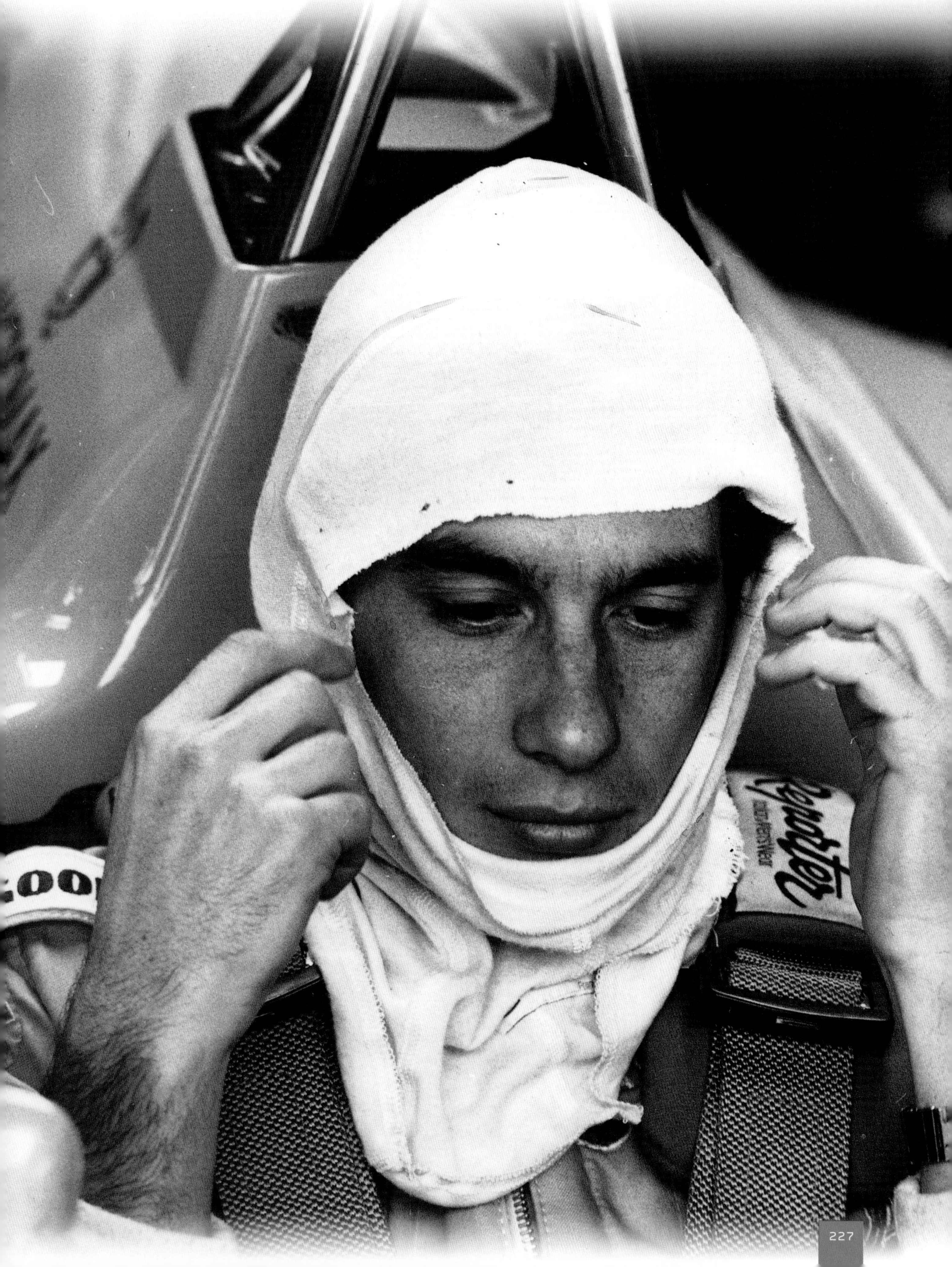

Senna and Prost dominate

Williams had had two highly successful years but 1988 would see a shift in favour of McLaren. The big problem for Williams was their change in engine, from the Honda to the unproven Judd. They still had Mansell and Riccardo Patrese as their main drivers, but neither had really impressed at the top level. McLaren meanwhile had signed Ayrton Senna, who was now partnering Prost under Honda power. They scored an immediate success, with Senna taking pole position. Prost followed by Senna achieved a one-two victory, but Senna was disqualified for having illegally switched cars at the start.

Senna made up for the error at Imola. He won, beating Prost into second place and leaving the rest of the pack a lap behind. Monaco was a different story; from the pole he led until lap sixty-seven. But then he hit the Armco before the tunnel and crashed out; Prost had been some distance behind but cashed in on the Brazilian's mistake, with Berger and Alboreto taking second and third places for Ferrari. The Italian outfit were experiencing a resurgence following the arrival of former McLaren designer John Barnard. Berger and Alboreto went on to finish third and fourth in Mexico, but they remained behind the McLarens.

Berger undermines McLaren

Senna demonstrated his daring skill in Canada when he took the lead from Prost in the nineteenth lap by overtaking on a left–right kink. Then he proved himself as worthy as Lauda and Moss by taking his sixth successive pole in Detroit, going on to win the race, again ahead of his team mate. The next race, at a wet Silverstone, was remarkable in that a slight chink in the McLaren armour revealed itself. Gerhard Berger took pole, with Alboreto's Ferrari beside him on the front row. Berger led for 13 laps – remarkable because it was the first time that anyone other than Prost or Senna had led at any stage at any race. Senna soon passed him, however, leading until the end. Mansell managed to break the McLaren grip by finishing in second, but in fact Prost had already retired with handling problems. At the halfway mark, the championship appeared to be heading McLaren's way; Prost led Senna by 54 points to 48.

Senna wins fourth in a row

Positions in the race for the championship were reversed when Senna beat Prost at a wet Hockenheim. Although the conditions were similar to those at the British Grand Prix, Prost had managed to finish, leading some to criticise his decision to retire from the race in France. The finish at the Hungaroring repeated this result, although the weather conditions were much improved. The real battle for third place, with Benetton's Boutsen vying with Berger for the honours. Senna equalled another achievement of the greats when he won at Spa; it was fourth victory in a row

and seventh of the season, only Jim Clark (1963) and Prost himself (1984) had performed the feat before.

It was finally Ferrari's turn to win at Monza; after both Senna and Prost retired from the race, Berger led Alboreto home for a Scuderia double celebration. But Estoril became yet another battleground for the McLaren duo. Their rivalry was most apparent here, and after the race, a victorious Prost openly criticised his team mate for what he considered to be recklessness; their cars had come perilously close to contact. The Spanish Grand Prix also belonged to Prost, who had led from the outset; Senna being held back by fuel concerns.

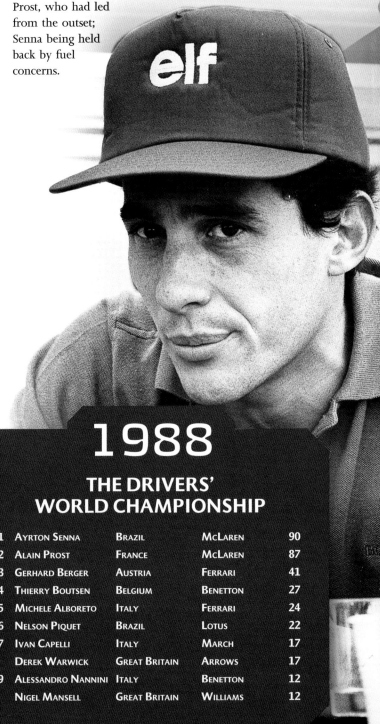

1988
THE DRIVERS' WORLD CHAMPIONSHIP

1	AYRTON SENNA	BRAZIL	MCLAREN	90
2	ALAIN PROST	FRANCE	MCLAREN	87
3	GERHARD BERGER	AUSTRIA	FERRARI	41
4	THIERRY BOUTSEN	BELGIUM	BENETTON	27
5	MICHELE ALBORETO	ITALY	FERRARI	24
6	NELSON PIQUET	BRAZIL	LOTUS	22
7	IVAN CAPELLI	ITALY	MARCH	17
	DEREK WARWICK	GREAT BRITAIN	ARROWS	17
9	ALESSANDRO NANNINI	ITALY	BENETTON	12
	NIGEL MANSELL	GREAT BRITAIN	WILLIAMS	12

Senna tour de force

Suzuka was a crucial win for Senna. With it came the guarantee of the title. It was a typical Senna tour de force; he had fought his way from a lowly fourteenth position at the start to lead by lap 27. With Prost's final win in Australia, McLaren had clearly emerged as the team to beat, with Senna and Prost enjoying world domination.

Champion in waiting

LEFT: Ayrton Senna joined McLaren in 1988. When he drove the Gordon Murray-designed MP4/4 with its Honda engine no one else on the grid could come close.

BELOW: Following his retirement from racing, Niki Lauda established his own airline.

OPPOSITE: Ayrton Senna: champion in waiting.

Senna contemplates tactics

OPPOSITE AND BELOW: Senna's mercurial and competitive nature on the track was in contrast to his character off it; he was enigmatic and deeply religious. Yet his fierce will to win when behind the wheel led to some spectacular victories, not least the decider at Suzuka, where he fought back from fourteenth place to take the victory.

LEFT: Alain Prost had welcomed his new team mate, but the two quickly became rivals. The two McLaren drivers dominated the season, and although Prost finally scored 11 more points than Senna, with only the 11 highest scores counting, Senna was the victor by three points.

Prost takes third championship

The previous season's domination by McLaren and its two rival drivers looked set to be under threat from Ferrari, with Gerhard Berger and new recruit Nigel Mansell back in contention. But most of the drama came, yet again, from the intense rivalry between Senna and Prost. The Frenchman considered Senna to be a danger on the circuit and their simmering tension turned to open hostility as the season progressed.

From the start in Brazil, Senna was embroiled in controversy. When Berger, Senna and Patrese approached the first corner abreast, the mercurial Senna refused to cede ground and his car and Berger's Ferrari touched. Berger retired on the spot and Senna finished far behind Mansell, the eventual winner.

Prost and Senna in dispute

Imola was a replay of many of the races of 1988; it was restarted after Berger crashed out at high speed. Prost lost ground to Senna on the first corner and the Brazilian held on to the finish. The drivers began an off-track quarrel, with Prost claiming that Senna had breached a McLaren missive that the leader at the first corner would not be challenged by the other driver. Senna won with less controversy in Monaco, where he converted pole position to victory with ease. He repeated the trick in Mexico, another career landmark; it was his thirty-third pole, equalling Jim Clark's record. A debut race at Phoenix saw Senna break the pole record, although the win here belonged to Prost.

The Canadian Grand Prix was run in torrential rain and as a result there were many retirements. The victory went to Boutsen, an acknowledged wet-weather specialist, and Patrese made it a one-two for Williams. Williams had recently struck a deal with Renault, an alliance that would eventually lift the team back into the top flight.

Senna suffered retirements in both France and Britain, which had an adverse effect on his score. He had suffered with gearbox trouble at the British Grand Prix, where Prost lead Mansell home. Mansell's popularity on home soil contrasted sharply with the crowd's response to Senna, whose retirement was greeted with cheers.

Mansell in fine win

Hockenheim saw Prost bow out with three laps to go and Senna powered past to win. Mansell had his fourth podium finish that day, but in Hungary he fared better. From twelfth on the grid, he fought his way through the field, overtook Senna on lap 58 and was nearly half a minute clear at

the flag. It was arguably his greatest performance.

Less than two seconds separated Senna, Prost and Mansell as they crossed the line in that order at Spa. Before Monza, Prost gave vent to his feelings of unequal treatment within the McLaren team. Dennis tried to paper over the cracks, but Prost revealed that he'd had enough and was off to Ferrari the following year. In the race Senna led for 44 laps, when his engine blew up. Prost stepped in to increase his lead in the championship. He paraded the trophy in front of the adoring Italian fans, creating wonderful PR with his future team in mind.

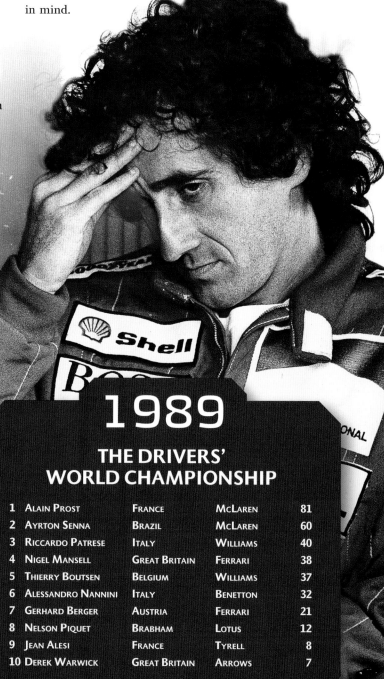

1989
THE DRIVERS' WORLD CHAMPIONSHIP

1	ALAIN PROST	FRANCE	McLAREN	81
2	AYRTON SENNA	BRAZIL	McLAREN	60
3	RICCARDO PATRESE	ITALY	WILLIAMS	40
4	NIGEL MANSELL	GREAT BRITAIN	FERRARI	38
5	THIERRY BOUTSEN	BELGIUM	WILLIAMS	37
6	ALESSANDRO NANNINI	ITALY	BENETTON	32
7	GERHARD BERGER	AUSTRIA	FERRARI	21
8	NELSON PIQUET	BRABHAM	LOTUS	12
9	JEAN ALESI	FRANCE	TYRELL	8
10	DEREK WARWICK	GREAT BRITAIN	ARROWS	7

Controversy at Suzuka

At Estoril, Mansell was penalised for having breached regulations by reversing into the pits and ignoring the black flag. He added insult to injury by colliding with Senna on the forty-eighth lap. Although Senna won comfortably in Spain, he now needed to win at both Suzuka and Adelaide in order to retain his title. It made for an exciting and controversial finish to the season; despite having pole position in Japan, Senna was outdone by Prost, who took the lead. An aggressive attempt to claw back the lead resulted in both cars spinning off; despite finishing the race, Senna was later disqualified for receiving assistance. Senna limped home again in Adelaide following a shunt with Brabham's Martin Brundle. The title went instead to Prost, for an historic third time.

McLarens go head to head

Opposite: Like the previous season, 1989 was a year in which the competition was focused on the rivalry between McLaren team mates Alain Prost and Ayrton Senna. Alain Prost took his third championship title in 1989, winning fewer races than his team mate Senna, but Senna's failure to finish or race in seven events meant that he lost valuable points.

Far left top, centre and below: Riccardo Patrese crashes out of the British Grand Prix at Silverstone. After he joined Williams, 1989 was Patrese's best year in Formula 1.

Left: Senna heads back to the pits after spinning off at Silverstone. Some sections of the crowd cheered the Brazilian's misfortune; his icy persona didn't endear him to all motor racing fans.

Bottom: Ayrton Senna on his way to yet another pole position in 1989. Senna took pole in 13 of the 16 races, converting six of them into victories.

Champion Prost moves to Ferrari

THIS PAGE: The rivalry between Prost and Senna reached a climax at the Japanese Grand Prix at Suzuka. A collision between the two forced both off the track, ending Prost's race. Although Senna took the victory, he was later disqualified as a result of the incident, and the title went to his rival. The matter remained a subject of debate for years to come.

OPPOSITE PAGE: Prost test drives the Ferrari 641. 5. Going into 1990, Prost and Mansell appeared very positive about each other and about their intention to unseat both Senna and McLaren.

Senna pushes for victory at Suzuka

The season almost began without the controversial figure of Senna within the fold; he had been under pressure from FISA to retract comments he had made about their handling of the Suzuka incident. Senna recanted, while maintaining his innocence; his fine was paid and McLaren was able to name him as their lead driver for 1990, but the Brazilian was to be the centre of further controversy as the season rolled on.

Senna won the first race at Phoenix, beating Jean Alesi into second place, but he complained about lack of motivation after the race. Yet by the time of his appearance in front of a home crowd it was clear that the desire was back. A collision with Nakajima couldn't prevent Senna from coming third, behind Prost and then his new team mate Berger. Imola was the setting for an early retirement following brake problems but the next two races, at Monaco and Montreal, were both victories. The win in Canada came as a result of Berger receiving a 60-second penalty for jumping the start. Mexico saw another retirement for Senna, a puncture ending his dominant lead this time.

Collision with Nannini

Senna returned to his winning ways at Hockenheim, but became embroiled in controversy at the Hungaroring when Boutsen was leading. Behind him battled Senna, Mansell, Berger and Nannini, and when Senna attempted to pass Nannini's Benetton at a corner on lap 64, their cars touched. Nannini may have been the wronged man in the manoeuvre but there was little natural justice; his car was pitched into the air, while Senna carried on, finishing second.

Controversial finale

The battle for the championship boiled down to Senna and Prost yet again. At Estoril, Senna won second place to Prost's third, and in doing extended his lead in the championship to 18 points. Prost had conceded too many wins to Senna during the season, the Brazilian having taken both Spa and Monza, and it looked as if Prost was simply going to hand his rival the coveted trophy. However, Prost did win the Spanish Grand Prix, which meant that it

was still possible for him to steal the title so long as Senna didn't fare too well in the next race: Suzuka. Prost got the better start, despite Senna's pole position. When the Brazilian attempted to take the lead they both ended up in the run-off area and the collision gave Senna the title.

Frustration for Mansell

Prost wasn't the only driver suffering this season, although according to his team mate, Nigel Mansell, Prost was having far too easy a run of things. Mansell, convinced that Ferrari were unfairly favouring their French driver, had reacted badly to an early retirement at Silverstone. He had tossed his gloves into the crowd and announced his retirement in a theatrical display of petulance. It was born out frustration; Mansell was desperate to win the title and he felt that playing second fiddle to Prost wasn't going to help his chances.

But Prost did not win the title this year either. Ferrari, incensed by what they saw as foul play by Senna at Suzuka, instigated an enquiry by FISA into 'tactical crashes' and in particular Senna's win in Japan. Much later Senna admitted to having deliberately caused the shunt which ended Prost's hopes.

1990

THE DRIVERS' WORLD CHAMPIONSHIP

1	AYRTON SENNA	BRAZIL	MCLAREN	78
2	ALAIN PROST	FRANCE	FERRARI	71
3	NELSON PIQUET	BRAZIL	BENETTON	43
	GERHARD BERGER	AUSTRIA	MCLAREN	43
5	NIGEL MANSELL	GREAT BRITAIN	FERRARI	37
6	THIERRY BOUTSEN	BELGIUM	WILLIAMS	34
7	RICCARDO PATRESE	ITALY	WILLIAMS	23
8	ALESSANDRO NANNINI	ITALY	BENETTON	21
9	JEAN ALESI	FRANCE	TYRELL	13
10	ROBERTO MORENO	BRAZIL	EUROBRUN, BENETTON	6
	IVAN CAPELLI	ITALY	MARCH	6
	AGURI SUZUKI	JAPAN	LOLA/LARROUSSE	6

A new line-up at Ferrari

OPPOSITE: Prost and Mansell were the new line-up at Ferrarri. Both drivers were keen to take point from Senna.

TOP LEFT: Senna started the year with a win in the US Grand Prix in Phoenix.

TOP RIGHT: Prost was left fuming when Senna's nudge at Suzuka pushed him out of the Japanese Grand Prix at the end of the 1989 season.

CENTRE LEFT: Gerhard Berger was Senna's new partner at McLaren following the departure of Alain Prost.

CENTRE RIGHT: Riccardo Patrese had been with Williams since the end of the 1987 season when he stood in for an injured Nigel Mansell in the last race of the season. In 1990 he won his first Grand Prix for seven years at Imola.

BOTTOM LEFT: Nigel Mansell endured another frustrating year with Ferrari in 1990.

BOTTOM RIGHT: Senna was a controversial figure throughout his career and 1990 was certainly no exception. Some believed his competitiveness was a sign of commitment, even genius; others considered him dangerous and untrustworthy.

Mansell set to retire

RIGHT ABOVE AND CENTRE: Nigel Mansell spins out of control in the forty-ninth lap of the season's opening race in Phoenix. A string of problems throughout the year led to his announcing that he would retire at the end of the season.

BELOW: Senna leads Mansell into the first corner at Silverstone. The race was eventually won by Prost after engine trouble caused Senna to grind to a halt with only eight laps to go.

OPPOSITE ABOVE: Mansell pictured at Silverstone during the weekend of the British Grand Prix. He is seen giving a lift to golfer Greg Norman (far right).

OPPOSITE BELOW: The Ferrari team share their tactic talk and lunch with the 'Great White Shark'.

Patrese and Berger perform solidly

RIGHT: The Williams FW13B, driven here by Riccardo Patrese.

BELOW: Gerhard Berger, McLaren's number two driver.

OPPOSITE ABOVE: Teamed up with the mercurial Senna, Berger strove to form an amicable relationship with his partner. He considered racing alongside the Brazilian to be an opportunity to hone his own driving skills.

OPPOSITE BELOW RIGHT: 1990 was Patrese's third full season with Williams. He and his team mate Thierry Boutsen won a race each in the 1990 season (San Marino and Hungary respectively). Patrese finished the season with 23 points, in seventh position, and Boutsen was in sixth place with 34 points.

OPPOSITE BELOW LEFT: Berger stepped onto the podium seven times in the 1990 season, accumulating enough points to secure third place in the final standings.

Ferrari favour Prost

RIGHT: Many felt that Ferrari failed Mansell during the 1990 season. The condition of the car was thought to be questionable and the Scuderia seemed to be putting all their effort into Prost.

BELOW: Mansell is checked over by medical staff. He managed to win only one Grand Prix – the Portuguese – in a season that was punctuated by seven retirements.

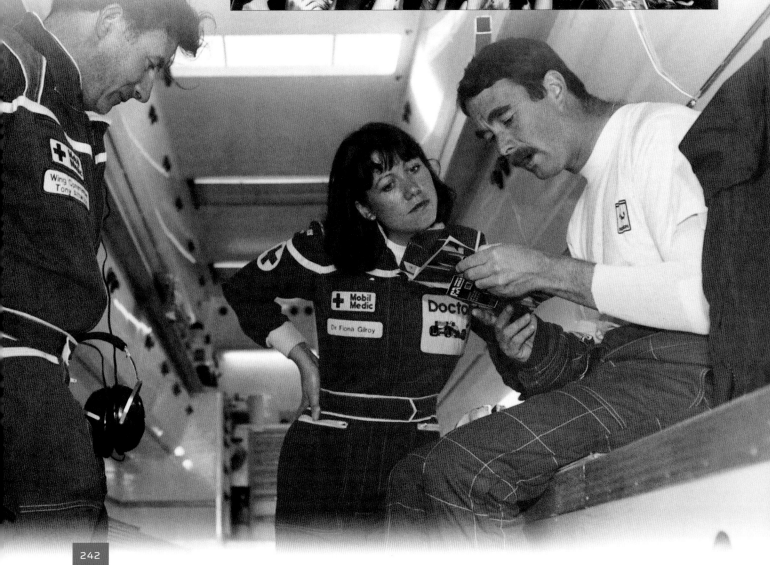

A new British talent waits in the wings

LEFT AND BELOW LEFT: David Coulthard aged 19. The young Scot enjoyed a successful apprenticeship on the karting circuit. By 1993 he would be test driving Formula 1 cars for Williams.

BELOW RIGHT: Martin Brundle is seen here with his young family. He decided to opt out of Formula 1 for 1990, concentrating instead on the sports car championship and the Le Mans 24-hour race.

BOTTOM: Mansell in his Ferrari at Silverstone. Mansell had been forced to retire from the race and, on learning that Prost had been given a superior car to drive, announced his retirement.

McLaren and Senna triumph again

McLaren and Senna looked all set for another memorable year as the 1991 season got under way. The cars were now powered by the new V12 Honda unit and the first four races were easy wins for the Brazilian. The statistics are impressive; there was a total of 282 laps in the four races and Senna led for 273 of them, taking pole in each one just for good measure. His main competition came from Patrese and Berger, both of whom put pressure on the Brazilian; less of a threat was Prost. The year was far less memorable for the Frenchman, who for the first time since 1980 failed to win a single Grand Prix. It was perhaps no surprise that this proved to be the last year that Prost raced for Ferrari. Senna's maximum haul for his effort was 40 points; a new points structure now meant 10 for a win. Another innovation this year, was that all 16 races counted towards the championship.

A fine run for Mansell

Mansell had been pulled back from the brink of retirement by Frank Williams and it looked as if he would finally end Senna's run of success in Montreal. He led the race from the start, but engine failure at the very end of the race meant that victory was snatched by Nelson Piquet. Senna himself had been absent at the end, having retired with alternator trouble, but in Mexico he suffered a full defeat. Patrese, followed by Mansell took a one-two win for Williams with the Brazilian in third place. The Briton went one better in France, winning at Magny-Cours. It was the start of a run of success. At Silverstone, Mansell beat Senna yet again and there was no frustrated outburst this year. Hockenheim saw him take his third win in a row, with Patrese's second yet more good news for Williams. Senna had run out of fuel on the penultimate lap, an expensive mistake as he watched his points lead drop to just eight.

The championship was becoming a battle between McLaren and Williams and the four main protagonists came out on top in the next race. Hungary saw Senna return to form; he had the quickest in practice at the Hungaroring and led all the way in the race, with Mansell crossing the line five seconds behind him. Patrese was third, ahead of Berger. The fastest lap in Hungary was set by Bertrand Gachot, driving the new Team 7-Up Jordan.

Schumacher makes his debut

Jordan might have had a dream first-season victory at Spa but their leading driver, de Cesaris retired with engine trouble when he was running second. This effort was overshadowed by the performance of his temporary team mate, the young German driver Michael Schumacher. Although Schumacher didn't finish the race, his performance was deemed exceptional and he was quickly snapped up by Benetton. The race in Belgium was won by Senna and Berger in a McLaren one-two. With Mansell failing to finish, the gap at the top of the table started to open up again.

At Monza, Mansell took first place ahead of of Senna, whose second place points score was crucial. Taking points in fifth place was Benetton's young prodigy Schumacher, who had beaten three-time world champion Nelson Piquet into the bargain. Senna was second again at Estoril, behind Patrese. It was a result that hurt Mansell, who was disqualified after a pit lane fiasco in which a wheel was changed in an illegal area.

Although Mansell hit back with a dramatic victory over Senna in Spain, the Brazilian's lead was still 16 points. Yet again, he clinched the title at Suzuka. With Mansell out of the race, Senna could even afford to sacrifice first place on the final lap, allowing Berger to come through for his sixth career win. It was another winning year for McLaren, but their run was at an end, and the Williams team was on the march.

1991
THE DRIVERS' WORLD CHAMPIONSHIP

1	AYRTON SENNA	BRAZIL	McLAREN	96
2	NIGEL MANSELL	GREAT BRITAIN	WILLIAMS	72
3	RICCARDO PATRESE	ITALY	WILLIAMS	53
4	GERHARD BERGER	AUSTRIA	McLAREN	43
5	ALAIN PROST	FRANCE	FERRARI	34
6	NELSON PIQUET	BRAZIL	BENETTON	26.5
7	JEAN ALESI	FRANCE	FERRARI	21
8	STEFANO MODENA	ITALY	TYRELL	10
9	ANDREA DE CESARIS	ITALY	JORDAN	9
10	ROBERTO MORENO	BRAZIL	BENETTON, JORDAN	8

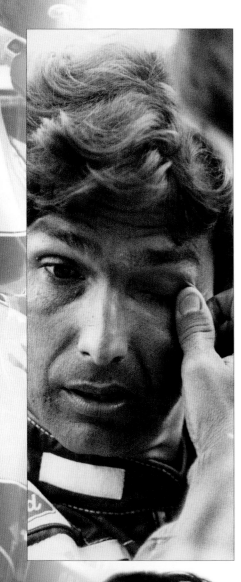

Mansell drives for Williams

OPPOSITE: Team Williams provide a pit stop service for their new recruit Nigel Mansell.

FAR LEFT: Nelson Piquet finished sixth in the Drivers' Championship in his first year with Benetton. He was about to be plunged into the shadow of his new young team mate, Michael Schumacher.

LEFT ABOVE AND CENTRE: Nigel Mansell with his family. Despite a declared intention to retire, Mansell had been tempted by Williams, who brought him on board to partner Patrese.

BELOW: Senna started eight races on pole position and had seven wins in 1991. It was a confident performance which brought a third crown for the Brazilian.

Family business

BELOW: Fathers and sons. Wilson Fittipaldi, Derek Bell and Jackie Stewart stand behind their sons, Christian, Justin and Paul. Damon Hill (far right) completes the quartet of young talent.

RIGHT: Senna prepares for the French Grand Prix by walking the track. He finished the race in third place behind Mansell's Williams and Prost in the Ferrari.

OPPOSITE, MAIN PICTURE: Riccardo Patrese finished third in the Drivers' Championship in 1991.Working alongside his partner Mansell, he had become a serious contender for the title.

OPPOSITE TOP: Mansell had more success with Williams, including winning at Silverstone in front of his home fans. However, disaster at Spa and Estoril ended his chances of the title.

OPPOSITE CENTRE: Four drivers crashed out of the British Grand Prix: De Cesaris, Alesi, Suzuki and Patrese.

OPPOSITE BOTTOM: Ayrton Senna at Silverstone, where he finished in second place behind Nigel Mansell.

Senna hitches a ride

BELOW: Nigel Mansell waves to the crowd during his victory lap at Silverstone. He had stopped to give Ayrton Senna a lift back to the pits because Senna had been stranded on the track after having run out of fuel.

LEFT: Nigel Mansell pictured with his wife Rosanne before the start of the French Grand Prix, the first of three consecutive wins for Mansell.

OPPOSITE ABOVE: Mansell celebrates a victory with a member of the Williams team.

OPPOSITE BELOW: The Williams FW14 with its Renault engine.

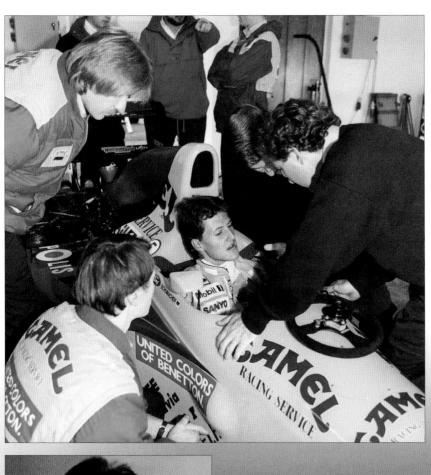

Schumacher: a new talent emerges

THIS PAGE: Michael Schumacher had been racing karts since the age of six. His Formula 1 racing career began with Jordan but he defected from Jordan to join Benetton in 1992 after just one race. An impressive debut season with Benetton was topped with a win at Spa.

OPPOSITE: Nigel Mansell seen here with Stirling Moss, 'one of the greatest drivers never to win the title'. Mansell, who had finished runner-up for the third time in 1991, was hoping not to earn the same accolade.

Mansell finally takes the title

1992 was the season that Nigel Mansell finally came good. It may have been due to his driving in the new Williams model, with its active suspension, but combined with Mansell's fierce determination to prove his critics wrong, the championship was now his for the taking. Just like Ayrton Senna in the previous season, Mansell dominated from the outset. He won the first five Grands Prix of the tournament, starting in pole position in each of the races. In four of the five – South Africa, Mexico, Spain and San Marino – Mansell led all the way, setting the first of a string of records during the year.

Williams could celebrate more than simply five straight victories, though as Patrese followed Mansell home, proving the might of the new car. Indeed, the only driver who prevented Williams from making it a clean sweep in all five races was Michael Schumacher, who came second to Mansell in Spain. Even then, Schumacher was helped by the fact that Patrese had spun out of the race early.

Mansell's grip broken

The man who broke Mansell's run was the reigning champion. Senna's season hadn't started well, he had only managed to finish third in two races. McLaren's new car, the MP4/7, couldn't compete with the Williams vehicle and Senna's victory at Monaco depended to some extent on Mansell having experienced a pit stop delay; the Britain still finished only 0.2 seconds behind Senna despite the lost time. Senna and Mansell were fast becoming fierce rivals; a spat in the Canadian race saw Mansell spin off, for which he later blamed the Brazilian. Neither Williams driver finished that day, Patrese having retired with gearbox trouble, and the victory went instead to Gerhard Berger.

Jackie Stewart's record broken

Williams were back on form in France, despite the rain, with Mansell leading Patrese home. His next win at Silverstone was both an event and a milestone, the victory before a huge home crowd was his 28th, beating Jackie Stewart's British record of 27. Yet despite the celebrations, rumours that Williams were considering bringing Alain Prost on board upset Mansell; their rivalry at Ferrari two years before had undermined the sensitive Englishman.

By August, the race for the championship was reaching an early conclusion. Having won again at Hockenheim, Mansell needed a first or second place at Hungary in order to gain an unassailable lead on points. Despite getting away fastest, Patrese's race was over by halfway as he spun off; Senna was leading with Mansell sitting comfortably on his tail. An unforseen pit stop pushed him down to sixth place, but he clawed his way back to regain second position and this finally clinched the championship for him.

There were signs of things to come in Schumacher's season. He scored his debut win in Belgium, but over the whole season he scored points in 11 races, stepping onto the podium an impressive eight times.

Bitter end to season

Mansell may have won the title, but there was another record to be broken; by winning at Estoril, he had achieved nine victories in one season. Despite this the season ended on a bitter note. Williams had signed Prost and Mansell agreed to partner the Frenchman again in 1993, but when Senna declared his intention to race with Williams, things turned sour. Williams made Mansell a demeaning offer, which the champion promptly refused. He decided that if Williams didn't want him and he couldn't defend his title in a competitive car, then he would walk away from the sport. Although Williams relented and put the original deal back on the table, it was too late and Mansell turned his back on Formula One.

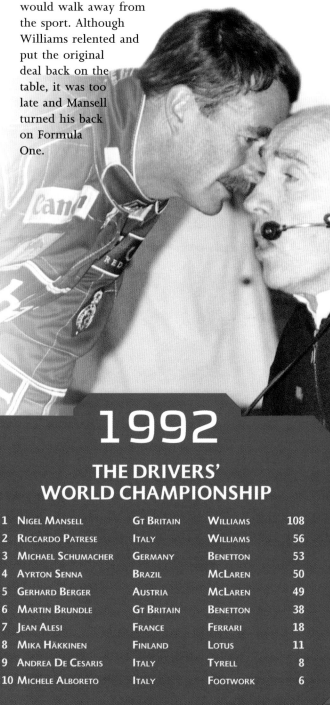

1992

THE DRIVERS' WORLD CHAMPIONSHIP

1	NIGEL MANSELL	GT BRITAIN	WILLIAMS	108
2	RICCARDO PATRESE	ITALY	WILLIAMS	56
3	MICHAEL SCHUMACHER	GERMANY	BENETTON	53
4	AYRTON SENNA	BRAZIL	MCLAREN	50
5	GERHARD BERGER	AUSTRIA	MCLAREN	49
6	MARTIN BRUNDLE	GT BRITAIN	BENETTON	38
7	JEAN ALESI	FRANCE	FERRARI	18
8	MIKA HÄKKINEN	FINLAND	LOTUS	11
9	ANDREA DE CESARIS	ITALY	TYRELL	8
10	MICHELE ALBORETO	ITALY	FOOTWORK	6

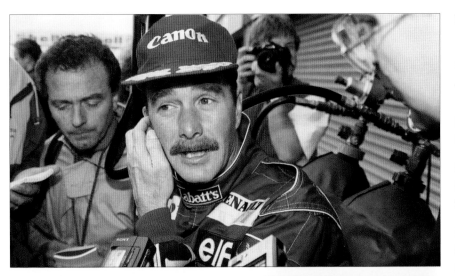

Williams and Mansell go all the way

Opposite: Nigel Mansell with team boss Frank Williams.

Left: Mansell prepares for the British Grand Prix, having secured pole position on the starting grid.

Left below: It was a start to finish lead for the British driver at Silverstone. Mansell won by a distance and threw in a record-breaking lap of 1 minute 22.539 seconds. Mansell in the new Williams model dominated the season.

Bottom: The Williams car with its new active suspension.

Clear finish for Mansell

Opposite top: Mansell's victory at the British Grand Prix gave him a 36 point lead just over half way through the season. He would eventually take the title by a margin of five points.

Opposite centre: Jean Alesi in the Ferrari F92A.

Opposite bottom: Patrese was the other Williams driver. The Italian was overshadowed by his team mate, but managed a career-best second placing in the championship.

Left: Senna at the wheel of his McLaren. The car struggled to match the performance of the Williams.

Below: The wreckage of Erik Comas' Ligier after a crash during practice at Silverstone.

Mansell is able to celebrate

Opposite above: The Mansell family have a cup of tea outside the trailor.

Opposite below: Nigel Mansell finished the 1992 season with a massive 108-point haul and a record-breaking nine wins.

Left: A winner at the table as well as on the track. Mansell's victorious campaign would be his last season in Formula 1.

Below: Nigel Mansell celebrates with champagne.

New British hopefuls

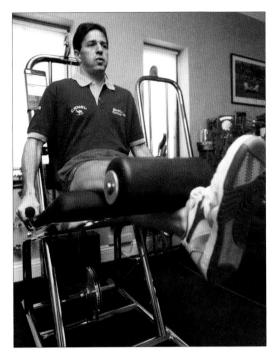

TOP LEFT AND RIGHT: Martin Brundle concentrates on his pre-season training. With the imminent departure of Mansell, Brundle was poised to become the British number one. Having had a somewhat mediocre seven years in Formula 1, his new place on the Benetton team appeared to provide the perfect opportunity to impress.

CENTRE AND BOTTOM: Williams had been quick to see the talent in Damon Hill and his role as a test driver put him behind the wheel of some of the finest cars on the circuit. However, his first taste of being a Formula 1 driver was in the seat of an uncompetitive Brabham.

Schumacher in the spotlight

RIGHT: By finishing the season with an impressive first haul of 53 points, Michael Schumacher had ensured that the media spotlight would now be fixed upon him as a possible future champion.

BELOW AND BOTTOM: Schumacher's bicycle had been an important tool during his first season. In preparation for his debut race at Spa for Jordan, Schumacher had cycled the circuit first in order to learn the track. He went on to qualify in seventh place but had to retire early from the actual race.

Golden season is tarnished for Mansell as Prost secures drive

OPPOSITE BELOW AND THIS PAGE: Alain Prost had spent a year on the sidelines but at the end of 1992 he was signed by Williams, keen to make the most of their technologically superior cars. The signing of Prost sounded the death knell for Mansell, who despite having won the championship felt undervalued by the team. He walked away from the sport that year.

OPPOSITE ABOVE: Mansell was awarded the BBC's Sports Personality of the Year trophy, seen here being held by heavyweight boxing champion Riddick Bowe.

Prost bows out with fourth title

Williams brought back Alain Prost from his year in the driving doldrums; the French number one joined as the team was celebrating its victorious 1992 campaign and it was a wise move. Patrese had also left the team at the end of 1992, moving to Benetton to partner Schumacher. In his place Williams elevated a test driver, Damon Hill, the son of former champion Graham Hill.

Senna on impressive form
The opening race in South Africa was won by Prost, who was more than a lap ahead of the rest of the field, apart from Senna, who was in second place. Although Senna won the next round, in Brazil, he knew that the MP4 carried an inferior Ford V8 engine. Prost and Hill had occupied the front row at Interlagos and Senna was easily able to outrun the inexperienced Hill and benefit from Prost spinning off.

Senna outsmarts the Williams duo
The European Grand Prix at Donington Park was the venue for another fine performance from the Brazilian. The Williams pair were again quickest in practice, but were outmanoeuvred by Senna despite the wet conditions. Although once keen to drive for Williams, Senna was now outsmarting the team. His luck ran out at Imola, however, when he was pulled up by a problem with his hydraulics. Initially the lead was with Hill, but Prost took over for the last 50 laps. Schumacher came in second. It was a near-repeat in Spain when Hill's early lead was brought to an end by engine failure, and again Prost beat Schumacher to the flag. Senna was back on form in Monaco, although it was Schumacher, in the lead, who was forced out with hydraulics problems.

Senna was now leading the title race, although the bubble was about to burst. Prost took four straight wins, in Canada, France, Britain and Germany, and in doing so came back into contention. His only threat had come from team mate Hill, but Prost was always one better. He now had seven wins from ten races.

Hill's luck turns
In contrast to Prost's great form, Hill was suffering a run of bad luck. He had been delayed in the pits at Magny-Cours, his engine then blew up at Silverstone, and, most cruelly of all, he suffered a puncture while leading at Hockenheim with just two laps to go. Fortune can change suddenly, though, and Hill's luck finally took a turn for the better as he took three successive wins of his own in Hungary, Belgium and Italy. At the Hungaroring he led from the start. Schumacher pushed him hard all the way to the line at Spa, a race in which Hill showed his mettle. He benefited from Prost's misfortune at Monza, inheriting the lead as the Frenchman's engine gave out five laps from home.

As consistent as ever, Schumacher had another podium-rich season, taking a place nine times. His best race was at Estoril, where he beat the Williams pair into second and third. But his victory was overshadowed by the success that second place afforded to Prost. Prost had secured his fourth world title with the points scored and with this he bowed out of the sport, having accumulated a record 51 wins from his 199 Grands Prix. Four championship wins put him second only to Fangio in the all-time list.

Prost's decision to retire may have been influenced by the news that Senna was leaving McLaren for Williams for 1994. In Senna's place, McLaren had signed Finnish driver Mika Hakkinen, who had been at Lotus. With Schumacher also carving out a position for himself as one of the top flight, the following season promised to be memorable. And it was, but for all the wrong reasons.

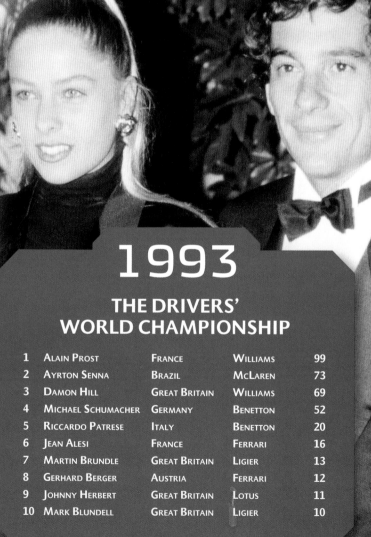

1993

THE DRIVERS' WORLD CHAMPIONSHIP

1	ALAIN PROST	FRANCE	WILLIAMS	99
2	AYRTON SENNA	BRAZIL	MCLAREN	73
3	DAMON HILL	GREAT BRITAIN	WILLIAMS	69
4	MICHAEL SCHUMACHER	GERMANY	BENETTON	52
5	RICCARDO PATRESE	ITALY	BENETTON	20
6	JEAN ALESI	FRANCE	FERRARI	16
7	MARTIN BRUNDLE	GREAT BRITAIN	LIGIER	13
8	GERHARD BERGER	AUSTRIA	FERRARI	12
9	JOHNNY HERBERT	GREAT BRITAIN	LOTUS	11
10	MARK BLUNDELL	GREAT BRITAIN	LIGIER	10

Senna considers his future

Far Left top and bottom left: Senna stands apart from the rest of the McLaren team. From the start of the season he had toyed with the possibility of leaving McLaren to join the now-dominant Williams team.

Left top: Senna had turned 33 in 1993 and was keen to wrest the title from the grasp of Prost, but the Frenchman and his Williams drive proved to be too good.

Centre: Michael Andretti (left), son of Mario, tried his hand at Formula 1 in 1993. After a rather uneventful year as Senna's number two at McLaren, Andretti returned to IndyCars.

Bottom right: Damon Hill with his young family at the outset of his first full year racing in Formula 1. It proved to be an impressive start to the Englishman's career.

Opposite: Ayrton Senna and girlfriend, captured at the Grand Prix Drivers' Gala at Monte Carlo, demonstrate the more glamourous side of Formula 1.

Hill overtakes the best of British

RIGHT: Martin Brundle and Mark Blundell (right) had been driving for Ligier. Despite some fine performances, their careers were on the decline. Brundle had been dropped from Benetton in favour of Patrese and overlooked by Williams who had decided to elevate Hill. Blundell secured two podium finishes with Ligier, but would find himself shifted over to Tyrrell in 1994.

BELOW: The cream of British talent (left–right): Johnny Herbert, Damon Hill, Derek Warwick, Mark Blundell and Martin Brundle.

OPPOSITE ABOVE LEFT: Damon Hill works on tactics with the Williams team.

OPPOSITE CENTRE AND OPPOSITE ABOVE RIGHT: Alain Prost en route to taking his fourth world crown. Alain Prost's incredibly consistent racing style earned him recognition as the most complete driver of his generation When he retired, after 12 years of racing, he had chalked up four Drivers' Championship titles and was runner-up on three occasions.

OPPOSITE BOTTOM: Senna's McLaren at Silverstone. The logo towards the rear of the car is that of Ford; the cars were no longer powered by Honda.

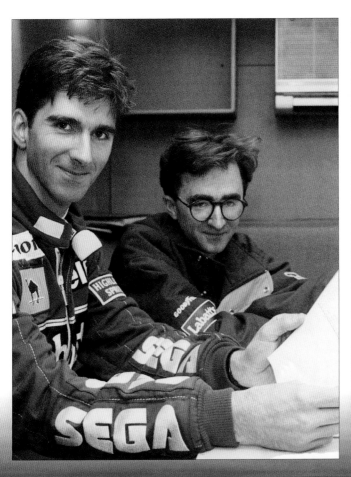

Senna wins at Monaco

Right: Senna is presented with the winner's trophy at Monte Carlo whilst McLaren receive the Constructor's cup.

Below: Despite accumulating five victories in the 1993 season, Senna was unable to prevent Prost from taking the title.

Bottom: Hill in practice at Silverstone. During the race he led for 41 laps, only for his engine to blow and thwart his chance of a home victory.

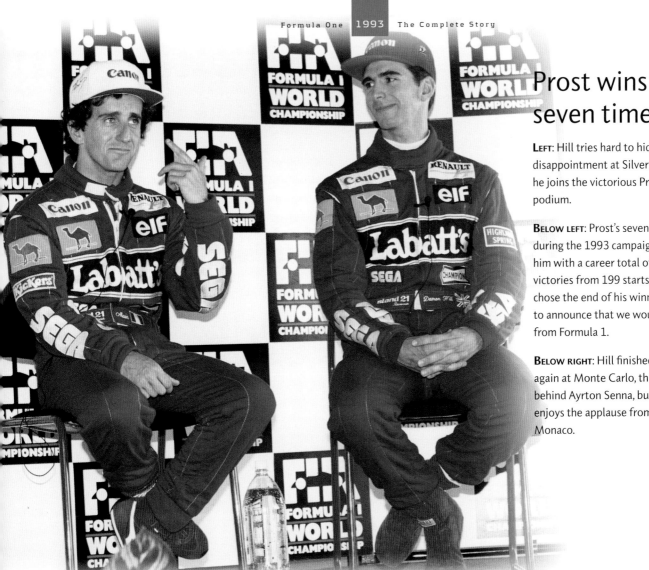

Prost wins seven times

LEFT: Hill tries hard to hide his disappointment at Silverstone as he joins the victorious Prost on the podium.

BELOW LEFT: Prost's seven wins during the 1993 campaign provided him with a career total of 51 victories from 199 starts. Prost chose the end of his winning season to announce that we would retire from Formula 1.

BELOW RIGHT: Hill finished second again at Monte Carlo, this time behind Ayrton Senna, but he still enjoys the applause from the fans in Monaco.

Tragedy at Imola

The 1994 season was to be marred by both tragedy and controversy, becoming one of the most unfortunate in Formula One history. Although safety standards appeared to have improved significantly since the death of Elio de Angelis in 1986, the sport was clearly still dangerous. During the the season, two drivers lost their lives, two were seriously injured and a host of spectators were caught by flying debris in a number of incidents. Meanwhile, controversy overshadowed the winning of the championship.

The Williams cars had made heroes of two of its drivers, Mansell in 1992, and Prost in 1993. Senna was now heading the team and he was determined that 1994 would be his. Although he took pole in the Brazilian opener, Schumacher's Benetton look the lead and kept it, despite Senna's best efforts. Second position went to Hill, Senna's team mate, but he had been a full lap behind the German. The new Pacific Grand Prix was next and Senna was again in pole position. Despite this, a nudge from Hakkinen's McLaren ended Senna's race and Schumacher won again.

Tragedy at San Marino

The San Marino Grand Prix at Imola was next and the weekend started badly. The Friday practice session ended when Rubens Barrichello had a brush with death following a high-speed crash. On the Saturday, Roland Ratzenberger, the Austrian driver who had begun his Formula One career only that season, was killed on the Villeneuve curve during qualifying when Simtek had crashed into the wall.

The actual race began with Senna in pole position again; he got away first, with Schumacher close behind. An early shunt then spread debris across the track and the safety car was brought out to clear up, reducing the speed of the cars. The race began again, but just two laps later, Senna's Williams crashed into a concrete wall at Tamburello Corner. The Brazilian was struck by part of the car's suspension and suffered massive head injuries; he was later pronounced dead at Bologna Hospital.

The death of a world champion in such circumstances had a huge impact on the sport, including the introduction of greater safety measures designed to slow down the cars, both in the vehicle engineering and in track design. In addition the active suspension units from which Williams had benefited were now banned by FIA.

The terrible loss of Senna now meant that the championship race was wide open and the driver who looked most likely to replace the Brazilian as the leader was Michael Schumacher. He had won the restarted San Marino race and then went on to claim a fourth win in Monaco two weeks later. His main threat came from Hill, who had won in Spain. Hill came second again at Montreal and was now four points behind the German. He needed Schumacher to miss out on points if he were to have any chance of beating him to the title.

Schumacher disqualified twice

The season began to follow a predictable pattern, Schumacher winning races and Hill coming second, even when Williams brought back Mansell to fill the vacuum left by Senna. Then, at Silverstone, Schumacher received a disqualification and a two-race ban for rule infringement and ignoring the subsequent black flag. His absence allowed Hill to pull back on points. On his return, the German continued to win high points, until he was disqualified again at Spa, this time for illegal skidblock wear.

Hill went on to win a further three races, bringing him within one point of Schumacher by the time of the final race at Adelaide. Schumacher led until lap 35, when he hit a wall and rebounded into Hill's path. With both contenders out of the race, Mansell won. Many accused Schumacher of deliberately taking out his rival; others thought Hill could have taken evasive action. His win was overshadowed by the controversy, but it was an important first title for Schumacher.

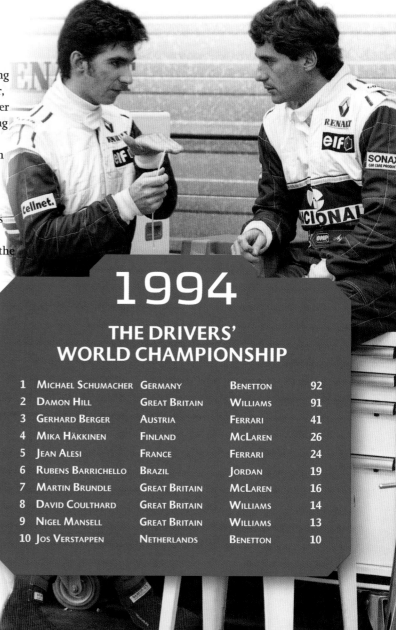

1994

THE DRIVERS' WORLD CHAMPIONSHIP

1	MICHAEL SCHUMACHER	GERMANY	BENETTON	92
2	DAMON HILL	GREAT BRITAIN	WILLIAMS	91
3	GERHARD BERGER	AUSTRIA	FERRARI	41
4	MIKA HÄKKINEN	FINLAND	McLAREN	26
5	JEAN ALESI	FRANCE	FERRARI	24
6	RUBENS BARRICHELLO	BRAZIL	JORDAN	19
7	MARTIN BRUNDLE	GREAT BRITAIN	McLAREN	16
8	DAVID COULTHARD	GREAT BRITAIN	WILLIAMS	14
9	NIGEL MANSELL	GREAT BRITAIN	WILLIAMS	13
10	JOS VERSTAPPEN	NETHERLANDS	BENETTON	10

Senna joins Williams and Hill

Opposite: Williams drivers Hill and Senna plan the new season. Senna started the year keen to capitalise on Williams' recent run of success.

Top left: Damon Hill with his wife, Georgie.

Top right: Both Damon Hill and Stirling Moss lend their support to a charity scheme which offers disabled children the opportunity to enjoy karting. They are pictured here with Hill's son Oliver, who has Down's Syndrome.

Left below: Following the loss of Senna at Imola, Hill assumed the mantle of Williams' number one driver.

Bottom: Hill in action at Silverstone, his second win of season. Schumacher had already noched up six wins by this point.

Schumacher seems unassailable

BOTTOM: The British Grand Prix was the half-way mark of the season and before the race Shumacher had held a seemingly unassailable 37-point advantage over Hill. The gap was narrowed by Schumacher's subsequent two-race ban, and a string of successed for Hill in the later part of the season.

RIGHT: The Australian GP was to be the deciding event, and Schumacher was leading Hill by a margin of one point going into the race. When the German rebounded into Hill's path after hitting a wall, Hill was forced to retire from the race. Hill's failure to score any points meant that the championship title went to Schumacher.

BELOW: Mika Hakkinen had risen from being the McLaren test driver in 1993 to their number one driver in 1994. He finished the season in fourth place with 26 points.

Consolation for Hill

BELOW: Damon Hill is voted the BBC Sports Personality of the Year – some consolation for his narrow defeat in the championship.

LEFT: Damon Hill attends the London Fashion Show with his wife Georgie.

BOTTOM RIGHT: The Palmers and the Brundles out on the town. Jonathan Palmer had long since decided that his racing days were over. Martin Brundle's form at Ligier in 1993 secured him a seat with McLaren in 1994.

BOTTOM LEFT: Ferrari's Gerhard Berger is accompanied by a glamorous girlfriend. The Austrian ace added a win at Hockenheim to his list of credits, but finished the year a distant third behind Schumacher and Hill.

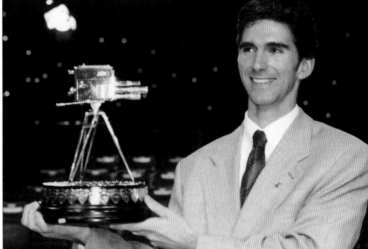

Schumacher by a distance

1994 had been a difficult year for the sport; the ramifications of the events at Imola led the FIA to introduce a battalion of new regulations and rules, aimed primarily at increasing safety. The initial effect of this could be seen in the confusions experienced by Benetton anf the two rule infringements that had resulted in Schumacher's disqualifications. In the wake of this, the 1995 season was therefore strangely calm. It was Schumacher's last year at Benetton; he would move on to Ferrari for the 1996 season. Hill was still with Williams. The two rivals provided the main drama as they battled for the title, although the outcome this time was less dramatic than in 1994.

Schumacher dominates

Schumacher won nine races during the season; he dominated the pack and it was his most impressive year so far. He won the first race at Interlagos, setting the tone for the season, although it was Hill who was victorious in the next two Grands Prix, in Argentina and San Marino. Schumacher and Johnny Herbert made it a one-two for Benetton at the Spanish Grand Prix; the marque had switched from Ford engines to the same Renault units that powered the Williams cars and with evenly matched hardware, success was now down to the skill of the driver. Schumacher was just too good.

Hill got the better of Schumacher in practice for Monaco, but the German took the victory when it counted. Montreal provided a surprise maiden victory for Jean Alesi, his first in eight years in Formula One. He had benefited from the absence of Hill and a delayed pit stop for Schumacher. Benetton were more careful with their pit stop at the French Grand Prix, where the German beat Hill again, but by less than a minute.

Bitter rivalry

Their rivalry took both Schumacher and Hill out of the British Grand Prix early, a shunt on Silverstone's Priory Corner meant that the Benetton–Williams battle was fought out by the number twos. It was Johnny Herbert who won for Benetton, after Coulthard was penalised for speeding in the pit lane.

Hill took a third successive pole position at Hockenheim, but crashed out again in the first lap; this time he had no one to blame but himself. With another win, Schumacher's lead was now 23 points ahead of Hill.

Thriller at Spa

The highlight of the season came at Spa, where Schumacher expertly climbed from an unlikely sixteenth place at the start in order to win from Hill. It was a thrilling race, with the pair fighting wheel to wheel on the straights. They had another spat at Monza with a collision on lap 23. The race was again won by Benetton, with Herbert beating Hakkinen and Frentzen this time. Schumacher had to work hard for his victory on home soil. He passed Alesi, who had dominated the race three laps from home, and crossed the line less than three seconds ahead of the Frenchman. Hill had crashed out in Germany for the fourth time and he now trailed Schumacher by 29 points with just three races to go. Schumacher's win at the TI circuit ended any possibility of Hill winning the title, and t there was no doubting who was the rightful recipient of the crown. Schumacher's ninth win of the year came at Suzuka. Hill did win Adelaide by two laps but he still finished the season 33 points adrift of Schumacher.

1995

THE DRIVERS' WORLD CHAMPIONSHIP

1	MICHAEL SCHUMACHER	GERMANY	BENETTON	102
2	DAMON HILL	GREAT BRITAIN	WILLIAMS	69
3	DAVID COULTHARD	GREAT BRITAIN	WILLIAMS	49
4	JOHNNY HERBERT	GREAT BRITAIN	BENETTON	45
5	JEAN ALESI	FRANCE	FERRARI	42
6	GERHARD BERGER	AUSTRIA	FERRARI	31
7	MIKA HÄKKINEN	FINLAND	McLAREN	17
8	OLIVIER PANIS	FRANCE	LIGIER	16
9	HEINZ-HARALD FRENTZEN	GERMANY	SAUBER	15
10	MARK BLUNDELL	GREAT BRITAIN	McLAREN	13

Reputations established

OPPOSITE: Although Schumacher was swiftly earning a reputation for being cold and aloof, those who knew him best didn't share this opinion.

LEFT AND BOTTOM: Keen perhaps to establish careers in the entertainment industry, several drivers indulge in some post-race rock karaoke. Hill takes lead guitar, while David Coulthard provides support with the maracas.

BELOW LEFT AND BELOW RIGHT: Coulthard's first full season in Formula 1 had promised much; he won pole position five times, was victorious in the Portuguese event and finished in the first three seven more times. Coulthard ended the season in third place. However, he was 20 points behind Damon Hill.

Imola one year on

RIGHT: The flowers and messages left at the Tamburello corner where Ayrton Senna died demonstrate how deeply the Brazilian's death had been felt by fans.

BELOW: Jacques Villeneuve, son of Gilles, test drives for Williams with a view to driving in Formula 1 in the next season. The Canadian had already made his mark on the IndyCar series.

Schumacher earns his second title

THIS PAGE: The posture of Michael Schumacher following a disappointing retirement (below left) contrasts with the obvious air of satisfaction at having won a second championship title. If his title in 1994 had been tarnished by the death of Senna and the controversy of the collision with Damon Hill at Adelaide, then his incredible success in 1995 more than made up for it. He had clocked up nine GP victories, despite driving with a run-of-the-mill Ford engine and had certainly earned the championship title.

Williams duo battle for title

The 1996 season produced yet another struggle between the teams, with the usual shuffle of drivers disrupting the balance. Schumacher left Benetton for Ferrari, which clearly hoped to cash in on his talent. The Scuderia had been without a championship title since Scheckter and Villeneuve finished first and second in 1979, and Jean Todt was keen to rebuild the former giant. Benetton received Jean Alesi and Gerhard Berger in exchange, but the loss of Schumacher marked the start of their decline, they would not retain the constructor's title this year. Ferrari was not quite ready to win either, although Schumacher's presence certainly improved matters. Instead, the team to beat was Williams, which still had Hill as its main driver and Jacques Villeneuve, son of Gilles, as the number two in place of Coulthard, who had departed for McLaren.

Damon equals Graham's career tally

The first three wins of the season went to Hill, at Melbourne, Interlagos and Buenos Aires. This time, Hill's main rival wasn't Schumacher, but his team mate. Villeneuve had taken pole position in his maiden race at Melbourne, but he was undone by the kerb on lap 33 and the win was Hill's. It was a milestone for the Englishman, his fourteenth win equalled his father's career tally. The race was memorable for driver Martin Brundle too. His Jordan rolled spectacularly through the air and landed on Johnny Herbert's Sauber before coming to rest in the sand. Brundle got out, dusted himself off and climbed into his spare car to finish the race.

Although he failed to finish in Brazil, Villeneuve came second to Hill in Argentina and went on to win in the fourth race of the season, the European Grand Prix. He led all the way, crossing the line less than a second ahead of Schumacher. It was an impressive first win; he had beaten the big guns, Coulthard, Hill, Barrichello, Brundle, Herbert, Hakkinen and Berger, all of whom had finished.

Schumacher's first win for Ferrari

Hill enjoyed a victory over Schumacher at Imola, made even sweeter since the German had started in pole position. Monaco was next and it was marred by a spate of accidents, leaving just four cars to finish the race; Olivier Panis in the Ligier was the victor. But by the Spanish Grand Prix, Ferrari and Schumacher were ready to stamp their mark on the tournament. The race was won in appalling weather conditions, Schumacher's skill in the rain earning him his first victory for Ferrari.

Rivalry at Williams

Schumacher was unable to build on the success at Catalunya, the car letting him down in the next three races. Instead, Williams took the victories: Hill won Montreal and Magny-Cours, beating Villeneuve, who took the third victory at Silverstone. Although Hill was leading on points, the Canadian was now only 15 points behind. Another win for Hill at Hockenheim extended his overall lead when Villeneuve finished in third place but it was a short-lived relief, as the Hungaroring race saw the Canadian win by a whisker. Their rivalry aside, the two had managed to secure the constructors' title for Williams by this stage.

Schumacher took the next two races, Spa and Monza, giving the tifosi plenty to celebrate. By Estoril, Hill led by only 13 points; he was undoubtedly the favourite, but with two races left an upset was always possible. The Williams pair slugged it out but Villeneuve eventually won by 20 seconds, slipping past a distracted Schumacher on the last corner.

The title was almost certainly Hill's as they went into the final race at Suzuka – he held a nine-point advantage. When Villeneuve crashed out on the 37th lap it was a done deal, it was almost immaterial that Hill won the race. Hill became the first son of a champion also to win the title for himself.

1996
THE DRIVERS' WORLD CHAMPIONSHIP

1	DAMON HILL	GREAT BRITAIN	WILLIAMS	97
2	JACQUES VILLENEUVE	CANADA	WILLIAMS	78
3	MICHAEL SCHUMACHER	GERMANY	FERRARI	59
4	JEAN ALESI	FRANCE	BENETTON	47
5	MIKA HÄKKINEN	FINLAND	MCLAREN	31
6	GERHARD BERGER	AUSTRIA	BENETTON	21
7	DAVID COULTHARD	GREAT BRITAIN	MCLAREN	18
8	RUBENS BARRICHELLO	BRAZIL	JORDAN	14
9	OLIVIER PANIS	FRANCE	LIGIER	13
10	EDDIE IRVINE	IRELAND	FERRARI	1

Hill fights back

Opposite: Hill was clearly focused on fighting back against Schumacher and Ferrari. In 1996 the Williams team would out race the Scuderia and their new star, Michael Schumacher.

Far left: Jacques Villeneuve had presented the only serious challenge to his team mate Hill during the season. He is shown here following his victory at Silverstone.

Left: Despite having led at Monza, Hill crashed out of the race.

Below left: Hill gives a dejected wave to fans at Silverstone following his early departure from the race. A lose wheel nut had forced him into a spin.

Below centre: Villeneuve in action at the British Grand Prix. He had impressed in his first season, with four victories and a second-place finish.

Below right: Frank Williams – always in control.

Villeneuve takes on Hill

LEFT: Villeneuve looks delighted at his victory at Estoril, whereas his team mate Hill seems less than impressed. The two had swiftly become rivals for the crown. By the last race of the season in Japan Hill was nine points ahead of his team mate. When Villeneuve crashed out of the race, the contest was over.

BELOW: In the practice race in Portugal Villeneuve had been happy to wave his team mate through, although things were rather different in the real event.

OPPOSITE BELOW: A view of the cars turning into the first corner at Silverstone and the eventual victor, Villeneuve, takes the lead.

OPPOSITE ABOVE: Tony and Cherie Blair visit the pits at Silverstone.

Villeneuve strikes back

In 1997 Williams was still the top team but its crown was under threat from a resurgent Ferrari. The Scuderia were now being sponsored by Marlboro, who had spent the past 23 years providing resources to McLaren. At the start of the year Ferrari unveiled its new car, the 310B, and they still had Schumacher. Williams and Hill had parted company and now Villeneuve was accompanied by Frentzen. Having been dismissed despite winning the championship, Hill moved to Arrows, with whom he was unable to achieve a single victory all season.

The drama in this year would be provided by Villeneuve and Schumacher, and yet again there would be controversy and tension. The opener seemed portentous; Eddie Irvine managed to take out both Villeneuve and Herbert as he tried to overtake at the first corner. Frentzen and Coulthard swapped the lead several times but Coulthard and McLaren took the win. Villeneuve won both of the next races, fighting off Berger at Interlagos and Irvine at Buenos Aires. In third position was Ralf Schumacher; this was his debut year in Formula One. Frentzen won at Imola, another victory for Williams, but it was Ferrari's turn in Monaco. The wet conditions in Monte Carlo meant that the race was dominated by Schumacher, who won well ahead of Barrichello.

Wins for Villeneuve and Schumacher

Spain fell to Villeneuve, who had failed to finish in the previous two races. But the see-sawing continued as Schumacher went on to win in Canada; he was declared winner after the Montreal race was stopped because Panis had smashed into the barriers and broken both his legs. It was an unlucky finish for Coulthard, who had been leading until his pit stop left him back in seventh place at the time of the crash. A more convincing win belonged to the German and Ferrari at Magny-Cours. But again luck favoured Villeneuve who won at Silverstone, despite Schumacher having led for some distance. The pattern was broken by Gerhard Berger, whose Benetton stormed home first at Hockenheim; it was the Austrian's final win in his final season.

Damon Hill could have won in Hungary had he not suffered clutch problems. More rain at Spa meant more success for Schumacher, who confounded the field by racing on intermediates rather than wets. A win at Monza for Ferrari was widely expected, but Schumacher was a disappointing sixth at the finish; instead Coulthard scored his and McLaren's second win of the season.

Penalties and disqualifications

With the title being so closely fought, the events in Austria proved disastrous for Schumacher. When Irvine and Alesi were involved in an accident that brought out the yellow flag, Schumacher found himself penalised for overtaking Frentzen.

He finished sixth, Villeneuve won and Schumacher's championship lead was reduced to just one point.

At the Luxembourg Grand Prix, staged at the Nürburgring, Schumacher was nudged out of the race by his younger brother, and the victory went to an uncontested Villeneuve once the McLarens of Hakkinen and Coulthard went out.

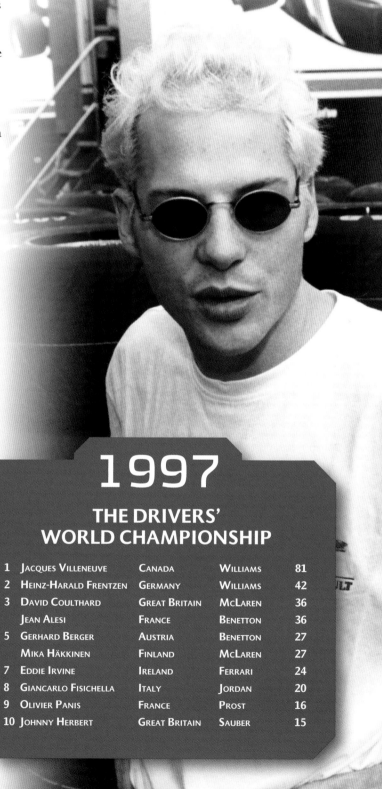

1997

THE DRIVERS' WORLD CHAMPIONSHIP

1	Jacques Villeneuve	Canada	Williams	81
2	Heinz-Harald Frentzen	Germany	Williams	42
3	David Coulthard	Great Britain	McLaren	36
	Jean Alesi	France	Benetton	36
5	Gerhard Berger	Austria	Benetton	27
	Mika Häkkinen	Finland	McLaren	27
7	Eddie Irvine	Ireland	Ferrari	24
8	Giancarlo Fisichella	Italy	Jordan	20
9	Olivier Panis	France	Prost	16
10	Johnny Herbert	Great Britain	Sauber	15

At Suzuka, it was Villeneuve's turn to be disqualified for a yellow flag infringement; so going into the final race at Jerez there was only one point separating the rivals. The two occupied the front row, with Villeneuve in pole position. By lap 48 Schumacher led, but only just. As Villeneuve dived through on the inside, Schumacher tried to shut him out, clipping the Williams and bouncing himself out of the race. Villeneuve managed to stay in the race for third place and it was enough. Villeneuve beat Schumacher by three points. As a punishment for causing the accident, Schumacher was stripped of all the championship points he had gained over the season.

Ambitious Villeneuve secures title

Opposite and left: A change of image but the intentions remained the same – Villeneuve was keen to emulate Hill's success of the previous season.

Below: Hill practices in the wet. He had moved to the Arrows team where he would score only seven points during the season.

Bottom: Taking the chequered flag for only the second time, Hill collects a point for sixth place.

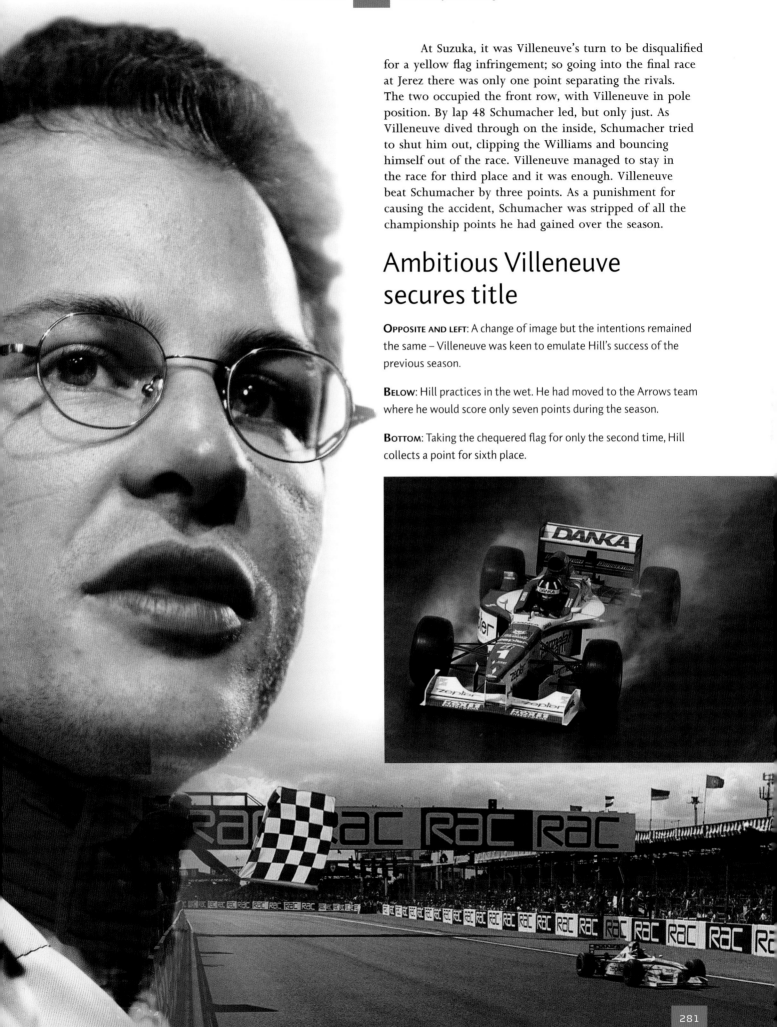

Schumacher stripped of points

Opposite: Going into the final race at Jerez only one point separated Schumacher and Villeneuve. Schumacher had looked set to take the title for a third time, leading until the forty-eighth lap. However, when he clipped Villeneuve's car, he not only bounced his own car out of the race but the FIA ruled that he should be stripped of all of his points. Villneuve became the champion and Frentzen was promoted to second place.

Right: Formula 1 boss Bernie Ecclestone looks strained as he leaves RAC Motorsports HQ.

Below: Schumacher and the impressive Ferrari leave the pits. Despite the teething problems of the previous season, the car had been much more consistent during 1997.

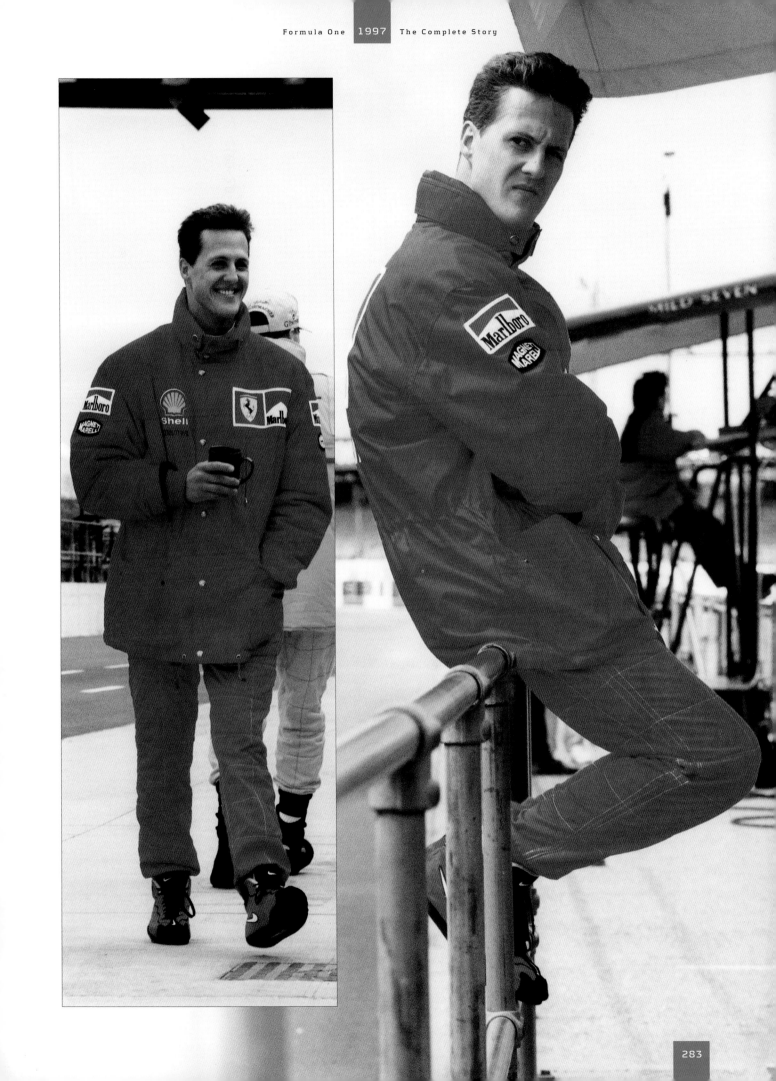

First win for 'Flying Finn'

Schumacher was back and raring to go for the 1998 season. His main rival for the title this year was Mika Hakkinen, who was still with McLaren. There was a series of rule changes; in particular, new tyre regulations were introduced and the cars were made narrower still to reduce down force and slow their speed even more. There were also some grumblings about the lack of possibilities for overtaking, with many complaining that the races were becoming mere processions with pit stops and retirements dictating placements. There were also the usual team changes at the start of the season; Renault had left the sport but Williams were keen to maintain their dominance without them, switching to a new engine company, Mecachrome. McLaren, meanwhile were in partnership with Mercedes and their new cars looked impressive.

McLaren off to a fine start

McLaren embraced the rule changes quickly, and won the first two races of the season convincingly. Hakkinen was handed the victory at Melbourne by his Scottish team mate, acting according to team protocol. For Coulthard, this supporting role continued throughout the season since it was Hakkinen who was expected to secure the driver's title for McLaren. Schumacher had been third that day, proving that he could compete well beyond the potential of the hardware he was given. He got the better of the McLarens in the next race in Argentina. Ferrari also saw Irvine finish third, but Hakkinen's second place gave him 26 points from three races.

Hakkinen was absent at Imola, so Coulthard was able to take what proved to be his only win of the year. The Finn was back for the Spanish event, taking his fourth win of the year. He was followed home again by Coulthard and Schumacher. Monaco provided even greater rewards; not only did Hakkinen finish first but his closest rivals failed to score any points. Schumacher had had an altercation with new Benetton driver, Alexander Wurz, and was declared tenth.

Failure on the grid kept Hakkinen out of the points at Montreal, where Schumacher took his second win of the year. Schumacher went on to make it a hat-trick of wins at Magny-Cours and then Silverstone. The Ferraris of Schumacher and Irvine managed to get ahead, and then stave off all challenges, the wet conditions at Silverstone helping the German to excel. Although Hakkinen and Coulthard hit back with successive one-two finishes in Austria and Germany, Schumacher was in the points in both races.

Jordan celebrate first victory

The reigning champion was not having such a good season; coming third at Hockenheim suddenly seemed like a triumph for the Williams number one. His FW20 simply could not compete.

Hakkinen, meanwhile, was still ahead of Schumacher on points after the Hungarian race, but only just. Schumacher had won at the Hungaroring, whereas the Finn had secured only one point; it was Hakkinen 77 points, Schumacher 70. Despite the rain, it was Damon Hill who won with the Jordan at Spa; a vital success for him since it proved that it he had the skill when the car was lacking.

Deserved win for Hakkinen

The battle between Schumacher and Hakkinen heated up towards the end; they were level on 80 points after Monza, then the Finn took the advantage at Luxembourg in a fine performance. The final round at Suzuka saw Schumacher fall at the last hurdle thanks to some poor luck. Having stalled on the grid he had to start from the back, then, after a brilliant battle up to third place his tyre was blown by track debris and the race was over for him. Hakkinen won the race, and with it he secured the title. It was well-earned, he had scored in each of the 13 races he finished, taking 9 poles, 6 fastest laps, 11 podium finishes and 8 fantastic victories.

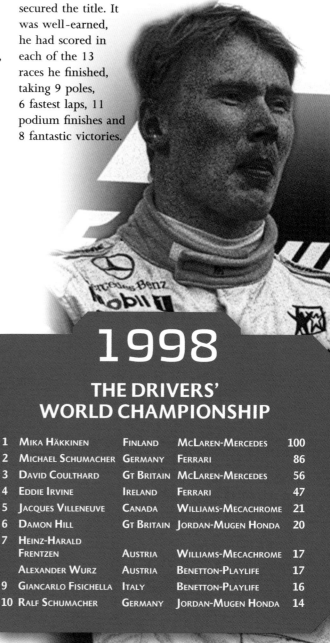

1998

THE DRIVERS' WORLD CHAMPIONSHIP

1	MIKA HÄKKINEN	FINLAND	McLAREN-MERCEDES	100
2	MICHAEL SCHUMACHER	GERMANY	FERRARI	86
3	DAVID COULTHARD	GT BRITAIN	McLAREN-MERCEDES	56
4	EDDIE IRVINE	IRELAND	FERRARI	47
5	JACQUES VILLENEUVE	CANADA	WILLIAMS-MECACHROME	21
6	DAMON HILL	GT BRITAIN	JORDAN-MUGEN HONDA	20
7	HEINZ-HARALD FRENTZEN	AUSTRIA	WILLIAMS-MECACHROME	17
	ALEXANDER WURZ	AUSTRIA	BENETTON-PLAYLIFE	17
9	GIANCARLO FISICHELLA	ITALY	BENETTON-PLAYLIFE	16
10	RALF SCHUMACHER	GERMANY	JORDAN-MUGEN HONDA	14

Hakkinen holds Schumacher at bay

OPPOSITE: Mika Hakkinen drove consistently all season, with eight victories spread over the year. He won the title at Suzuka when Schumacher's tyre blew, but his was a deserved title victory.

TOP LEFT: Schumacher's disappointment at losing out on the title again is clear to see.

TOP RIGHT AND CENTRE LEFT: David Coulthard had played an effective supporting role to his team mate Hakinnen at McLaren. He earned third place in the process.

BELOW: The British Grand Prix attracts its share of celebrities: James Major, Emma Noble and Anthea Turner.

BOTTOM: Damon Hill had moved to Jordan for the 1998 season, where he enjoyed some success again, including a win at Spa in appalling weather conditions. He is shown here after spinning out of the British Grand Prix at Silverstone.

Schumacher triumphs in the rain

OPPOSITE ABOVE LEFT AND BELOW RIGHT:
Schumacher celebrates victory at
Silverstone. The weather conditions at the
Britsh circuit were atrocious, but the Ferrari
driver was renowned for his handling in
wet conditions.

RIGHT: Eddie Irvine takes third place in a
race at Silverstone that was finished by
only nine drivers.

BELOW: The safety car leads during the
downpour at Silverstone.

BOTTOM: Schumacher's Ferrari glides
through the water.

OPPOSITE ABOVE RIGHT: Hill is dejected after
spinning off on lap 13.

OPPOSITE BELOW: Schumacher's pit stop
at Silverstone earned him a ten second
penalty, but he still managed to win the
race.

Hakkinen's second successive title

During the practice for the Australian curtain raiser the McLaren cars dominated yet again and it appeared that Hakkinen and Coulthard would be keeping Ferrari at bay for another year. It certainly proved to be a McLaren–Ferrari battle, but there would be no repeat of the rivalry of the previous season, instead Eddy Irvine had to carry the colours for the Maranello team when Schumacher's season was dramatically cut short by injury.

When Hakkinen and Coulthard disappeared into the distance at the start of the race in Melbourne, things looked ominous for everyone else. But although the McLarens were fast, they were still unreliable and both Coulthard and Hakkinen had to retire. Irvine inherited the lead and held it to the end, taking his first Grand Prix victory from 82 starts. Frentzen, now racing with Jordan, finished just a second behind.

Ferrari start well

On home territory at Interlagos, Rubens Barichello gave the crowds something to cheer when he pulled away first, but a costly pit stop gave Schumacher an opportunity he was quick to take. Even quicker, however, was Hakkinen, who manoeuvred his way to a fine win. It appeared to be a season for leaders to crash out; at Imola it was Hakkinen's turn to retire having held a comfortable lead. Coulthard missed the chance this time, losing his inherited lead to Schumacher. The German dominated at Monaco and Irvine's second place finish gave Ferrari their first one-two of the season.

It was McLaren's turn to take the one-two at Barcelona when Hakkinen and Coulthard were followed home by the two Ferraris; the season was clearly shaping up to be a see-saw battle between the giants. When Schumacher crashed out at Montreal, Hakkinen scored his third win, thus edging ahead of the German by four points.

Schumacher breaks leg at Silverstone

The crash at Montreal wasn't serious, but Frenzen had sustained a fractured leg during the race. Despite this he went on to win in the next event at Magny-Cours. It was a second victory for Jordan, which looked to be a possible new contender in a field that was dominated by just two teams. The last few seasons had seen the gradual decline of constructors like Brabham and Williams, which was becoming a matter of concern for many. Another crash at Silverstone proved to be more disastrous for Schumacher, as his broken leg kept him out of the next six races and so out of contention for the title. The British Grand Prix was won by David Coulthard, his first success since Imola the year before.

Irvine makes a play for the title

With Schumacher out, Irvine was number one for Ferrari, and he rose to the challenge by winning in Austria, beating the McLarens. Hockenheim was another victory for the Ulsterman, with team mate Mika Salo in second. It was Hakkinen's eighth pole position but he lost the advantage when a tyre blew out.

Irvine now led the championship by eight points, but McLaren responded with a one-two in Hungary. The lead in the points race became frenetic. Hakkinen spun out while leading at Monza, where Coulthard and Irvine only managed fifth and sixth respectively. Frentzen could easily have made 60 points had he won the European Grand Prix, which he had led before retiring. Instead Johnny Herbert came through to give the Stewart team its first success. Hakkinen crossed the line in fifth place, taking a 2-point advantage into the penultimate round.

1999

THE DRIVERS' WORLD CHAMPIONSHIP

1	MIKA HÄKKINEN	FINLAND	MCLAREN-MERCEDES	76
2	EDDIE IRVINE	GT BRITAIN	FERRARI	74
3	HEINZ-HARALD FRENTZEN	GERMANY	JORDAN-MUGEN HONDA	55
4	DAVID COULTHARD	GT BRITAIN	MCLAREN-MERCEDES	48
5	MICHAEL SCHUMACHER	GERMANY	FERRARI	44
6	RALF SCHUMACHER	GERMANY	WILLIAMS-SUPERTEC	35
7	RUBENS BARRICHELLO	BRAZIL	STEWART-FORD	21
8	JOHNNY HERBERT	GT BRITAIN	STEWART-FORD	15
9	GIANCARLO FISICHELLA	ITALY	BENETTON-PLAYLIFE	13
10	MIKA SALO	FINLAND	FERRARI	10

Schumacher, with a metal plate in his leg, was back for the Malaysian Grand Prix. He took pole position, but now needed to provide support for Irvine. He did so perfectly, lying second and acting as a buffer between Irvine and Hakkinen, who was behind. A post-race dispute almost saw the Ferraris disqualified, but the original result was upheld.

Irvine went into the final race at Suzuka with a four-point lead. Hakkinen was on top form and won the race comfortably, with Irvine a distant third. So with only two points between them Hakkinen had become the seventh man in the history of Formula One to win back-to-back titles.

A royal appointment

LEFT AND CENTRE: Prince Charles meets McLaren boss Ron Dennis (left) and the team drivers, Coulthard and Hakkinen, while a young Prince Harry imagines life in the driving seat of a Formula 1 car (bottom centre).

BOTTOM LEFT AND BOTTOM RIGHT: A triumphant David Coulthard in Belgium. He finished the season in fourth place with a respectable 48 points.

OPPOSITE: Mika Hakkinen poses with model Sophie Dahl at a charity event. The Finn secured his second title following a fierce contest with Ferrari driver Eddie Irvine.

Hakkinen wins title in the final round

OPPOSITE ABOVE: Schumacher in practice at Silverstone. He was injured in a crash caused by brake failure and spent the next six races on the sidelines.

OPPOSITE BELOW: Despite having had a difficult season, Hill finished the British Grand Prix in fifth place.

LEFT: Eddie Irvine preparing to drive. 1999 was to be his best season in formula 1, with four victories he was a serious contender for the title.

BELOW: The rear wheel of Hakkinen's McLaren-Mercedes rolls away, taking with it any hope of winning the British Grand Prix. But Hakkinen eventually won his second consecutive championship title in a car less reliable than the one that had taken him to victory in 1998.

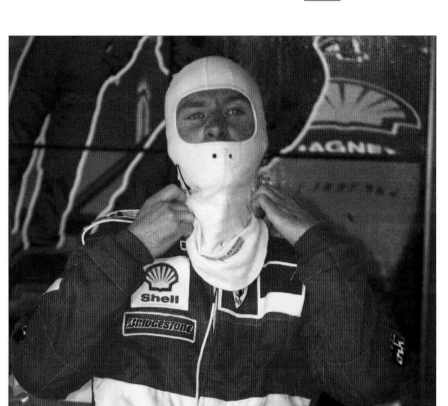

Ferrari bite back

It was business as usual for Ferrari and McLaren as the 2000 season got underway; the two giants were set to dominate the sport again, winning between them 332 of the 442 points available. There would be some input from the lesser teams, though; partnership with BMW meant that Williams would begin to reassert itself again, with Ralf Schumacher and fresh new talent Jenson Button on their books. Jordan and Benetton were also still in contention, although they looked far from threatening to the top two.

Ferrari had acquired the driving skills of Rubens Barrichello for its campaign, having parted with Eddie Irvine. Michael Schumacher and Barrichello made it a one-two win for Ferrari at the opener in Melbourne, despite Hakkinen having taken pole.

At Interlagos the McLarens gambled on a heavy load whereas Ferrari opted for speed and an extra stop. The Ferraris sped out in front but Barrichello's engine eventually blew. Schumacher kept his sizeable lead, and Button managed to acquire his first point despite finishing in seventh place; Coulthard, who had finished in third, was disqualified after the race for a rule infringement. Hakkinen and Coulthard both got away well at Imola, but eventually they were beaten into second and third by Schumacher, who was yet again on fine form.

Coulthard threatening
It was a win for Coulthard at Silverstone, made all the better because he had suffered gearbox problems. At Barcelona the balance shifted, however, when Hakkinen took the flag 16 seconds ahead of the Scot.

The Rainmeister won convincingly at the European Grand Prix, only Hakkinen finishing on the same lap as Schumacher. It looked as if Schumacher would win in Monaco, but a cracked exhaust caused upset and Coulthard profited with a win. Jaguar won their first points when Irvine came home in fourth.

It seemed as if Coulthard was becoming Schumacher's greatest threat when he won at Magny-Cours, in spite of the German's attempts to block him. With Hakkinen coming in second, McLaren had their one-two win.

BAR-Honda driver Ricardo Zonta took Schumacher out of the Austrian Grand Prix at the first corner. His exit was McLaren's bonus; Hakkinen won easily, with Coulthard second. Then, after seven years and 123 races, Barrichello finally won a Grand Prix; the venue was Hockenheim. Schumacher failed to finish in the next three races, but by Hungary he was back in the points, taking six behind Hakkinen's third win of the season. The points tally was no longer in his favour; Schumacher was six points adrift of Coulthard, at the top with 61. A brilliant final four rounds would reverse matters. Schumacher beat Hakkinen at Monza, a race which was marred by the death of a fire marshal who was hit by debris from a shunt between the Jordans.

Schumacher then cruised to victory at Indianapolis. It was his 42nd win, and put him ahead of Senna in the Drivers' Championship. It was all over at the Japanese Grand Prix, when another win gave Schumacher an unassailable lead. It was a prize that Ferrari had sought for 21 years. With a final victory for Schumacher at Kuala Lumpur, the Maranello-based team won the Constructors' title. Scuderia-Ferrari could finally emerge from the shadow of their last dual win in 1979.

2000
THE DRIVERS' WORLD CHAMPIONSHIP

1	MICHAEL SCHUMACHER	GERMANY	FERRARI	108
2	MIKA HÄKKINEN	FINLAND	McLAREN-MERCEDES	89
3	DAVID COULTHARD	GT BRITAIN	McLAREN-MERCEDES	73
4	RUBENS BARRICHELLO	BRAZIL	FERRARI	62
5	RALF SCHUMACHER	GERMANY	WILLIAMS - BMW	24
6	GIANCARLO FISICHELLA	ITALY	BENETTON-PLAYLIFE	18
7	JACQUES VILLENEUVE	CANADA	BAR-HONDA	17
8	JENSON BUTTON	GT BRITAIN	WILLIAMS-BMW	12
9	HEINZ-HARALD FRENTZEN	GERMANY	JORDAN-MUGEN HONDA	11
10	JARNO TRULLI	ITALY	JORDAN-MUGEN HONDA	6

Schumacher equals Senna's record

OPPOSITE: The first year of the new millennium saw Schumacher battling for supremacy with his closest rival Mika Häkkinen. Schumacher was initially successful, winning the first three races of the season at Melbourne, Interlagos and Imola. However, he failed to win the next two, allowing the Finn to close the gap between them.

LEFT: Super-fit Schumacher runs back to his truck at Silverstone. At the Italian Grand Prix Schumacher fended off his opponents, finishing first and equalling Ayrton Senna's record number of 41 wins. The delight at matching his idol's record reduced Schumacher to tears at the press conference after the race.

BELOW: The crucial challenge of 2000 proved to be the Japanese Grand Prix in October. Schumacher lost his early lead but managed to get back to the head of the field after a pit stop and finally emerged the triumphant winner of the race and the Championship. Two weeks later he consolidated his success by winning the last race of the season at Kuala Lumpur, bringing the total number wins that year to nine. A jubilant Ferrari had won the Constructors' Championship after a 21-year wait.

Sir Stirling Moss

RIGHT: Accompanied by his wife Susie and children Allison and Elliott, former racing driver Sir Stirling Moss beaming outside Buckingham Palace after receiving his knighthood from the Prince of Wales. Moss had previously been awarded an OBE in 1959 and was often referred to as 'the greatest driver never to win the World Championship'.

OPPOSITE ABOVE RIGHT: At the age of 77, Murray Walker finally announced that he would be retiring at the end of the following year. He had been commentating on the sport for 51 years, working with both the BBC and ITV, and had been christened 'the voice of Formula One'.

BELOW: Accompanied by his then fiancée Heidi Wichlinski, David Coulthard attends a gala dinner for the Prince's Foundation in Shoreditch, London. During the season, Coulthard had won the races held in Britain, France and Monaco, and finished third in the Drivers' Championships.

BELOW LEFT: Owner of Jordan Grand Prix, Eddie Jordan, receives the famous red book from Michael Aspel at the end of 'This Is Your Life'.

BELOW RIGHT: Frank Williams, founder and manager of the Williams Formula One racing team. Despite being paralysed in a car accident in France in 1986, he continues to be passionate about Formula One racing and is one of the most well-respected characters on the circuit. He was awarded the CBE in 1987 and in 1999 was knighted by the Queen.

Schumacher wins again

The goal for Ferrari was now to maintain their position at the top. The gulf between the rest of the pack and the two premier outfits seemed to have widened but during the course of the season, McLaren would suffer disappointment, while the resurgence of Williams would continue. The Oxfordshire outfit loaned Jenson Button to Benetton for the year and replaced him with Juan Pablo Montoya, who would go on to take one of Williams' victories during the season. Benetton were also aided by a new partnership with Renault, who had returned to the sport.

After Melbourne, however, it looked as though the year would belong to Michael Schumacher yet again. The German led from the first corner and was never seriously challenged. Hakkinen had crashed out on lap 26 and so Coulthard was left to take the spoils for McLaren; in this instance it was second place. As at Monza the previous year, the race was marred by the death of a marshal, this one also hit by flying tyre debris following a crash involving Ralf Schumacher and Jacques Villeneuve.

Montoya impresses

The Malaysian Grand Prix was a wet affair, and typically it was Schumacher who took the flag, despite having slipped into the gravel and having endured a mishandled pit stop. Brazil was the venue for McLaren's first success of the 2001 season, when Coulthard out-manoeuvred Schumacher with panache to seal his first victory of the season. The race was also notable for the impression Montoya made when he aggressively passed the German, forcing him momentarily onto the grass, but the Columbian CART champion was himself forced to retire after a bump from Jos Verstappen.

Winning Schumachers

San Marino saw another Schumacher win, but this time it was younger brother Ralf who took the place at the centre of the podium. It was his maiden win and also a significant victory for the Williams team, the first since 1997 when Villeneuve had won at Luxembourg. It had not been a good race for Ferrari, as the McLarens had dominated the front row at the start, with Coulthard on pole and Michael Schumacher forced to make his first retirement with suspension problems. He was back on form for the next meeting at Barcelona, though, taking pole position, setting the fastest lap time and winning the race. The victory came at a price for Hakkinen, who had been leading into the penultimate lap when a hydraulics failure put him out.

At the Austrian Grand Prix it was Coulthard for McLaren who was again first to the flag. The race had to be restarted following a debacle at the start when four cars stalled on the grid. Montoya and Schumacher clashed yet again, with both

temporarily coming off the track, although Schumacher battled back to third position. As they approached the final lap, Barrichello, lying in second was forced to pull back and let his team-mate slip ahead to secure second place; Schumacher was now on target to take the title. In fourth place that day was the young Finn Kimi Räikkönen; although this was his first season he now had a total of four points, having already scored one in Melbourne. He would finish the season with nine.

2001

THE DRIVERS' WORLD CHAMPIONSHIP

1	MICHAEL SCHUMACHER	GERMANY	FERRARI	123
2	DAVID COULTHARD	GT BRITAIN	MCLAREN - MERCEDES	65
3	RUBENS BARRICHELLO	BRAZIL	FERRARI	56
4	RALF SCHUMACHER	GERMANY	WILLIAMS - BMW	49
5	MIKA HÄKKINEN	FINLAND	MCLAREN - MERCEDES	37
6	JUAN PABLO MONTOYA	COLOMBIA	WILLIAMS - BMW	31
7	JACQUES VILLENEUVE	CANADA	BAR - HONDA	12
	NICK HEIDFELD	GERMANY	SAUBER - PETRONAS	12
	JARNO TRULLI	ITALY	JORDAN - HONDA	12
10	KIMI RÄIKKÖNEN	FINLAND	SAUBER - PETRONAS	9

Schumacher makes history

Schumacher went on to win a further six Grand Prix races, although arguably the most important one was the Hungarian at the Hungaroring in August. His victory there marked his 51st victory, equalling Alain Prost's record for the most wins in Formula One. He also secured the Championship title with this race, tying with Nigel Mansell for the earliest title win in a season. The points margin between him and second-placed Coulthard was impressive; the German scored a total of 123, while the Scot took 65. It was also Schumacher's fourth title and so another milestone was reached; he had equalled Prost's Championship tally and was now only one Championship win behind the great Fangio.

Ralf and Michael first and second in Canada

OPPOSITE: Mika Häkkinen pictured with tennis champion Boris Becker. 2001 proved to be Häkkinen's last year in Formula One. At the end of the season he initially planned to take a sabbatical but the following summer announced his retirement to spend more time with his young family.

LEFT AND BELOW: Jenson Button puts his Benetton car to the test in wet conditions in preparation for the coming season. It proved to be a useful session as in the second round of the Championship in Kuala Lumpur there was a tropical rainstorm on the second lap.

ABOVE: Rubens Barrichello watches as Mika Häkkinen celebrates his win at the British Grand Prix in July 2001. Earlier in the year, at Barcelona, Häkkinen was set to capture the Spanish Grand Prix for the fourth year in succession until his car's hydraulics failed on the penultimate lap. He then went on to win the United States Grand Prix at Indianapolis in September and finished the season in fifth position

BELOW RIGHT: Schumacher again dominated the season winning on nine separate occasions, securing his fourth Drivers' Championship with 123 points, 58 points ahead of runner-up David Coulthard. At the Canadian Grand Prix Michael came second to brother Ralf, setting a new statistic in Formula One racing, with two brothers taking the first and second positions in a race.

Jenson with Benetton

ABOVE: British-born Jenson Button first raced in Formula 1 in 2000 for the Williams team and finished eighth in the championship. In 2001, although still under a contract with the Williams team, he was loaned to Benetton but did not have such a successful season. His best placing was fifth in the German Grand Prix but he ended the year a disappointing seventeenth in the Drivers' Championship.

OPPOSITE ABOVE AND LEFT: 2001 proved to be a successful year for Coulthard. He finished second in the Drivers' Championship with wins in Austria and Brazil.

OPPOSITE BELOW: Rubens Barrichello with David Coulthard. Barrichello had been signed up by Ferrari in 2000 and he finished the 2001 season in third place with ten podium places and a total of 56 points. He had also supported both Schumacher to win another Drivers' Championship and Ferrari, as they took the Constructors' Championship for the third year in succession.

Ferrari and Schumacher untouchable

Ferrari was ever-dominant in 2002, with Schumacher and Barrichello clocking up 221 points between them, bettering the previous year's total by 33. No one else could come close to threatening the Ferrari duo, who took first position in 15 of the 17 races, although there were some all too familiar controversies to be had along the way.

Raikkonen emerges

The traditional Melbourne opener was the venue for a spectacular pile-up which put Barrichello out of contention. Schumacher was followed home by Montoya and Raikkonen. The latter had joined McLaren following the departure of Hakkinen and not only did he secure a place on the podium but he also took the honours for fastest lap. Australian Mark Webber enjoyed a successful debut in front of a home crowd; he came in at fifth for Minardi.

Montoya frustrated

Montoya was forced into second again at Sepang, although many felt he should have taken the win; he had been penalised for an early crash with Michael Schumacher, whose brother went on to take first place for a Williams' one-two. Britain's Jenson Button was forced to endure the agony of his ailing Renault being passed by the world champion on the final lap, which kept him off the podium. The third place position for Michael Schumacher was his lowest of the season; he would finish either first or second in every other race.

Ferrari clean sweep

In Brazil, Montoya engaged in another first-lap spat with Schumacher, but there was no penalty outcome this time and he finished an uncontentious fifth. It was the first of four successive wins for Schumacher, now driving the new Ferrari. Barrichello had lost his lead in Brazil to his team-mate when his engine failed, but he was back on form at Imola, where a Ferrari clean sweep left many bemoaning the lack of excitement. It was a charge which Montoya did his best to refute in Spain, where he took six points, but his second place came at the expense of a retired Barrichello.

Team orders cause contention

Austria saw a blatant example of team orders cynically determining the winning line-up when Barrichello handed victory to his team-mate at the final corner. It seemed to contravene the spirit of racing and at the end of the year FIA moved to bring an end to team orders. Although Schumacher had insisted upon Barrichello joining him on top of the podium, the crowd showed its displeasure and the German's reputation was further tarnished.

McLaren occupied the front row at Monaco, but both Montoya and Coulthard were outclassed; the Colombian was forced to retire and Coulthard lost to Schumacher. The Scot managed to split the Ferraris in Montreal, but after this the season turned into a Maranello juggernaut. Canada saw Ferrari's 150th Grand Prix victory, and they would take nine more in the season. Barrichello enjoyed victory at the European Grand Prix; he was followed home by Schumacher and the lack of orders from Jean Todt was a sensible decision in the face of a FIA hearing on events in Austria. Joining Ferrari on the podium was Kimi Raikkonen, showing yet more promise.

2002
THE DRIVERS' WORLD CHAMPIONSHIP

1	MICHAEL SCHUMACHER	GERMANY	FERRARI	144
2	RUBENS BARRICHELLO	BRAZIL	FERRARI	77
3	JUAN PABLO MONTOYA	COLOMBIA	WILLIAMS - BMW	50
4	RALF SCHUMACHER	GERMANY	WILLIAMS - BMW	42
5	DAVID COULTHARD	GT BRITAIN	MCLAREN - MERCEDES	41
6	KIMI RÄIKKÖNEN	FINLAND	MCLAREN - MERCEDES	24
7	JENSON BUTTON	GT BRITAIN	RENAULT	14
8	JARNO TRULLI	ITALY	RENAULT	9
9	EDDIE IRVINE	GT BRITAIN	JAGUAR - FORD	8
10	NICK HEIDFELD	GERMANY	SAUBER PETRONAS	7
	GIANCARLO FISICHELLA	ITALY	JORDAN - HONDA	7

Fantastic haul for Schumacher

Schumacher's victories during the 2002 season saw him pass milestones and smash records. He enjoyed his 60th career win at Silverstone, and victory at Magny-Cours secured a fifth Championship crown, with which he equalled Fangio's record. His 11 victories during the season beat the record of nine that he had held jointly with Nigel Mansell, and he also became the first man in Formula One's history to record a podium finish in every race. Schumacher was now well on his way to becoming the sport's most decorated driver.

The Red Baron

ABOVE AND OPPOSITE: A triumphant Schumacher claims the trophy after winning the British Grand Prix at Silverstone in July 2002, which was also the 60th victory of his career. Team-mate Rubens Barrichello was second, giving the top two slots to Ferrari while Juan Pablo Montoya was third in a Williams BMW. By the end of the season Schumacher had successfully retained his Drivers' Championship, finishing 67 points ahead of Barrichello.

LEFT: Ralf Schumacher, younger brother of Michael, joined the Williams racing team in 1999. In 2002 he won the Malaysian Grand Prix but was behind team-mate Juan Pablo Montoya in the Championship, in fourth position with 42 points. The two team members contributed to Williams coming second in the Constructors' Championship that year.

Orange Arrows

RIGHT: Mechanics from the Orange Arrows team wait around the garage at Silverstone as their future hangs in the balance. The team, formed in 1977 in Milton Keynes, was initially called the Arrows but changed to Footwork in 1991 after investment by a Japanese businessman. They changed to back to the Arrows five years later. In March 1996 Tom Walkinshaw bought into the team and signed up Damon Hill who came second in the Hungarian Grand Prix the following year. In 2002 the team were hit with three litigation cases and eventually ran out of money. The company failed to complete all the races in the season and were forced into liquidation.

RIGHT: Although there was no shortage of tyres, Ford were refusing to supply engines until the company's debts had been paid off.

BELOW: One of the team's mechanics slumps in despair against Heinz Harald Frentzen's car. All the vehicles had been put into the garage while company boss Tom Walkinshaw negotiated to try to prevent the team from going out of business.

Difficult season for Coulthard

LEFT: Coulthard's helmet receives a final polish before a practice. During 2002 he continued to race for McLaren, along with team-mate Kimi Räikkönen. His only win was at the Monaco Grand Prix and by the end of the season he was placed fifth in the Drivers' Championship with 41 points.

BELOW: Coulthard surrounded by mechanics as he makes his fourth pit stop at Silverstone. He ended the race in tenth position.

Schumacher beats Fangio's record

At the San Marino Grand Prix during the 2002 season, many had expressed their discontent at the lack of excitement borne out of yet another Ferrari clean sweep. The way that season panned out had done little to quiet those voices of discontent. With this in mind, the FIA decided to act before the sport lost too much of its appeal; so it was out with team orders and telemetry and in with new qualifying rules, points scoring and a prohibition on topping-up the fuel tank after qualifying. The changes had an instant effect during the 2003 season, as eight different drivers topped the podium and the fight for the Championship title went right to the wire.

It was David Coulthard who took the first win of the year, at Melbourne. The Ferraris had started well but Barrichello crashed out and Schumacher damaged his F2002 after a run-in with the kerb. The new Renault driver Fernando Alonso also finished in the points, coming in at seventh. He went on to become the youngest driver to take pole position for the Malaysia event, and ended the race on the podium, below winner Kimi Raikkonen and Barrichello in second. The young Spaniard was clearly one to watch.

Drama at Interlagos

The Brazilian Grand Prix proved to be the dramatic highlight of the year. The Interlagos circuit was dogged by pouring rain and when Mark Webber crashed his Jaguar, Alonso struck the debris, sending the wall of tyres onto the track as he hit the barrier. The race had to be red-flagged, and victory was initially awarded to Raikkonen, but an appeal from Jordan over a timing error led to Giancarlo Fisichella taking the trophy from the Finn a week later.

Four of the next five rounds were won by Michael Schumacher. In San Marino, Spain and Austria, the defending champion converted poles into victories. His win at Imola was poignant, coming just hours after he learnt of the death of his mother. The battle was between Schumacher and Raikonnen at Barcelona, where Ferrari unveiled their new 2003 car, giving the German the necessary edge. He brushed aside a pit-lane fire to notch up another win at the A1-Ring.

Montoya victories

Monaco was the venue for Montoya's second Formula One victory, but it was a close finish; less than two seconds separated him from Raikonnen and Schumacher. The season's traditional half-way venue, Spa, had been dropped following a row over tobacco advertising and so it was the win at Montreal which saw Schumacher top the table for the first time in the season. Younger brother Ralf led a Williams' one-two at the European Grand Prix, a race which seemed to belong to Raikkonen

– until his engine expired. Ralf Schumacher took a second successive victory for Williams at the French Grand Prix, but the Ferraris were back on form for the British event. Despite winning pole, fastest lap and the flag, Barrichello's victory was somewhat overshadowed by the death-defying protest of a kilted spectator. A first lap shunt at Hockenheim took Raikkonen, Barrichello and Ralf Schumacher out of contention for the German Grand Prix, leaving the way open for Montoya to finish first, over a minute ahead of Coulthard.

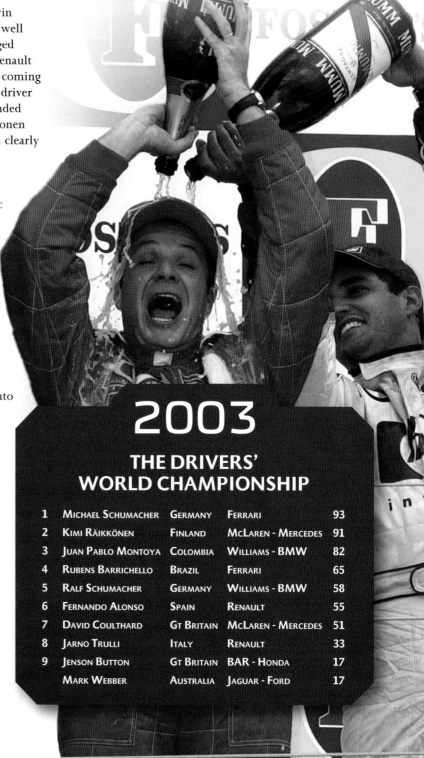

2003
THE DRIVERS' WORLD CHAMPIONSHIP

1	MICHAEL SCHUMACHER	GERMANY	FERRARI	93
2	KIMI RÄIKKÖNEN	FINLAND	McLAREN - MERCEDES	91
3	JUAN PABLO MONTOYA	COLOMBIA	WILLIAMS - BMW	82
4	RUBENS BARRICHELLO	BRAZIL	FERRARI	65
5	RALF SCHUMACHER	GERMANY	WILLIAMS - BMW	58
6	FERNANDO ALONSO	SPAIN	RENAULT	55
7	DAVID COULTHARD	GT BRITAIN	McLAREN - MERCEDES	51
8	JARNO TRULLI	ITALY	RENAULT	33
9	JENSON BUTTON	GT BRITAIN	BAR - HONDA	17
	MARK WEBBER	AUSTRALIA	JAGUAR - FORD	17

Alonso becomes youngest-ever winner

When Fernando Alonso, aged 22 years and 26 days, won at Hungary, he broke Bruce McLaren's record as the youngest-ever winner of a Grand Prix. He led from start to finish and, significantly, it was Renault's first win for 20 years. The revamped Hungaroring circuit had already sent off more seasoned drivers, such as Barrichello. Schumacher, leading Montoya by a single point, went on to take back-to-back wins at Monza and Indianapolis. Going into the Japanese event he was leading the Championship table but the title was not safe; in serious contention were Raikonnen and Montoya, although both needed the German not to finish. In the event, Schumacher's eighth place was enough to secure his sixth title; he had finally beaten Fangio's 46-year-old record.

Ferrari dream team

Opposite: A jubilant Rubens Barrichello celebrates his win at the British Grand Prix and is joined on the podium for a dousing by Juan Pablo Montoya. Barrichello later went on to win the Japanese Grand Prix and finished the season in fourth place, assisting Ferrari and Schumacher to win their respective titles once again. Montoya, a title contender at the beginning of the year, eventually finished in third place and announced he would be driving for McLaren in 2005.

Above left: Ross Brawn joined Scuderia Ferrari as technical director in 1997. He had previously worked with Williams, Jaguar and Benetton and was instrumental in helping Ferrari achieve their six successive Constructors' titles and Schumacher his five consecutive Drivers' Championships, making him a vital member of the Ferrari 'dream team'.

Left: Schumacher clinched his sixth Drivers' Championship, finally breaking Fangio's record of five wins and finishing the season with 93 points.

Closely contested

OPPOSITE LEFT: After being replaced at Renault F1 (formerly named Benetton) by the young Spanish driver Fernando Alonso, Jenson Button joined the British American Racing team to drive alongside Jacques Villeneuve. Although Button crashed during a practice at Monaco and was unable to take part in the race, he had a successful year and finished fourth in both the Austrian and Japanese Grand Prix.

OPPOSITE RIGHT AND BELOW: Coulthard was an opponent of the single-lap qualifying format introduced in 2003 and the new ruling had an impact on his results. He finished first in the Australian Grand Prix and second in Germany but ended the year in seventh place.

LEFT: Kimi Räikkönen closed the season as runner-up to Schumacher by only two points. The Constructors' Championship was similarly keenly fought, with Williams only twelve points behind Ferrari and McLaren a very near third. The changes in FIA rules had successfully made it a much more closely contested year.

Formula One goes global

As the 2004 season got underway the only real contenders to Ferrari's domination were McLaren and Williams. However, the Scuderia would not be easily turned over, in fact they would not really be challenged at all during a season which saw them comfortably win both the constructor's title and the driver's Championship. With the introduction of two new races, in Bahrain and China, the competition had finally become truly global; there were now 18 Grand Prix to be contested and from these Ferrari would take an incredible 15 wins.

Button climbs the podium

The season opener at Melbourne was won by Schumacher, followed by Barrichello, in a Ferrari one-two. This performance was followed by another victory at Sepang and a repeat one-two at the Bahrain inaugural Grand Prix. Schumacher and Barrichello had looked dangerous from the outset and both the McLarens and the Williams cars had struggled to match the power of the scarlets. At Sepang it was BAR-Honda who showed they were 'the best of the rest' when Jenson Button, in his first season with the Lucky Strike-sponsored outfit, took third place, the first of a total of ten podium finishes that season. This was an achievement which would earn him third place in the overall Championship. He went on to take pole in San Marino, but was finally beaten to the finish by Schumacher. The young Briton could be satisfied with a clear second place, ahead of Montoya.

Schumacher makes it five out of five

Schumacher took the triple in Spain, winning pole position, fastest lap and the victory. It was an impressive seventy-fifth win, as he had to contend with a damaged exhaust for much of the race. It was also his fifth consecutive victory, a milestone which saw him equal Nigel Mansell's 1992 record. Ferrari and Schumacher were finally overhauled at the sixth event, in Monaco. A clash between Alonso and Schumacher in the tunnel dashed any hopes of a perfect season, although it was Schumacher's only retirement of the year and his first in 19 races. The victory went instead to Renault's Jarno Trulli, who had begun on pole and led for periods at the start and the finish.Only half a second behind him was Jenson Button, his attempts to pass having been foiled by the twisting street circuit.

McLaren's season had so far been a nightmare, with Raikkonen enduring a series of engine failures and only once finishing in the points, coming eighth at Imola. At the European Grand Prix his car was beset by engine problems again, retiring after just nine laps. The race was won convincingly by Schumacher, 17 seconds ahead of Barrichello in second. Coulthard, meanwhile, had managed to finish more often, but had only accumulated points in the lower

rankings, if at all. Instead, Ferrari were having all the luck; Schumacher won again in Montreal, despite having qualified only sixth – stopping for fuel just twice was a strategy that worked perfectly. Williams were sharing McLaren's pain, but for them it was frustration at having Ralf Schumacher and Montoya finish second and fifth only to lose out on a technical infringement. Renault had hoped for a home victory at Magny-Cours, but their plans were thwarted by Ferrari's clever four-stop strategy. Alonso at least had the consolation of splitting the Maranello pair and taking eight points.

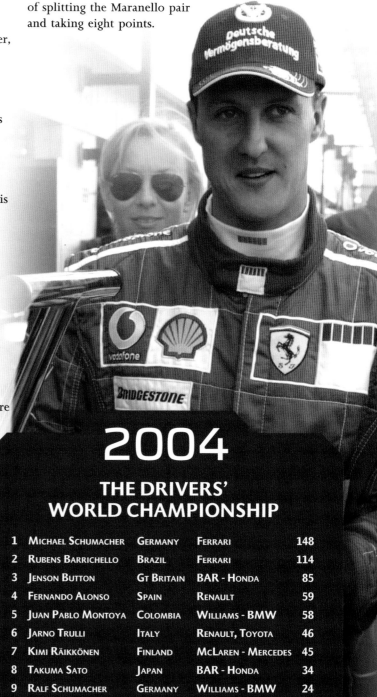

2004

THE DRIVERS' WORLD CHAMPIONSHIP

1	MICHAEL SCHUMACHER	GERMANY	FERRARI	148
2	RUBENS BARRICHELLO	BRAZIL	FERRARI	114
3	JENSON BUTTON	GT BRITAIN	BAR - HONDA	85
4	FERNANDO ALONSO	SPAIN	RENAULT	59
5	JUAN PABLO MONTOYA	COLOMBIA	WILLIAMS - BMW	58
6	JARNO TRULLI	ITALY	RENAULT, TOYOTA	46
7	KIMI RÄIKKÖNEN	FINLAND	McLAREN - MERCEDES	45
8	TAKUMA SATO	JAPAN	BAR - HONDA	34
9	RALF SCHUMACHER	GERMANY	WILLIAMS - BMW	24
	DAVID COULTHARD	GT BRITAIN	McLAREN - MERCEDES	24

Silverstone saw Schumacher claim his tenth victory of the season, but McLaren finally had something to cheer about as Raikkonen came in second. The German Grand Prix could have gone to Button but he fell foul of the new rule that dropped a driver ten places down the grid if the car needed a replacement engine, so the victory went to the Ferrari number one again. With a further one-two for Ferrari in Hungary, both titles were finally secured. Although McLaren at last made the MP4-19 a winner at Spa, Schumacher's second place had sealed his seventh title. His 13th win at Suzuka was almost academic, but it perfectly rounded off another searing campaign.

Record wins for Schumacher

OPPOSITE: Schumacher had a blistering start to the 2004 season and, with the exception of Monaco, had twelve successive wins, giving him the necessary points to claim his seventh Drivers' Championship. The title was clinched at the Belgian Grand Prix, in August, in a race won by the improving Kimi Räikkönen. By the end of the year Schumacher had set a new record of thirteen wins out of a potential eighteen.

BELOW: Schumacher enjoyed his tenth win of the season at the British Grand Prix, with Räikkönen taking second place to give McLaren their much-needed first podium position of the season.

Best of British

OPPOSITE TOP LEFT: Jenson Button receives some words of advice from former three times World Champion and President of the British Racing Drivers' Club, Jackie Stewart. Button had a successful season achieving his first podium place when he finished third in the Malaysian Grand Prix. At the end of the year he was in third position overall, with BAR runners-up in the Constructors' Championship.

OPPOSITE TOP RIGHT AND BOTTOM: Jenson Button during practice sessions for the British Grand Prix. He was sporting a new Cross of St. George on his helmet in preparation for the race. He eventually crossed the line in fourth place.

ABOVE LEFT: British drivers David Coulthard and Jenson Button. Coulthard finished the season in tenth position alongside Ralf Schumacher but it proved to be his last year driving for McLaren who had just taken on Juan-Pablo Montoya. The following season Coulthard signed for Red Bull Racing who wanted to add his experience to their team.

LEFT BELOW: Bernie Ecclestone is often referred to as the 'F1 Supremo'. In October 2004 he and Jackie Stewart were unable to reach an agreement over the future of the British Grand Prix, resulting in the race being dropped from the following year's calendar. However, the heads of the ten racing teams met and agreed to cut costs which officially reinstated the race and a contract was signed guaranteeing the event would take place for the next five years.

BELOW: Schumacher's income in 2004 was estimated to be $80 million but he is renown for being a very generous benefactor to various charities. In the same year he gave $10 million to assist victims from the Indian Ocean earthquake.

Ferrari give way to Renault

The five-year-long domination of Formula One by Ferrari and Schumacher finally came to an end in 2005 with the two producing only one winning performance all season, at the US Grand Prix in Indianapolis. Instead the battle for the crown raged between Renault and McLaren, with Fernando Alonso and Kimi Raikkonen in close contention for the Drivers' title. The series now ran to a record-breaking 19 races, with the addition of the new Turkish event in Istanbul, but the title was decided with two rounds to spare; at 24 years and 58 days, Fernando Alonso became the youngest champion in the event's 56-year history.

Alonso rises to the challenge

The season got off to a blistering start for Renault; they had Giancarlo Fisichella in pole behind the wheel of the much-vaunted new R25 at Melbourne. The Italian converted his start into a fine win, but it was Alonso who set the fastest lap time, and came in third behind Barrichello. The next three races all went Alonso's way; at Sepang he beat Jarno Trulli, now driving for Toyota, into second position. It was a key first podium for the new outfit. Bahrain had been run in scorching heat and it was a short-lived race for the Ferrari team. They had been prompted to hasten the introduction of their new car by their lacklustre start to the season, but a hydraulics failure forced the seven-times champion to retire for the first time in four years.

Alonso's run of fortune was put on hold by Raikkonen, who scored successive wins in Barcelona and Monaco The McLaren would prove to be the more powerful car, but unfortunately it suffered a number of teething problems and at the European Grand Prix at the Nürburgring, its suspension failed within sight of victory. Raikkonen was forced to hand victory over to the Spaniard who claimed his fourth of the season. With a return victory from the Finn at Montreal the gauntlet was clearly being thrown, but again Raikkonen was thwarted by the unreliability of the car; three blown engines at Magny-Cours, Silverstone and Monza proved costly to his Championship hopes. Alonso's win in France gave Renault their first home victory since Alain Prost's 1983 triumph.

Button in contract dispute

It would be a disappointing year for BAR after finishing second to Ferrari in 2004. Collecting his first points of the year in France, Jenson Button had come fourth, having already seen a third place at Imola chalked off for a technical infringement and then been hit with a two-race ban. Yet before the season was out, Button nailed his long-term colours firmly to the team's mast. Despite being contracted to Williams until 2006, Button controversially decided to remain with BAR; he was reported to have stumped up over £10 million to buy himself out of the deal with Williams.

With a win for McLaren at Silverstone, Montoya put his name on the points board, beating Alonso and Raikkonen into second and third, but it was another ten points for Alonso at Hockenheim – a race that Raikkonen had been leading until his engine gave out.

Going into the Hungarian event, Alonso had a 36-point cushion, although this was swiftly cut to 26 when the Finn scored maximum points, while Alonso failed to score any.

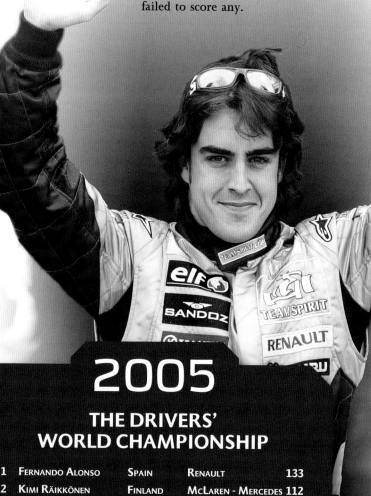

2005
THE DRIVERS' WORLD CHAMPIONSHIP

1	FERNANDO ALONSO	SPAIN	RENAULT	133
2	KIMI RÄIKKÖNEN	FINLAND	MCLAREN - MERCEDES	112
3	MICHAEL SCHUMACHER	GERMANY	FERRARI	62
4	JUAN PABLO MONTOYA	COLOMBIA	MCLAREN - MERCEDES	60
5	GIANCARLO FISICHELLA	ITALY	RENAULT	58
6	RALF SCHUMACHER	GERMANY	TOYOTA	45
7	JARNO TRULLI	ITALY	TOYOTA	43
8	RUBENS BARRICHELLO	BRAZIL	FERRARI	38
9	JENSON BUTTON	GT BRITAIN	BAR - HONDA	37
10	MARK WEBBER	AUSTRALIA	WILLIAMS - BMW	36

The battle between the pair was taken to Istanbul, where Alonso capitalised on a Montoya mistake to snatch second behind Raikkonen's victory. It was the same result again at Spa, which kept Alonso far enough ahead on points. His third place at Interlagos made the title secure, and he now beat the record long held by Emerson Fittipaldi to become the youngest-ever Formula One champion.

The youngest champion

OPPOSITE: On September 25, 2005, after finishing in third position at the Brazilian Grand Prix, Fernando Alonso became the youngest World Drivers' Champion, aged 24 years and 58 days, breaking the record set by Emerson Fittipaldi and finally ending Schumacher's five-year hold on the title. At the Chinese Grand Prix Alonso finished third and Renault F1 triumphantly claimed the Constructors' Championship, also ending Ferrari's six-year run.

LEFT: Ron Dennis, principal of McLaren. The company was runner up in the Constructors' Championships in 2005.

BELOW: Jenson Button was disqualified from the San Marino Grand Prix in April because of the car's fuel system which resulted in a two-race ban for the team. Ironically this enabled Button to make his debut as a commentator for the Monaco Grand Prix. This poor start to the season was compounded by a crash on the 46th lap in Montreal.

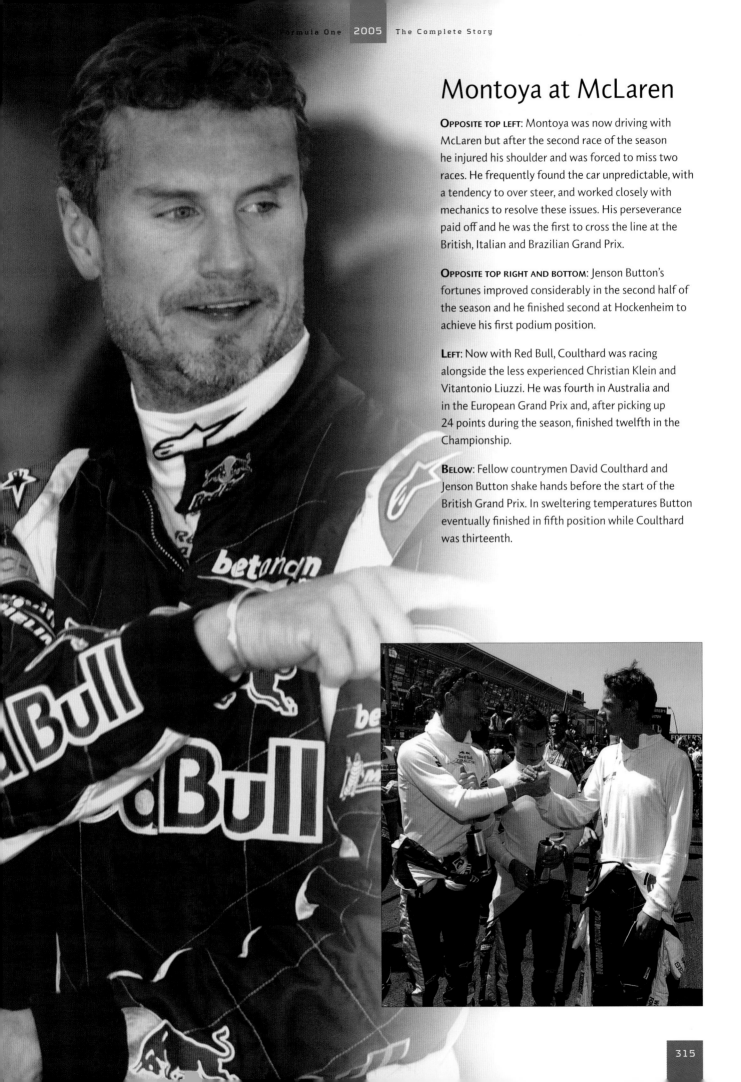

Montoya at McLaren

OPPOSITE TOP LEFT: Montoya was now driving with McLaren but after the second race of the season he injured his shoulder and was forced to miss two races. He frequently found the car unpredictable, with a tendency to over steer, and worked closely with mechanics to resolve these issues. His perseverance paid off and he was the first to cross the line at the British, Italian and Brazilian Grand Prix.

OPPOSITE TOP RIGHT AND BOTTOM: Jenson Button's fortunes improved considerably in the second half of the season and he finished second at Hockenheim to achieve his first podium position.

LEFT: Now with Red Bull, Coulthard was racing alongside the less experienced Christian Klein and Vitantonio Liuzzi. He was fourth in Australia and in the European Grand Prix and, after picking up 24 points during the season, finished twelfth in the Championship.

BELOW: Fellow countrymen David Coulthard and Jenson Button shake hands before the start of the British Grand Prix. In sweltering temperatures Button eventually finished in fifth position while Coulthard was thirteenth.

Schumacher bows out

As the 2005 season had not been a good one for Ferrari or their number one driver, going into 2006 there was some expectation of a return to form. As it turned out, 2006 was defined by the rivalry between Schumacher and Alonso, who won seven Grand Prix apiece. Ferrari and Renault were consistently the best outfits at each event, and only one race would be won by a driver in a different car; Jenson Button took his first victory at the Hungaroring with his BAR-Honda. Key changes at the start of the season included the loss of the Belgian Grand Prix, as alterations to the Spa circuit had not been completed. But perhaps the most significant change was the announcement after the Italian Grand Prix that Michael Schumacher was to retire at the end of the season.

Ferrari proved that they had returned to form in the early stages of the season with wins for Schumacher at Imola and at the European Grand Prix at Nurburgring; he later celebrated three consecutive wins in America, France and Germany. In contrast, Renault's fortunes began to change for the worse. Fernando Alonso had started well, winning in Bahrain and securing a run of victories in the Spanish, Monaco, British and Canadian races. However, several FIA rulings went against Renault and from July, Alonso faced a dry spell, finishing fifth in Indianapolis and Hochenheim, and retiring altogether at the Hungaroring.

Alonso and Schumacher battle it out

The see-sawing between the two drivers continued as Schumacher took over from Alonso to win at the US, French and German events, and the gap between them in the race for the Drivers' Championship began to close, with Alonso just ahead of his rival. Alonso was beset by further difficulties, including being controversially penalised for obstructing Massa in qualifying for the Italian Grand Prix. Ultimately the penalty was academic; the Spaniard was forced to retire from the race with engine trouble. Schumacher went on to win the race and as he took his place on the podium, Ferrari announced their driver's intention to withdraw from Formula One at the end of the season.

Three weeks later, in Shanghai, Alonso gained pole position with Schumacher back in sixth. The race was full of excitement, with Schumacher fighting back to push Alonso into second place. Schumacher's victory put the pair level on points, although the German's greater number of wins placed him in first position. There were only two events to go and Schumacher's last season was proving to be one of the most nail-biting. As it was, Alonso was handed victory at Suzuka when Schumacher's engine trouble forced him to retire. Now with ten points in hand, Alonso looked set to win in Brazil; Schumacher needed a victory and for Alonso to fail to earn any

points. As it was, neither man won; victory went instead to the Brazilian Felipe Massa, scoring a first home victory at Sao Paolo since Ayrton Senna won the 1993 race.

Alonso had sealed victory in the Drivers' contest in Brazil and his win had also secured the Constructors' Championship for Renault. It was an impressive second consecutive title for the young Spaniard, but he was not destined to remain with the French team. Instead he would begin 2007 with McLaren, replacing Montoya who had decided to leave Formula One following a disappointing run of seasons. Montoya was accompanied in his departure by former champion Jacques Villeneuve, who had sustained injuries at Hochenheim and decided to hang up his helmet at the end of the year. But it was the departure of 37-year-old Michael Schumacher which was the defining event of the year. Having won the Drivers' title seven times, achieved 91 wins out of 250 Grand Prix races, taken the podium 154 times and amassed a total of 1,369 points, he is arguably the greatest driver the sport has ever seen.

2006
THE DRIVERS' WORLD CHAMPIONSHIP

1	FERNANDO ALONSO	SPAIN	RENAULT	134
2	MICHAEL SCHUMACHER	GERMANY	FERRARI	121
3	FELIPE MASSA	BRAZIL	FERRARI	80
4	GIANCARLO FISICHELLA	ITALY	RENAULT	72
5	KIMI RÄIKKÖNEN	FINLAND	MCLAREN - MERCEDES	65
6	JENSON BUTTON	GT BRITAIN	HONDA	56
7	RUBENS BARRICHELLO	BRAZIL	HONDA	30
8	JUAN PABLO MONTOYA	COLOMBIA	MCLAREN - MERCEDES	26
9	NICK HEIDFELD	GERMANY	SAUBER - BMW	23
10	RALF SCHUMACHER	GERMANY	TOYOTA	20

Most successful driver

OPPOSITE: After the Italian Grand Prix Ferrari announced that Michael Schumacher, the most successful driver in the history of Formula One, would be retiring from racing at the end of the season. He still planned to work for the team but in a managerial capacity, assisting the CEO select future drivers.

LEFT: Ferrari simultaneously announced that Räikkönen would be joining the team the following year. During his last season with McLaren-Mercedes Räikkönen had a mixed year; he retired from six races due to mechanical problems but claimed six podium positions.

BELOW: In Barcelona, David Coulthard completed his 200th Grand Prix, joining the prestigious Formula One '200 club'.

Alonso's Hat Trick

OPPOSITE ABOVE: Fernando Alonso celebrates his win at the British Grand Prix taking the fastest lap, pole and win; the youngest driver to achieve the Hat Trick. He beat Schumacher and Räikkönen into second and third place. From the season's eighteen races Alonso had seven wins and gained a total of fourteen podium places.

OPPOSITE BELOW: Schumacher's last race of his Formula 1 racing career took place in Brazil. Before the race he was presented with a trophy by footballer Pelé for his years of dedication to the sport.

LEFT AND BELOW: At the beginning of the season BAR Honda was purchased by Honda and thus changed their name to the Honda Racing F1 Team. Jenson Button gained his first Grand Prix win in Hungary, crossing the line in atrocious conditions forty seconds ahead of the runner-up. Thirteen years earlier, Damon Hill had claimed his first F1 win on the same track.

Welcome Lewis

RIGHT: At the age of ten Lewis Hamilton had approached Ron Dennis, asking if he could race for him in the future. Twelve years later, when Hamilton was approaching his 22nd birthday, it was announced he would be racing for the McLaren Formula 1 team the following year, partnering Alonso.

BELOW AND OPPOSITE BELOW: Alonso leading the British Grand Prix. He had already announced a move to McLaren in 2007 but Renault allowed him to test drive for McLaren on the Jerez circuit for one day in December 2006. It was also revealed that he would be partnering the young British driver Lewis Hamilton. Alonso was to be paid a reported £20 million for the coming season.

OPPOSITE ABOVE LEFT: In the last six races of the season Button scored a total of thirty-five points, more than any other driver. He was destined to end the year in sixth place, amassing 56 points in total, achieving three podium positions.

OPPOSITE ABOVE RIGHT: Schumacher's contribution to the racing world has also been recognised by renaming the eighth and ninth turns at Nürburgring as the 'Schumacher 8'. He also received a gold medal for Motor Sport from the FIA in 2006 to honour his achievements.

A season of change

Inevitably the departure of Schumacher left space at the top for new talent to shine. Alonso looked to be ready to take on the mantle as the driver to beat, but when Raikkonen moved from McLaren to fill the void left at Ferrari, it became apparent that Alonso had serious competition. Back at McLaren the seat left vacant by the Finn was to be filled by a 22-year-old from Stevenage who made an even bigger impact than the German ace had managed in his rookie year; in 2007, Lewis Hamilton would prove himself to be a rising star.

Several established teams had disappeared at the end of the 2006 season, including Sauber which sold out to BMW; Jordan, which became Spyker; and BAR ,which became Honda following a takcover. Meanwhile, the end of the concord agreement between the constructors' association and Bernie Ecclestone had seen threats of a splinter competition away from Formula One; threats which were eventually subdued. The season itself consisted of 17 rounds, with a revamped Spa back on the fixture list but the German Grand Prix had gone and, after a quarter of a century on the roster, the San Marino Grand Prix was also dropped. 2007 was a year in which the Drivers' title went to the wire, with only one point in it for the victor, while the Constructors' title was dogged by controversy and scandal as McLaren were accused of having spied on Ferrari when their chief designer was found to be in possession of the Scuderia's technical data.

Lewis Hamilton debuts in style

Hamilton made an immediate impression in Formula One by stepping up on the podium on his debut; he had come in third behind Raikkonen and Alonso. The Finn had dominated the opening race, leading all the way from the lights to the flag. Alonso won the next event, in Malaysia, with Hamilton moving up to second position. The rookie was to manage nine consecutive podium finishes, a record performance for a newcomer in the history of the Championship. McLaren looked set to dominate as their pair went on to secure a one-two at Monaco, but only after Felipe Massa had already taken the Bahrain and Spanish Grands Prix.

Ferrari versus McLaren

Ferrari were by no means out of contention, however; whenever a McLaren failed to win the title, it was a scarlet car that took the honours, and ultimately Ferrari recorded nine wins to McLaren's eight. Canada was the scene of Hamilton's maiden triumph, with Nick Heidfeld and Alex Wurz taking the minor placings. Alonso had been handed a ten-second penalty for pitting when the safety car was out, and Massa was disqualified for a rule infringement. Heidfeld was the only driver outside the big four to claim another top-three spot, bringing his BMW-Sauber home behind

Hamilton and Räikkönen in Hungary. During qualifying, a ruck between Alonso and his team-mate, and now rival, had placed the Spaniard back at sixth place on the grid. Australian Mark Webber went on to take third at the European Grand Prix, after Räikkönen retired and Hamilton slid off in a downpour that claimed several victims.

2007
THE DRIVERS' WORLD CHAMPIONSHIP

1	Kimi Räikkönen	Finland	Ferrari	110
2	Lewis Hamilton	Gt Britain	McLaren - Mercedes	109
	Fernando Alonso	Spain	McLaren - Mercedes	109
4	Felipe Massa	Brazil	Ferrari	94
5	Nick Heidfeld	Germany	Sauber - BMW	61
6	Robert Kubica	Poland	Sauber - BMW	39
7	Heikki Kovalainen	Finland	Renault	30
8	Giancarlo Fisichella	Italy	Renault	21
9	Nico Rosberg	Germany	Williams	20
10	David Coulthard	Gt Britain	Red Bull	14

Raikkonen wins crown

Another impressive rookie, Renault's Heikki Kovalainen, finished second to Hamilton in Japan from 11th on the grid, keeping his head as a string of drivers hit trouble. He held off his compatriot, Räikkönen, to secure his first podium in Formula One.

By the time of the final race in Brazil, Hamilton held a four-point lead over Alonso and a seven-point advantage over Räikkönen. Although Massa looked good for a home victory after leading for much of the race,

he made way for his Ferrari team-mate. Alonso had to settle for third, while Hamilton battled on with a faulty gearbox to finish seventh; fifth place would have won him the title. McLaren appealed over irregularities involving the cars that finished ahead of Hamilton but it came to nothing and Räikkönen became the third Finnish driver to don the crown. He had gone to Brazil in third position, and by winning, he emulated Farina's victory in the inaugural Formula One Championship.

Record for rookie

OPPOSITE AND BELOW: Lewis Hamilton followed up a third-place finish in the first race of the season in Australia with eight consecutive podium finishes, a record performance in the 58-year history of the championship for a driver in his first year.

LEFT: Alonso finished the season level on points with Hamiltion and just one point behind Räikkönen in one of the most closely fought contests in the history of Formula One.

Born racer

OPPOSITE: Hamilton's love of racing began when, at the age of six, his father bought him a radio-controlled car. He came second in the BRCA championship the following year, regularly beating adults. His father then bought him a go-kart and promised to help him as long as Hamilton worked hard at school. At the age of thirteen Ron Dennis signed him up to the McLaren driver development programme where he progressed through the ranks, reaching the Formula Three Euro series by the age of nineteen. In 2006 he won the GP2 Championship which led to the offer of a contract with McLaren.

BELOW: Hamilton's father Anthony watches as his son is surrounded by mechanics. Anthony Hamilton has supported his son throughout his career, taking on extra jobs when necessary to provide the financial support. He acts as Lewis's full-time manager and attends every race along with his younger son Nicholas.

BOTTOM: At the Chinese Grand Prix Hamilton took pole position but eventually made his first retirement from a race after excess wear on the tyres caused him to run into the gravel trap during a pit stop.

Friction at McLaren

BELOW: During the qualifying rounds of the Hungarian Grand Prix Alonso delayed leaving the pit, slowing Hamilton's departure and causing friction between the two young drivers. It then emerged that Alonso had access to confidential Ferrari data. As his relations with the team broke down it was announced that Alonso's contract with McLaren had been mutually terminated. A month later Alonso announced his intention to return to Renault the following year.

RIGHT ABOVE AND BELOW: Hamilton gets ready to leave the garage for his first practice session at Silverstone.

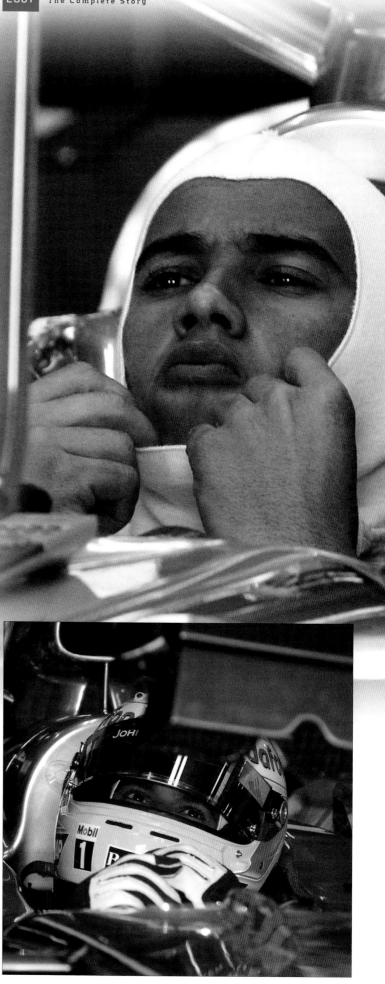

Button to team up with Barrichello

LEFT AND BELOW: Button continued to race for Honda but had a somewhat poor season. He had sustained two fractures to the ribs and was unable to take part in the winter testing. During the season he retired from six races and failed to achieve any podium positions, only claiming a final six points. He became very frustrated with the way the car handled which proved to have problems with the aerodynamics. He did, however, confirm that he would remain with Honda and continue to partner Rubens Barrichello the following year.

Twelve podiums for Hamilton

Below: By the end of the season Hamilton had taken twelve podium positions, amassed 109 points and was the eventual joint runner-up in the Drivers' Championship only one point behind the winner, Kimi Räikkönen.

McLaren and Ferrari battle it out

2008 saw an end to launch and traction control, the addition of two new street circuits to the schedule - Valencia and Singapore – and a new name on the grid. Indian billionaire Vijay Mallya bought out Spyker and rebranded the team as Force India. As one new player entered the fray, another relative newcomer was losing its battle to survive in a sport requiring cavernously deep pockets. Financial pressures led to Super Aguri's withdrawal in May 2008, after barely two years at motor sport's top table.

Lewis off the mark

Lewis Hamilton wasted no time in putting the disappointment of 2007 behind him. He got his and McLaren's campaign off to a flying start with a victory in the Melbourne curtain-raiser. Five cars were taken out in a first-lap melee, but Hamilton stayed clear of trouble and drove imperiously, the only threat to his lead coming from two further safety car outings. Nick Heidfeld took second for BMW Sauber, while Nico Rosberg stepped onto the podium for the first time after bringing his Williams home in third. Neither Ferrari was among the six finishers in an attritional race. Reigning champion Kimi Raikkonen gave the Scuderia a solitary point, classified seventh though his car gave out five laps from home.

Raikkonen edges in front

Kimi hit back with a crushing win in Sepang, but the chance of a Ferrari clean sweep disappeared when pole sitter Felipe Massa spun out at the halfway mark. BMW Sauber showed that 2008 was to be no duopoly by again taking second, this time through Robert Kubica in a career-best finish. McLaren took the other podium spot, but it was Heikki Kovaleinen spraying the bubbly; Hamilton was left ruing the time lost as mechanics wrestled with a wheel nut, the 12-second delay costing him a top-three spot. He crossed the line fifth, a respectable return for the McLaren duo, who were each docked five grid places for qualifying misdemeanours.

If technical gremlins had stymied Hamilton in Malaysia, it was the driver who held up his hand after losing seven places in a disastrous start at Bahrain. He then tangled with Alonso's Renault, losing his nose cone in the process, and by the time he'd limped into the pits for repairs, he was a minute behind the leader, Massa. The Brazilian must have been relieved to take the chequered flag after two error-strewn races. Raikkonen tracked his teammate to the line in a fairly comfortable victory parade, though the hard-charging BMWs meant they couldn't totally relax. Kubica and Heidfeld's solid showing put the team on top of the constructors pile for the first time in its history.

Raikkonen headed the championship after three rounds, and extended his lead to nine points with a regulation win from pole in Barcelona. This time it was Massa playing second fiddle as Ferrari made it back-to-back one-twos. Hamilton got his campaign back on track by finishing third, but the edge was taken off McLaren's weekend as Kovaleinen took a big hit when his MP4-23 ploughed into a tyre wall. The Finn was lucky to escape with minor injuries.

Massa hat-trick

Massa notched up a hat-trick of wins in Istanbul, finishing ahead of title rivals Hamilton and Raikkonen. Lewis, on a three-stop strategy to prevent tyre degradation, led briefly during the middle part of the race when he was running lighter, but the Brazilian went on to turn pole position into ten points. Hamilton had to settle for splitting the Ferraris.

Lewis survived an early puncture at Tabac to score a magnificent first win in Monte Carlo. It was a serendipitous mistake, for the unscheduled stop afforded him the opportunity to change from intermediates to dry weather tyres on an improving track, and also to top up the tank. Kubica and Massa took the minor placings, but it was a miserable outing for Raikkonen, who finished out of the points following a drive-through penalty and a shunt which took out Force India's Adrian Sutil. The 25-year-old German was inconsolable at having a career-best fourth place snatched from his grasp.

Robert Kubica recorded his and BMW Sauber's maiden victory in Montreal, while Heidfeld took second to make it a red-letter day for the team emerging as

2008
THE DRIVERS'
WORLD CHAMPIONSHIP

likely to threaten Ferrari-McLaren dominance. The Pole profitted from a lapse by Hamiltton, who had made a dream start from the front of the grid, only to clatter into a disgruntled Raikkonen in the pit lane under safety car conditions. The Briton's failure to spot a red light put both men out of contention. After a flurry of pit stops which saw the lead change hands several times, the BMW pair took up the running, with David Coulthard bringing his Red Bull home third, a marvellous effort from 13th on the grid. DC's first podium for two years came just before he announced his retirement from F1 at the end of the season. The result catapulted Kubica to the top of the leader board on 42 points, four clear of Hamilton and Massa.

Home win for Hamailton

Hamilton was demoted ten places on the Magny-Cours grid for his Montreal blunder, and a drive-through penalty for taking a short cut through Nurburgring chicane to pass Sebastian Vettel ensured he left France empty handed. Ferrari, meanwhile, was back on song, Massa claiming his third win of the year to sit on the top of the championship for the first time in his career. He capitalised on the misfortune of Raikkonen, who looked set for victory until his F2008 sustained a broken exhaust. The Iceman limped home a distant second, with Jarno Trulli putting Toyota in

the frame for the first time since 2006.

The British Grand Prix, which marked the halfway point in the championship, was run in changeable conditions that made tyre selection a matter of tactical nous, crystal ball gazing and pure chance. Hamilton proved himself equal to anything the heavens could throw at the track, crossing the line over a minute ahead of Heidfeld and Barrichello. Of his main rivals, only fourth-placed Raikkonen finished in the points. The Finn said the decision not to change to fresh inters at his first stop cost him any hope of victory. He stayed out on his original rubber and struggled for grip as the rain returned. By contrast, Honda's technical and tactical wizard Ross Brawn pulled Barrichello in for full wets, a decision that helped the veteran driver to record his first podium finish for three years.

But the day belonged to Hamilton. He had hailed his Monaco performance as the high point of his career, but becoming the first Briton to win his home Grand Prix for eight years eclipsed his accomplishments in Monte Carlo.

The Silverstone result left the title race wide open, Hamilton, Raikkonen and Massa sharing a three-way lead going into the second half of the season, with Kubica only two points adrift.

Lewis off to a flying start

OPPOSITE AND RIGHT: In January 2008 Hamilton signed a new five-year contract with McLaren-Mercedes and began the new year partnering Finnish driver Heikki Kovalainen. The season began well when he won the Australian Grand Prix from pole position.

ABOVE LEFT: Coulthard started the season poorly but managed to capture third place at the Canadian Grand Prix with his 62nd podium finish. Just prior to the start of the British Grand Prix Coulthard announced his planned retirement from Formula 1 racing at the end of the year.

LEFT: Home from home on the circuit with McLaren.

Back to back victories put McLaren ahead

PREVIOUS PAGE OPPOSITE: At the British Grand Prix in July, Hamilton started fourth on the grid but went on to produce a stunning performance, winning the race in very wet and hazardous conditions. He later declared that this win had meant more to him than any others.

BELOW: A decisive victory in Germany gave Hamilton a clear lead in the World Championship title race.